LEADING WITH LOVE

C000157715

As business becomes more automated, power more concentrated, and the forces of competition and consumption seem to dominate our lives, we are in danger of losing what it is to be human. Work for many can be a soulless activity, creating feelings of disempowerment, alienation, and depression. Learning to lead with love is a counterforce to the instrumentalisation of the person.

This book presents original research based on leaders who were nominated by their people for leading with love. It shows how they learned to lead with love for the benefit of themselves, their organisations, and their people. It shows that leading with love is something that is practised by leaders who are more emotionally, morally, and spiritually mature. Leading with love is a sign of psychological maturity, whilst leading with fear is a sign of hindered emotional and spiritual development. Based on this research, this book presents a simple framework to help leaders who wish to develop their psychological maturity and apply practices which will enable them to successfully lead with love.

Karen Blakeley was formerly Programme Leader for the DBA and Head of the Centre for Responsible Management at Winchester Business School. She has published widely in the area of responsible leadership. Karen also spent 20 years as a leadership development consultant and now works as a writer, teacher, and coach.

Chris Blakeley has run a successful leadership development consultancy, Waverley Learning, for over 20 years and is Programme Director for the Society of Leadership Fellows at St George's House, Windsor Castle. Chris is also a Lay Benedictine and works as a Spiritual Director and Retreat Guide alongside his leadership work.

LEADING WITH LOVE

Rehumanising the Workplace

Karen Blakeley and Chris Blakeley

Routledge
Taylor & Francis Group

LONDON AND NEW YORK

First published 2022
by Routledge
2 Park Square, Milton Park, Abingdon, Oxon OX14 4RN

and by Routledge
605 Third Avenue, New York, NY 10158

Routledge is an imprint of the Taylor & Francis Group, an informa business

British Library Cataloguing-in-Publication Data
A catalogue record for this book is available from the British Library

Library of Congress Cataloging-in-Publication Data
Names: Blakeley, Karen, author. | Blakeley, Chris, author.
Title: Leading with love: rehumanising the workplace/Karen Blakeley and
Chris Blakeley.
Description: New York: Routledge, 2021. | Includes bibliographical
references and index. |
Identifiers: LCCN 2020053743 (print) | LCCN 2020053744 (ebook) |
ISBN 9780367234263 (hardback) | ISBN 9780367234287 (paperback) |
ISBN 9780429279812 (ebook)
Subjects: LCSH: Leadership. | Leadership–Psychological aspects.
Classification: LCC BF637.L4 B53 2021 (print) | LCC BF637.L4 (ebook) |
DDC 158/.4–dc23
LC record available at https://lccn.loc.gov/2020053743
LC ebook record available at https://lccn.loc.gov/2020053744

ISBN: 978-0-367-23426-3 (hbk)
ISBN: 978-0-367-23428-7 (pbk)
ISBN: 978-0-429-27981-2 (ebk)

Typeset in Bembo
by Deanta Global Publishing Services Chennai India

To our two children, Grace and Eliot Blakeley, who have taught us the most about love.

CONTENTS

PREFACE

The story of this book is unusual on many levels. It has taken me on a journey of discovery, not only intellectually but personally and spiritually. I will try to unravel this journey as I write the story of how the book came about, how it evolved and how it ended up taking the shape it did.

What originally inspired me to begin this project was a growing sense of unease at the quality of organisational life. As I began researching the background to this book I realised how few people really enjoyed their work. For many people work was becoming more and more oppressive, stressful, repetitive, unrelenting, and joyless. Whilst this was not new, and some authors have been writing about work intensification for 30 years or so, it seemed that this intensification and growing intrusion of work into people's private lives was becoming accepted as the norm. When asked if they minded working unsociable hours, long days, whilst being monitored 24/7 via electronic devices and constant customer feedback, more and more people just seemed to shrug – that's how it is. It did not seem to matter whether I spoke to taxi drivers, financiers earning millions of pounds, teachers, or senior managers in multinational corporations – everyone was stressed and striving to meet targets or to earn enough to get by and, whatever the level in the hierarchy, work was sucking the joy out of life. In addition, the regular stream of corporate scandals that emerged in the media started to include stories of bullying, intimidation, and gross exploitation. Something was going deeply awry in the workplace.

Many managers and their staff responded by going into survival mode. But some managers seemed to be able to withstand the pressures and create an atmosphere of trust, co-operation and enjoyment amongst their teams. At the time I was head of the Centre for Responsible Management at the University of Winchester Business School and I hosted a series of talks by leaders who were passionate about responsible management. I loved listening to these people who were often humble, despite their position, and I became intrigued by the role played by qualities such as empathy and compassion in their unique ability to forge trust and community in organisations driven by targets, measurement, and the constant drive for growth.

A conversation about this kind of leadership with an academic colleague, Chris Mabey, who was then Professor of Leadership at Middlesex University, led to us submitting a proposal for a book called 'Leading with Love' drawing on the notion of agape – selfless love – which was often used in a Christian context. We felt that there was a lot of academic literature which drew on eastern notions of spirituality and leadership but not enough which drew on western notions, specifically Christian views.

Our experience of working with leaders on our MBA and DBA programmes, as well as my role as head of the Centre for Responsible Leadership, gave us access to a lot of leaders at all levels and within all types of organisations. We decided the book would be based on the stories of leaders who led with love. Who were these people and how did they lead with love? Together with Chris (Blakeley) we started to ask around our networks and asked if anyone could nominate a leader who they felt led with love. We came up with nine people and these extraordinary people formed the basis of our research.

Our research participants were senior managers in large corporates, inter-national and national not-for-profit organisations and entrepreneurs who had set up thriving medium-sized businesses. All but one were nominated by direct reports and/or peers as people who noticeably led with love. In addition, they were happy to be interviewed about this topic. These were people who under-stood that, although the term 'love' was unusual in a commercial or professional context (and they often redefined the concept as kindness or empathy or emo-tional intelligence) they knew, on some level, that 'love' was what they were doing. I am very grateful to these men and women who took a risk in being interviewed and associated with this book.

At this point Chris Mabey decided to retire and withdrew from writing the book. I conducted the research and what I learned from our participants was illuminating. On one level, their leadership styles were 'simple' – there was no magic potion that they had distilled to give them the extraordinary abilities that shone through in their organisations. In fact, we have known for over 100 years, particularly through academic research going back to the 1930s, what good lead-ership looks like. The issue is that most leaders do not enact this kind of leader-ship – despite research showing its benefits for organisational performance and personal wellbeing. Our research participants, however, had learned how to put these ideas into practice often in difficult and sometimes hostile environments, and I realised that what enabled them to do this was what developmental psy-chology termed 'adult psychological maturity'. Our leaders were psychologically mature individuals and it was this that enabled them to implement outstanding leadership. What's more, when I looked into ideas around *how* to become a psy-chologically mature adult, I repeatedly came across ideas from eastern spirituality.

The East, it seemed, had made a more than two-millennium study of this very subject – how to become a psychologically mature adult.

It is important also at this point to bring in a bit of personal background to explain how the book came to take the shape it did.

At the time of the research, I was beginning to feel alienated in my own organisation. The joy of teaching started to diminish and I increasingly felt like a cog in a machine – I was experiencing the phenomenon I was writing about in my book! I felt adrift as if I had forgotten who I was and why I was doing what I was doing. So, I engaged a transpersonal coach who was trained in the Diamond Approach, established by A.H. Almaas who drew on eastern ideas based in Sufism, Hinduism and Buddhism as well as western psychology.

As a by-product of this process, I gave up my Christian faith of 25 years and started to explore eastern ideas of love and spiritual growth, investigating the connections between spiritual growth and psychological maturity. I also started to collaborate more with Chris, my partner. Chris was guiding senior corporate leaders using practical techniques related to many of the ideas we were exploring in the book. Although he did not term his approach as developing psychological or spiritual maturity, this is one way of viewing what he was doing. As I started to realise that the development of psychological maturity and spiritual maturity were connected in some way, and that both were central to leading with love, Chris's contribution became more important. His experience of helping leaders to implement these ideas enabled us to identify the techniques that really worked in practice. It is important to note that Chris is steeped in Christian mysticism as well as more contemporary approaches to spiritual development and these have informed his contributions to this book.

So, I can honestly say that what we are writing about in this book, I have experienced personally in my own life. I hope I have managed to lead with love in my role at Winchester, though I know I have failed many times. I have been through the processes of self-awakening, self-knowledge, self-acceptance, and self-expression I talk about in the chapter on self-love. I have practised self-remembering, presence, self-inquiry, and all of the practices we outline in the book. And I am freer, calmer, happier and more present than I have ever been. This is not just an academic book – it is a book rooted in deep personal experience. But it is also a book for everyone! Firstly, it is very practical, and it is the experience of leaders leading in complex organisations that forms the backbone of the book. You will see how ordinary people put leading with love into practice – what they do, what they say, how they resolved dilemmas, how they led in difficult and tough times. Overwhelmingly this is a practical book.

The COVID-19 pandemic hit just as we were putting the finishing touches to this book and it has been humbling and heartening to see many of the aspects of leading with love, playing out so prominently as people have stepped forward to do what is needed in times such as this. Our hope is that, despite the horror and the suffering that COVID has caused, it will change forever the dynamics of performativity and instrumentalism that we describe in the early chapters of the book and usher in an era in which leading with love becomes part of the 'new normal'. Secondly, despite the mention of spirituality, you do not need to have a faith or even a sense of spirituality to enjoy and benefit from the lessons derived from our research participants. Only a few of our leaders had an explicit faith and whilst most had a sense of 'something bigger' in life, the role of faith and spirituality did not play an explicit role in the leadership of the majority of our participants. What our participants did have was a freedom and a lightness of being that are characteristics that come with adult psychological maturity and of course, spiritual maturity. And this maturity often bestows a sense of wisdom, positivity and resilience. This does not mean that our leaders did not experience stress or sadness or anxiety, but rather that they had managed to discover some sense of peace within themselves that helped in their personal lives and in their leadership. We also realised that, for those interested in claiming this peace, the East has a lot to teach us.

Thirdly, the idea of developmental maturity (whether you call it psychological or spiritual maturity) seems to be crucial for the development of our future leaders. As I said, we have known for over 100 years what good leadership looks like. We may call it democratic leadership (Lewin et al. 1939), Theory Y leadership (McGregor 1960), team leadership (Blake and Mouton 1964), contingency leadership (Fiedler 1967; Hersey and Blanchard 1988; Goleman 2000), transformational leadership (Bass 1990), authentic leadership (Gardner et al. 2005), responsible leadership (Pless and Maak 2009), or spiritual leadership (Benefiel 2005), but we don't do it! This book explores why we do not do it and focuses on the emotional, cognitive, and spiritual maturity that needs to take place before leaders are able to put these ideas into practice. This has practical implications for how we select and develop leaders in all our organisations and communities – whether local, national or global; whether commercial, not-for-profit, public or transnational. Today more than ever, we need leaders with psychological and spiritual maturity. We hope this book contributes to the debate about how this can come about.

Karen Blakeley

References

Bass, B.M. (1990) From transactional to transformational leadership: Learning to share the vision. *Organizational Dynamics*, 18(3), 19–31.

Benefiel, M. (2005) The second half of the journey: Spiritual leadership for organizational transformation. *The Leadership Quarterly*, 16(5), 723–747.

Blake, R.R. and Mouton, J.S. (1964) *The Managerial Grid*. Houston, TX: Gulf.

Fiedler, F.E. (1967) *A Theory of Leadership Effectiveness*. New York: McGraw Hill.

Gardner, W.L., Avolio, B.J., Luthans, F., May, D.R. and Walumbwa, F. (2005) Can you see the real me? A self-based model of authentic leader and follower development. *The Leadership Quarterly*, 16(3), 343–372.

Goleman, D. (2000) Leadership that gets results. *Harvard Business Review*, 78(2), 78–90.

Hersey, P. and Blanchard, K. (1988) *Management of Organizational Behavior* [5th ed.]. New Jersey: Prentice Hall.

Lewin, K., Lippit, R., and White, R.K. (1939) Patterns of aggressive behaviour in experimentally created social climates. *Journal of Social Psychology* 10, 271–301.

McGregor, D. (1960) *The Human Side of Enterprise*. New York: McGraw Hill.

Pless, N. and Maak, T. (2009) Responsible leaders as agents of world benefit: Learnings from 'Project Ulysses'. *Journal of Business Ethics*, 85, Supplement 1: 14th Annual Vinventian International Conference on Justice for the Poor: A Global Business Ethics, 59–71.

ACKNOWLEDGEMENTS

We would like to acknowledge the leaders who have inspired us and contributed to this book, either directly through the interviews or indirectly through our interactions with them both personally and professionally. Thank you to Clive Adams, Martin Pluves, Nigel Taylor, Paul Holland, Sarah Corbett, David Cousins, Mark Chegwidden, Leigh Lafever Ayer, Nickie Hills, and Simon Mitchell. Thank you to all the guest speakers at the Centre for Responsible Leadership at Winchester University Business School, particularly John Timpson, Jonathon Porritt, Keith Abel, Paul Drechsler, Guy Watson, Alex Beasley, Jonathan Gosling, Carolyn Fairbairn, Justin Byworth, David McCullough, Andy Stanford-Clark, Sue Hollingsworth, Wayne Visser, Marylyn Carrigan, Kami Lakanan, Claire Genkai, Duncan Exley, Sophie Graham, Steve Holmes, Christine Adshead, Ralph Schneider, Alan Smith, Amanda Mackenzie, Paul Maiteny, Gopal Krishnamurthy, Richard Parker, Tom Anderson, and a very special thank you to Michael Coleman.

I, Karen, would like to thank some particularly inspiring academic colleagues: Adam Palmer, Carole Parkes, Roz Sunley, Tammi Sinha, Karen Cripps, Richard Bolden, Terry Biddington, Kim Bradley-Cole, Katrina Easterling, Lindsay Birthwhistle, Adrienne Marsden, and a special thank you to Professor Chris Mabey who started this project with me many years ago.

Thanks to those who have helped me (Karen) on my personal journey: Dominic Liber my personal coach and guide from the Ridhwan School, Bodhi Shapiro, Heather Heaton, Gene Dilworth, John Beeney, David Petheridge, Sue Iacobucci, Paul McMullen, Abi Hucker, Anne and Steve Hemmings, Elise Ace, Tessa and Richard Elphick, Karen Firbank, Jane Gilmore, Elizabeth and Mel Thomas, and Karen Woodhouse.

In addition, Chris would like to thank the many people who have supported him in the development of his practice, without which his contribution to this book would not have been possible. In particular his co-directors at Waverley Learning, Karen Stefanyszyn and Tim Richardson: Karen for her endless fascination with what it means to be human in the 21st century, and Tim for his passionate advocacy of responsible leadership. Beyond that, the whole Waverley Learning Community – our associates who have worked alongside us as we have piloted our approaches and those who have supported us on annual retreats for over 20 years to help us stay true to our foundations. Thanks in particular to Jani Rubery for all her support over the years and for loaning us her cottage in Wales for the writing of this book! Thanks go also to our clients at Waverley who have been willing to give us their trust, however unusual our approach may have seemed! You know who you are – thank you! With particular thanks to Roger Thomas, Dan Gresham, Karen Brown, Judith Payne, and Hueston Finlay. Thanks are also due to Russ Hudson, Jason Stern, Marie Flynn, and Martha Eskew for the inspirational Inner Work retreats in Dublin. Finally Chris would like to express a special debt of gratitude to the Benedictine Brothers at Alton Abbey who have been the source of so much support and wisdom over many years, and in particular to the late Dom Nicholas Seymour who was his guide and mentor for over 15 years.

Finally, very special thanks to our loving and inspiring friend Charles Platel and soul-mate Michelle Machin-Jefferies, who leads with love in everything she does.

1

WHY LEADING WITH LOVE IS NEEDED NOW

Organisations are rarely places of love. Organisations are the spaces in which goals are pursued, both shared and contested, and where people are put to work in pursuit of these goals. Of course, there is nothing wrong with the communal pursuit of shared goals – where would we be without hospitals, large companies that provide for a range of our needs, charities that care for the vulnerable, and government institutions that take responsibility for our safety, health, education, and environment? However, in our shared pursuit of organisational goals, perhaps we have lost a sense of whom organisations are meant to serve, and what function they should play in our lives?

Let us meet some people who work for organisations.

Adam is an options trader who works for a bank. He never stops working. He spends at least 14 hours a day at work and constantly checks the markets to ensure his trading positions are exactly where he wants them to be. He is wealthy beyond most people's dreams. As a result of his obsession with work, he recently divorced, and rarely sees his children. So now there is no respite from work even if he wanted it, as he must maintain two households and three children at private school. He is trapped. He is anxious: the bank he works for has been underperforming and they have invited in a professional services company to 'rationalise' his operation. He is scared of losing his job and sometimes feels suicidal.

Jackie works for the professional services company that is consulting to Adam's bank. She specialises in cost-cutting and re-engineering. She regularly spends 12 hours a day at work. She has no partner or family as she has never found the time to get out and meet people. When she gets home she still has work to do; with no time to cook, she orders a meal that is delivered by a local food delivery service. The man who hands over her meal is on a zero-hour contract and is working ten hours a day, hours that are scattered around the early morning, lunchtime, and early and late evening. For those hours where there is less demand and therefore no work, he is not paid, but there is nothing else for him to do but wait until he is called. He has no job security and is living off an income that barely covers his expenses: there is no pension or sick pay and he is constantly afraid of getting ill or of not being given any work. On his days off – normally Monday and Wednesday (he rarely gets a full two days' rest) – he relaxes with his video games ordered from an online retailer.

Sonya works for that retailer in one of their giant warehouses; she is also on a zero-hour contract. In fact, Sonya does not work directly for the retailer but for a contractor who rarely pays her on time and often pays her the wrong money (always less than she is owed). Sonya always works with a monitor strapped around her wrist to measure how long it takes her to pick the customer's item and place it in the right despatch point. She walks at least ten miles a day around the warehouse picking and sorting items that have been ordered by customers online. There is no time to go to the toilet (the time would be included in the time she takes to collect an item) and lunch breaks are limited to half an hour. Every day she is assessed to see if she has met her time targets: if she misses her target on too many occasions, she will lose her job. Sonya is one of the working poor – i.e. she does not earn enough money to cover the expenses incurred by her and her family – so she has to deal with the government office that dispenses her top-up payment.

At that office she has recently come into contact with Mark, whose role is so broad following the government cutbacks that he is constantly stressed and unable to deal with the queries and complaints that come his way. He eventually sees his doctor about his stress and feelings of depression. His doctor, Janine, is given a maximum of ten minutes to deal with each patient. She has seen many people like Mark – in fact, the number is increasing – but she cannot go into any depth about his complaint and dispenses some antidepressants to help him in the short term. When she gets home, she realises that it is parents' evening and she has an appointment to see her daughter's teacher. The teacher, Paul, informs her that her daughter is not thriving at school and seems somewhat anxious: this is affecting her test scores and maybe she will have to drop a couple of subjects as the school cannot afford to have too many pupils attaining poor grades because it will affect their rankings.

* * *

We seem to have reached a situation where human beings are serving organisations rather than organisations serving human beings. People are becoming instrumentalised by the objects of their own creation. Some may be benefiting – and we will come to that point later – but many are simply suffering: from anxiety, exhaustion, meaninglessness, anger, and fear.

In fact, there is a short but poignant Zen tale that encapsulates the condition in which we find ourselves: the story of Zumbach the tailor.

Zumbach the tailor

A man went to Zumbach the tailor to have a new suit made. When the suit was ready, the man tried it on to check the fit. Strangely, he noticed the right arm of the suit was too short so he asked Zumbach to lengthen it.

'The sleeve is not too short,' Zumbach replied. 'Your arm is too long. Just pull your arm up a bit and you'll see the sleeve fits perfectly.' The man did as Zumbach told him and the sleeve seemed to fit much better, but holding his arm like this rumpled the collar of the jacket.

'Okay, so the sleeve looks fine but the collar is all wrong,' the man complained. 'There's nothing wrong with the collar,' Zumbach replied. 'You need to raise your left shoulder up a bit more.' The man raised his shoulder and it seemed to do the job, but now the bottom of the jacket rested too high up his back.

'This is hopeless,' the man insisted, 'the jacket is halfway up my back.' 'No problem,' Zumbach replied. 'Lower your head and bend your knees so the jacket sits on your hips.' The man did as Zumbach suggested and it worked: the suit fitted him perfectly and was beautifully stylish.

So the man walked out of the shop in a highly contorted and uncomfortable manner but feeling like he was wearing the most beautiful suit in the world.

He got onto a bus and the person next to him looked at his suit. 'What a lovely suit,' he said, 'I bet you got that suit from Zumbach the tailor.' 'How did you know?' the man asked.

'Because only the brilliant Zumbach could cut a suit to fit a body as distorted as yours.'

The organisation as Zumbach's suit: the performativity culture

We are contorting ourselves and incapacitating our bodies and minds in order to fit into our own version of Zumbach's suit: the organisations we work for.

We already know that work can have a major negative impact on our mental health. While being out of work very often has severe negative consequences, the wrong type of work can also lead to mental disorders such as stress, anxiety, and depression. Recent evidence has shown that the workplace is one of the main sources of stress we experience in our lives. According to research quoted by Pfeffer and Carney (2018: 75), 'almost half of US workers experience[ed] work-related stress and one-quarter of respondents claim[ed] that the work-place was their single biggest source of stress.' A recent survey in the United Kingdom demonstrated that 60% of UK employees experienced poor mental health due to work-related conditions (BITC 2017). Factors causing psychological stress include experiencing a lack of control over one's work, low social support, the behaviour of one's line manager, increased work intensification, and even linking pay to time (whether hourly paid manual work or hourly billed professional work) (Pfeffer and Carney 2018).

It has been shown that alleviating workplace stress *increases* productivity (Jackson, Alexander, and Frame, 2018), and yet advances in technology are increasingly tempting senior management into upping their levels of observation and control of employees' actions in order to maximise the effort they can extract. And, in doing so, stress levels go up. We saw in the example above how warehouses monitor employees' movements to ensure that every step they take is efficiently dedicated to locating and sorting stock, limiting toilet and refreshment breaks, and threatening dismissal if the required targets are not met. We will also see how performance is measured with increasing frequency and intensity throughout a range of industry sectors, leading to people going from 'hero' to 'zero' on a month-by-month basis. And we will also see how 'performativity cultures' lead to excessive working hours, family breakdowns and burnout. Performativity cultures are those in which there is a normative acceptance that the sole purpose of the organisation is to extract from its employees the maximum performance possible often by recourse to extensive and intrusive controls, targets, and measures.[1]

Of course, productivity/GDP, partly as a result of these technological advancements, has soared since 1980, so perhaps this emphasis on performance is no bad thing (Boushey 2019). One could argue that this increase in our ability to monitor efficiency ultimately leads to increases in wealth (and, for those on the breadline, increases in income that could ease their stress). However, the increase in productivity over the past 40 years has not led to an equivalent rise in wages (Ghilarducci 2018). According to labour economist Teresa Ghilarducci, in the United States (which is the most extreme example), '[f]rom 1973 to 2013, hourly compensation of a typical worker rose just 9 percent while productivity increased 74 percent' (Ghilarducci 2018). Similar trends, decoupling productivity from wages, can be seen in Europe and other industrialised countries (Piketty 2014).

In essence, workers from all socioeconomic backgrounds are being controlled to an increasingly sophisticated extent in order to maximise the amount of work it is possible to extract from a human being. Most of these workers are experiencing high levels of stress as a result, and very few are receiving any significant financial benefit from their increased efficiency. Even those who are privileged enough to enjoy some of the monetary rewards from their efforts (i.e. the small percentage of top earners who receive bonuses in the form of shares and other financial assets) suffer from a lack of family and leisure time and the accompanying social and psychological problems.

For many, if not most, workers in industrialised countries, the quality of working life (and therefore the quality of life in general) has diminished, the main causes being fear of job loss, fear of missing targets, excessive working hours/insufficient working hours, stagnant income, loss of pensions and other security-enhancing systems, and increasing control being exercised over their every move (McDowall and Kinman 2017).

According to the UK government's report on Sports Direct, a company that epitomises this approach, the kinds of working practices commonly seen represent:

> an arrogance and a contempt, actually, at the very highest level of this business. We have it described to us as a gulag, as Victorian, as a workhouse, not a warehouse. We believe that there is no place for these kinds of 19th century working practices in 21st century Britain.
>
> *(House of Commons Business, Innovation and*
> *Skills Committee 2016: 8)*

The report went on to say that this increased work intensification and the instrumentalisation of the workforce (at all levels) is in danger of becoming the norm.

The business model described here – which focuses on extracting the maximum work possible from every employee while withholding financial compensation, employment rights, pension rights, and rights to union representation – is underpinned by fear.

Another Sports Direct witness stated:

> The problem with this is when you have people under that much fear, they come into work ill. When you get presenteeism in the workplace that creates a significant health and safety risk, because these people are now not only at risk to themselves but they are at risk to those they are working with.
>
> *(House of Commons Business, Innovation and*
> *Skills Committee 2016: 8)*

According to *Forbes* magazine, worker fear is something that government and industry leaders consciously use in their economic and monetary policy. In 1997, despite high employment, the US government recognised that work insecurity was high and workers were afraid of abandoning their jobs in search of better ones; this allowed them to make policy decisions in the knowledge that inflation would not be boosted by demands for higher wages. The same article claims that, in 2018, 'people feel just as likely to lose their jobs now, when the unemployment rate is 4%, as they did in 1991 when the unemployment rate was over 7%' (Ghilarducci 2018).

Going back to the tale of Zumbach the tailor, it appears we are all like Zumbach's customer. We are contorting our psyches to fit the demands of an increasingly powerful machine. We may find the naivety of Zumbach's customer amusing, but it is not so funny when we recognise that large swathes of the population are walking around with twisted psyches, feeling fear or inadequacy, and worrying whether they will meet their targets at work or whether they will be facing admonishment, sanctions, or dismissal.

Part of the problem lies in the secrecy of our private worlds. We do not share our anxieties with our peers and managers and end up defensive, anxious, and stressed. We in turn then become Zumbachs: imposing measurements, controls, and contortions on our staff just as they are imposed on us. We can find ourselves shouting at our staff, demanding or threatening others, focusing purely on our numbers, and having little energy or attention for the humanity of our staff and colleagues.

Workplace bullying, a major source of workplace stress, has risen by 19% in the past 11 years (Robinson 2019). A senior executive coach we know has reported a massive increase in cases that involve bosses bullying their staff or colleagues ganging up on victims.

Viewing the problem through a psycho-spiritual lens

Clearly, there is a political dimension to this, which concerns how power and wealth are distributed in society: for example, the well-known dynamics of increasing productivity and stagnant wages leading to a massive concentration of wealth in the hands of the top 1%. While sympathetic to these economic and political concerns, this book focuses more on the spiritual and psychological dynamics. The reason for this is that there are many interweaving political and economic arguments explaining the growing inequality in our society and the diminishment in the quality of working life, and they are mostly well rehearsed and understood. They include globalisation, the growth in outsourcing, competition with low-wage economies, and the growing power of capital vis-à-vis labour; the financialisation of large swathes of our economy (i.e. treating homes, property, and companies as financial assets to be invested in and disposed of at will by global economic elites); technological change and the Fourth Industrial Revolution; and the rise of new economic powers such as India and China (Brewer 2019). The various forces identified by these arguments appear to have led to increasing divisions in our societies which are spread across political, economic, and social lines. We are all hurting; as a result, we lash out against the 'other,' blaming social and ethnic groups – who are often suffering just as much if not more – for our problems. These divisions have already led to increasing social strife and will continue to generate yet more suffering. Unless we can learn to cooperate, listen, and respect the other, any solutions on offer can never be successfully implemented.

Another way of understanding our problems (*which is in no way to disregard the economic, social, and political forces at play*) is that our performativity culture is also creating a psycho-spiritual malaise, i.e. a sickness in the human heart and spirit. This culture leaves us no time to consider, reflect, or challenge our sense-making; connect deeply with each other; tune in to our deeper longings (e.g. for meaning and purpose); and ask ourselves what we really want for our lives (and for our organisations and societies). We are exhausted and fearful and find ourselves automatically reacting to every stimulus that comes our way. We go from day to day, with the same routine, acting out our place in a system that rewards only the very few, distorting ourselves into our organisational 'suits,' reacting to the various frustrations and anxieties, pleasures and reliefs we experience, articulating words and beliefs that are not our own.

According to research by Bains (2007), people want work that feels worthwhile and meaningful, work that gives them the opportunity to make a difference. In a similar vein, Jim Clifton, Chairman and CEO of the Gallup organisation, which conducts regular polls on workplace engagement, argues that one way of addressing low engagement and productivity is to build workplace cultures that deliver mission and purpose (Gallup 2017). Millennials in particular are looking for work that feels meaningful (Desimone 2020). Yet regular Gallup polls tell us that engagement at work is extremely low, with only 15% of people worldwide actively engaged in their jobs (Gallup 2017). In a more recent survey (from 2019), the figure for engaged employees in the United States rose to 35% (Harter 2020). Nonetheless, 52% remained not engaged (psychologically unattached – not putting any energy or passion into work) and 11% actively disengaged (likely to consciously undermine their company's performance). In Western Europe, the latest data are from Gallup's 2017 report, where levels of engagement ranged from 17% in Norway (highest) to 5% in Italy (lowest). In the United Kingdom, 11% of employees were engaged. Even in Norway, that left 75% of employees not engaged and 8% actively disengaged; the corresponding figures for Italy were 64% and 30% respectively, and 68% and 21% for the United Kingdom (Gallup 2017). According to Jim Clifton, 'stress and clinical burnout and subsequent suicide rates in Japan have caused the government to intervene. The current practice of management is now destroying their culture – a staggering 94% of Japanese workers are not engaged at work' (Clifton 2017). There is a Japanese term, *inemuri*, which refers to the notion of 'sleeping while present,' and it is not unusual to observe the Japanese sleeping in public spaces such as on the street, on park benches, on trains and even at work during meetings or at one's desk. Yielding to *inemuri* is actually seen as a positive sign: that the sleeper has been working extremely long hours and has sacrificed personal and home life, even to the point of sacrificing sleep, in order to dedicate their time to the company (see Steger 2016). Like the Japanese worker who engages in *inemuri*, we are sleepwalking through our lives.

Ironically, this performativity mind-set eventually undermines the very efficiency it is intended to promote. It is not simply that employees take more days off as a result of stress – and various reports can show how money can be saved by organisations investing in stress management programmes – but rather that decision-making in organisations suffers when people are stressed and worked to their maximum limit.

The Future of Work unit at ESADE, Spain, recently reported on trends resulting from the powerful, parallel forces of globalisation, digitalisation/virtualisation, and knowledge creation-innovation (Dolan et al. 2015).[2] The authors characterise the contemporary work space as being 'a continual search for quick fixes and lives that are distanced – while causing us to give up the "high-touch" aspects of life that give our lives meaning, hope, fear and longing, love, forgiveness, nature and spirituality' (Dolan et al. 2015: 5).

Our proposition is that while we recognise and acknowledge the systemic nature of these issues, we will never be able to address them until we can transform the nature of the consciousness that originally gave birth to them. A popular saying, often attributed to Einstein, claims that no problem can be solved using the same level of thinking that created it.[3] Einstein also argued that:

> If we want to improve the world we cannot do it with scientific knowledge but with ideals. … We must begin with the heart of man – with his conscience – and the values of conscience can only be manifested by selfless service to mankind.[4]

We argue in this book that the problems outlined here are, in part at least, psycho-spiritual in nature and we need a transformation in consciousness in order to address them. If we do not change our beliefs, our values, and our hearts, our solutions to the systemic ills that face us will be no better than the problems they attempt to address. The main difference between a purely psychological and a psycho-spiritual approach is that psychologists seek to equip their patients with a 'normal' level of ego-functioning, while psycho-spiritual approaches draw on both Western psychology and ancient spiritual traditions to equip their followers with the ability to transcend the ego – another point made by Einstein: 'I believe the main task of the spirit is to free man from his ego.'[5]

Focusing on a psycho-spiritual diagnosis helps us to go deeper into a problem which in part lies in our own fears, egocentricity, need for personal survival, competitiveness, greed, pride, envy, individualism, and narcissism. We are all humans and we all share these aspects of our being – this is recognised by each and every psychological and spiritual tradition on the earth. However, we also share a capacity for love, compassion, empathy, tenderness, and mutual support, as well as sharing needs: for passion, purpose, meaning, vision, creativity, and transcendence.

Unfortunately, our performativity cultures tend to cultivate the former qualities – and our fear or exhaustion or anxiety leads us into doing as we are told. As long as we all stay on this treadmill, we will be controlled and exploited and continue to sleepwalk through our lives.

There is no shortage of business books that urge us to tap into our deepest potential, to combat our fears, to demonstrate compassion and empathy for others, to inspire people to dedicate their creativity and passion to their work, to care for others and bring out their best so that they give their all. We may read these books and agree with them – yet we do not change our behaviour. And that is mainly because new behaviours such as these are rarely rewarded in the organisational systems that we inhabit. We are damned if we do and damned if we don't; the power struggle is unequal. The reality of life is this: comply and conform or suffer the consequences. This is the hard-nosed question this book needs to address: why should I bother? What's in it for me?

This book is founded on research undertaken with leaders in a range of organisations who were nominated by their direct reports as leaders who led with love. Our fascination in writing this book was to discover people, ordinary leaders in ordinary roles, who bucked the trend – who somehow, despite all the negative forces described above, managed to create a 'space,' an atmosphere around them, where kindness, compassion, and love were able to breathe, ripple out, and refresh the people working in the very systems that tend to squeeze such feelings out.

In seeking nominations for people to feature in this book, one of the most striking things was the reaction when people were asked if they could identify anyone who genuinely led with love in their organisations. Many laughed, then thought about it, then gave up with a sigh. But a few were able to identify individuals who came immediately to mind. They just stood out. They stood out because love stands out, not as a management technique but as a genuine expression of the human spirit. In the next section, we explore what this means and delve a little deeper into the role that love can play in the workplace and in our leading of others.

* * *

Love

There is an interesting marketing experiment that looked at the effects of love in terms of how it affected people's charitable donations (Cavanaugh et al. 2015). A general assumption in marketing is that the experience of positive emotions triggers a desire to do good: if I feel good, I will do good.[6] But do different kinds of positive emotions trigger different kinds of prosocial behaviours?

In the experiment, each participant was shown a series of pictures that each conjured up a different emotion, while a control group was exposed to pictures that provoked no particular emotion. The researchers then asked each participant, having been exposed to a picture and its relevant emotion, how they would use an unexpected financial bonus. They could donate to a local cause, to an international cause, or keep it for themselves. We have found some similar pictures to those used in the experiment and encourage you to take part in this exercise before you read what happened in the actual experiment. As you look at each picture, try to notice what kinds of physical sensations, emotions, thoughts, and desires you are experiencing.

FIGURE 1.1

Any physical sensations, emotions, thoughts, or desires ...?

FIGURE 1.2

Any physical sensations, emotions, thoughts, or desires ...?

FIGURE 1.3

Any physical sensations, emotions, thoughts, or desires …?

FIGURE 1.4

Any physical sensations, emotions, thoughts, or desires …?

The different emotions that the marketing experiment aimed to trigger were compassion (here Figure 1.1), pride (here Figure 1.2), hope (here Figure 1.3), and love (here Figure 1.4), or else no emotion (control group).

Before reading on, consider the responses you had to the four pictures above. Compare and contrast these responses, paying particular attention to any physical sensations you experienced.

In the marketing experiment, the researchers offered participants a distinction between giving to local charities and giving to international charities – what they referred to as giving to 'distant others.' Each picture was designed to trigger either pride, hope, compassion, love, or no emotion. Of the emotions triggered, they found that only love encouraged giving to international charities – to 'distant others.' They concluded:

> whereas positive emotions (vs. neutral emotional states) typically enhance prosocial behavior aimed at close others, only love (not hope, pride, or compassion) enhances prosocial behaviors aimed at distant others ... love is distinct from hope and pride in that it also generates feelings of social connection, enhancing consumers' propensity to feel caring and exhibit concern toward those with whom they are not related (i.e., others with whom psychological and physical proximity are not shared). Thus, love ultimately changes the boundary of caring and concern to include more distant others.
>
> *(Cavanaugh et al. 2015: 658)*

Why does love have this effect? Take a look at the picture designed to provoke love. It depicts a baby – beautiful, innocent, vulnerable, and ultimately non-threatening. A baby, like pictures of kittens and puppies, melts us – it melts our ego defences (after all, a baby cannot harm us) and triggers a profound, heart-shifting, energetic desire to protect and care. Our need to judge, or criticise, or explain or assert our ego needs dissolves a little and we feel safe and happy when this happens. Did you notice your heart soften? Did you feel yourself relax a little when you saw this picture? Did you notice some feelings or sensations in your heart area? Love involves a movement of the heart which gives rise to a desire for the flourishing of others, even those who are unlike ourselves – distant others. According to the research, unlike compassion or even empathy, love involves a long-term desire to see everyone flourish, grow, succeed, and contribute, even if they are very different to us. Paul Bloom, in his book *Against Empathy* (2016), shows how we are more likely to empathise with those who look like us and more likely to find it difficult to empathise with 'distant others.' We can empathise with someone when they go through difficult times, we can feel compassion for those who are suffering, but when someone has won the lottery, we tend not to feel compassion or even empathy. Love, however, delights in seeing others flourish and wants only what is good for them (as long as it does not harm others). This is why it is easy to love our partners or children: it is natural to want only what is good for them.

What relevance does this have to the workplace? Well, if we take the foregoing argument, it would seem that the workplace is designed to stimulate anxiety and self-protection, which does not in any way allow for the melting of our hearts, the suspension of our ego needs, and the experience of love for our fellow human beings. While we may try our utmost to express kindness and compassion for others, we may do this in opposition to the systems that drive organisational behaviour and often find ourselves burned out in the process. And yet the experience of love is heart-warming, stress-reducing, happiness-inducing. We love feeling love! And it is good for our health; therefore, unfortunately, we are killing ourselves in the process of protecting ourselves. The question then becomes: How do we keep love alive when every part of our being wants to deny it and shut it out? Because it is too painful, vulnerable, naive, unproductive, sentimental – whatever your reason.

Outline of the research and the structure of the book

If you feel curious or motivated to continue reading, we close this chapter with a few practical points to give you a sense of where we are headed: firstly, a brief description of the research we conducted to underpin our analysis, followed by an outline of the main argument of the book and how the following chapters develop it.

The research

It was our conviction that if we were going to write a book on leading with love, it had to be informed by people who in some way were putting this into practice in hard-nosed, tough working environments. But the question was: how to find them? Both of us had access to people leading in organisations: Chris through his highly successful leadership development consultancy Waverley Learning, and Karen through her Winchester University roles as Head of the Centre for Responsible Leadership, Programme Leader for the Doctorate of Business Administration, and as a teacher on the MBA programme. We decided that the best way to find people who led with love was to ask others in our networks to nominate those who they felt fit the description. As a result, nine leaders were nominated, either by their direct reports or by their peers, and these included senior leaders in global corporates, successful entrepreneurs, and senior leaders or founders of charities. More information on the research and on the backgrounds of the interviewees can be found in Chapter 5.

The interviews provided information that was vital to the integrity and power of the arguments presented in the book. Firstly, we conducted a thematic analysis of the interviews which contributed towards the practical model of how to lead with love presented in Chapter 5. Secondly, we used quotes from the interviews in order to illustrate and bring to life the points we make throughout the book, showing how the ideas we explore are being lived out on a daily basis by leaders in highly competitive workplaces.

You will notice that the two authors each bring a somewhat different lens to this book, and you will probably become aware of this as you read. Chris brings a practical focus based on his role as an executive coach to many senior leaders in business and as an organisational development specialist consulting organisational change. Karen brings a more academic focus, although in the past she too has been an executive coach and a consultant to organisations. The way the book set out to some extent reflects this partnership between academic research and executive practice.

Outline of the book

Chapter 2 concentrates on definitions in order to bring greater clarity to what we mean by 'leading,' 'love,' and 'leading with love,'

Chapter 3 introduces the context for the book and looks at economic, technological, and sociological trends within the workplace, which help to explain why the need for leading with love has become so urgent.

Chapter 4 argues that the ability to lead with love embodies the highest level of human maturity, while leading with fear, reactivity, and defensiveness demonstrates a far lower level of maturity. It argues that we should expect our leaders, who today hold so much power, to act with such maturity.

Chapter 5 describes the research that informs the framework around how to lead with love. It describes the backgrounds of the interviewees, how the data was analysed, and the themes derived from the analysis.

Chapter 6 moves the book to a more developmental focus, inviting the reader to reflect on whether leading with love is really for you.

If this is the case, Chapters 7–10 present a framework and practical tips for how to expand your capacity to lead with love.

Chapter 11 explores the question of how we develop self-love as an important foundation for leading with love.

Chapter 12 offers case examples of leaders leading with love in global organisations, exploring what it takes to consciously learn to lead with love in pressured, visible leadership roles.

Finally, Chapter 13 presents our summary and conclusions. It brings together the large themes that we have explored throughout the book and presents some suggestions as to how to move forward – on a societal, organisational, and individual level.

We hope you enjoy the journey!

Notes

1 We are aware of the postmodern term 'performativity' referring to the process by which language creates the phenomenon it describes. We are being somewhat bold in coining this new meaning but it speaks very well into what we are discussing and reads much better than 'a culture that promotes excessive emphasis on performance' or even a 'performance culture,' which does not have the same overtones.

2 The work of the Centre is reported in a paper by Dolan et al. (2015), which probes what is needed to develop people, companies, and ecosystems to flourish in a high-tech, high-touch, and high-growth work reality while resisting the possibilities of strategic implosion. It is an example of a growing number of reports that are questioning a drive for performance that fails to consider the human, social, and environmental costs.

3 This quote can be found widely in books and across the internet but without a source attached. It may be that Einstein said that no problem can be solved using the same level of thinking that created it, and Ram Dass paraphrased the sentiment and changed the word 'thinking' to 'consciousness.'

4 https://en.wikiquote.org/wiki/Albert_Einstein.

5 https://en.wikiquote.org/wiki/Albert_Einstein, From Hermanns 1983.

6 This also implies the converse: i.e. if I feel bad, I will behave badly – which is what we increasingly see within organisations and society as a whole.

References

Bains, G. (2007) *Meaning Inc.* London: Profile Books.

Bloom, P. (2016) *Against Empathy: The Case for Rational Compassion.* New York: Ecco Press.

Boushey (2019) The economy isn't getting better for most Americans. But there is a fix. https://www.brookings.edu/opinions/the-economy-isnt-getting-better-for-most -americans-but-there-is-a-fix/ (accessed 3 April 2020).

Brewer, M. (2019) *What Do We Know and What Should We Do about Inequality?* London: SAGE.

Business in the Community (2017) *Mental Health at Work Report: National Employee Mental Wellbeing Survey Findings 2017.* London: BITC.

Cavanaugh, L.L., Bettman, J.R. and Luce, M.F. (2015) Feeling love and doing more for distant others: Specific positive emotions differentially affect prosocial consumption. *Journal of Marketing Research*, 52(5), 657–673.

Clifton, J. (2017) The world's broken workplace. *Gallup*, 13 June 2017. http://www .gallup.com/opinion/chairman/212045/world-broken-workplace.aspx?g_source= &g_medium=&g_campaign=tiles (accessed 4 August 2017).

Desimone, R. (2020) Employees want work that matters -- Managers can help. https:// www.gallup.com/workplace/275417/employees-work-matters-managers-help.aspx (accessed 2 April 2020).

Dolan, S., Makarevich, A. and Karamura, K. (2015) Are you and your company prepared for the future of work. *European Business Review*, July–August, 5–12.

Gallup (2017) State of the global workplace. https://www.gallup.com/workplace /238079/state-global-workplace-2017.aspx (accessed 2 April 2020).

Ghilarducci, T. (2018) Why wages won't rise when unemployment falls. *Forbes*, 18 July 2018. https://www.forbes.com/sites/teresaghilarducci/2018/07/18/why -wages-wont-rise-when-unemployment-falls/#33f387e25d9d (accessed 14 July 2020).

Harter, J. (2020) 4 factors driving record high employee engagement in US. https:// www.gallup.com/workplace/284180/factors-driving-record-high-employee -engagement.aspx (accessed 2 April 2020).

House of Commons Business, Innovation and Skills Committee (2016) Employment practices at sports direct: Third report of session 2016–17. *HC 219*, 22 July 2016. https://publications.parliament.uk/pa/cm201617/cmselect/cmbis/219/219.pdf (accessed 14 July 2020).

Jackson, A. and Frame, M. (2018) Stress, health, and job performance: What do we know? *Journal of Applied Biobehavioral Research*, 23(4), 1071–2089.

McDowall, A. and Kinman, G. (2017) Health and work–life balance in times of austerity. In Lewis, S., Anderson, D., Lyonette, C., Payne, N. and Wood, S. (eds.), *Work–Life Balance in Times of Recession, Austerity and Beyond* (pp. 23–44). London: Routledge.

Pfeffer, J. and Carney, D.R. (2018) The economic evaluation of time can cause stress. *Academy of Management Discussions*, 4(1), 74–93.

Piketty, T. (2014) *Capital in the Twenty-First Century*. Boston, MA: President and Fellows of Harvard College (translated by Arthur Goldhammer).

Robinson, B. (2019) New study says workplace bullying on the rise: What can you do during national bullying prevention month. https://www.forbes.com/sites/ bryanrobinson/2019/10/11/new-study-says-workplace-bullying-on-rise-what-can -you-do-during-national-bullying-prevention-month/#1c31b18b2a0d (Accessed 3 April 2020).

Steger, B. (2016) The Japanese art of (not) sleeping. *BBC*, 6 May 2016. http://www.bbc .com/future/story/20160506-the-japanese-art-of-not-sleeping (accessed 26 August 2018).

2

WHAT IS 'LEADING WITH LOVE'?

This chapter looks more deeply at the central hypothesis of this book: unpacking our definition of 'leading with love' and asking whether it is possible, let alone reasonable, for anyone to lead in this way.

Firstly, we will look at 'leading,' followed by a more in-depth investigation of what we mean by 'love.' Can a leader really have any significant agency in the face of the complex and powerful forces at play in today's world? Can any individual make a real difference, or are we all just products of the system we inhabit? Can love play a role in resisting instrumentalising forces, or is it simply an invitation to suppress conflict in favour of harmony and acceptance?

Leading

We see leading as a process of mutual influence exercised in human interaction which focuses efforts on realising an intention or outcome. Leadership always involves the exercise of some kind of power. Sometimes the power being exercised draws on formal hierarchical structures and roles: people 'follow' or comply as a result of role expectations. But influence is exercised both by followers over leaders and leaders over followers. Followers offer their trust to those leading in the hope that leaders will represent their perceived interests, values, and ideals. However, if leaders fail in this task, followers may withdraw their trust and followership. If leaders are exercising power through the mechanisms of formal hierarchy, direct reports may comply but may withhold commitment or trust. Social identity theory maintains that followers 'choose' their leaders, selecting those who most closely match the group's prototype of an ideal leader (Hogg et al. 2012). It is worth reiterating at this point that the leaders we interviewed for this book were nominated by their direct reports and/or peers as outstanding leaders who led with love. Taking social identity theory as our reference point, they could therefore be said to represent an ideal leader prototype for those who nominated them.

In recent years, there has been a shift of emphasis from leaders as individuals to *leadership* as a process within which all of us exercise some degree of influence. This reflects an evolution in the understanding of what effective leadership in the twenty-first century might look like. At the end of the twentieth century there was a movement to reject the 'heroic' forms of leadership that attribute leadership to the actions of a single, powerful, and usually charismatic individual. This rejection stems in part from an acknowledgement of the complexity of the leadership process. For example, change within large, global organisations – and the systems within which they are embedded – relies on leadership being distributed widely throughout the system. Leadership emerges as large numbers of people coordinate and construct change both in their actions and in their on-going sense-making. In this view, it is overly simplistic to focus on leaders as individuals; rather, we should be focusing on leadership as a collective property of a group of people within a system. Moreover, an excessive focus on individual leaders 'romanticises' such leaders and grossly exaggerates their impact on organisational outcomes and change processes. Crucially, such romanticisation means that 'concerns relating to power tend to disappear from view, replaced by a focus on the language of "natural" harmony and conciliation' (Collinson et al. 2018: 1,626).

Another reason for rejecting heroic models of leadership relates to the ethical implications of investing so much power in, and attention on, one individual. Following a series of corporate scandals, culminating in the financial crash, those who assume leadership roles in the corporate world are increasingly viewed by the public with disillusionment and scepticism. With senior corporate leaders having benefited disproportionately from the intensifying inequality of the past four decades, there has been a decline in deference and in trust. In the World Economic Forum's *Outlook on the Global Agenda* of 2015, 86% of survey respondents agreed that the world was facing a leadership crisis. Leaders in all spheres were viewed as playing politics and pursuing selfish interests while what was needed was 'a prioritization of social justice and wellbeing over financial growth; empathy; courage; morality; and a collaborative nature' (World Economic Forum 2015; Shahid 2014).

We feel the need to respond to these critiques because our approach is one that explores leadership as something embodied in individuals – but, importantly, individuals who are not detached from context, systems, ideologies, or societal processes. In focusing on individuals in leadership, rather than group processes, we could invite criticism for both romanticising and 'essentialising' leadership, i.e. locating leadership within individuals (and their hearts and bodies) rather than viewing leadership as a process distributed throughout the system.

We are sympathetic to such arguments. Our aim is neither to disregard the forces that instrumentalise people nor to promote an impossible ideal to which individuals should aspire. On the contrary, we believe that those who lead with love can be relatively free from the fear that causes us to tolerate what we know is wrong. While the rise of instrumentalisation, measurement, and performativity in organisations seems relentless, it is our belief that if enough of us change our aware-ness and practices, freeing ourselves from the fear that keeps us compliant, we can effect beneficial change. For us, individual change links to wider systemic change.

Moreover, we have some great examples. The powerful knowledge workers of Google are organising collectively to challenge their senior leaders' policies that sup-port the censored web development in China, which is used to spy on its own citi-zens (Kowitt 2019). Workers at Sports Direct in the United Kingdom successfully drew attention to their predicament, which led to a government investigation into their company's dehumanising practices. It *is* possible to effect change when indi-viduals with shared values come together to exercise collective leadership, and we believe individual change and personal growth play an important role in this process. Some of the most successful movements for social change have been spearheaded by those who led with love – Gandhi and Martin Luther King are just two examples.

And we have our own examples to inspire us. The subjects of our case studies in this book offer genuine real-world instances of leading with love – all within the context of the performativity and the work intensification agenda we have high-lighted. These leaders don't draw attention to themselves and certainly provide no vision statements about leading with love. In fact, you have to be quite humble to lead with love – because you can never 'succeed' at it. You just do it, and in the process you will make mistakes and succumb to the faults that characterise all humanity. But you carry on anyway. Our leaders led with love, on an everyday basis, because, despite their mistakes, they thought it was the right thing to do.

So leading with love is both an individual and a collective choice, and it is a choice that is made within a unique and particular context. Every person is free to exercise kindness in their relationships with others. Admittedly, this is much more difficult when not on the receiving end of kindness, but it is still possible.

We also acknowledge that if leading with love is to be successful on a larger scale, it has to be part of a social movement in management and leadership. This is beyond the scope of this book, although we will allude to it in the concluding chapter. When we acknowledge the power of the forces for instrumentalisation and dehumanisation, we believe it is clear that leading with love can be a unify-ing basis for a collective movement for change. We *all* have to make a stand to reject ineffective and intolerable leadership of our organisations. And, of course, such a movement has to be led – individually and collectively!

Now let us turn to a deeper understanding of what we mean by 'love.'

* * *

A definition of love and the influences we draw upon

In constructing this part of the book's narrative, we needed to find a clear defini-tion of what we meant by 'love' – something we perceive as much as a state of consciousness as an emotion. It was a daunting task. It is a topic that has been addressed by some of the greatest minds throughout human history; philosophical, theological, religious, sociological, and scientific traditions spanning thousands of years have explored the meaning of love (May 2012). What ideas were we going to draw on? How could we write about love without recourse to all the great philosophers, poets, spiritual writers, novelists, and playwrights? We had to narrow down our reference points. We also wanted to draw on some of the world's greatest spiritual wisdom, but this, too, was a daunting task. While Chris is predominantly Christian in his outlook, Karen has recently explored Eastern, particularly Vedic, spiritualities as well as indigenous, shamanic traditions. These influences will be made manifest throughout this work, but we make the disclaimer here that our knowledge of these traditions is limited and we do not pretend to be experts. And it is important to point out that, despite these spiritual influences, we wanted to make our writing accessible to all, regardless of any spiritual, religious, or philosophical position.

On the other hand, any discussion of love had to make sense in the context of the workplace. We wanted to draw on our interviewees' real experience of leading with love and make our definition practical and applicable to working life. We recognised that this was not the place to go into great depth regarding the subtleties, complexities, paradoxes, and arguments concerning love. Readers are referred to the excellent works by Simon May or Thomas Oord if they are interested in pursuing this path.

In our explorations of the writings on love, the definition by Thomas Jay Oord stood out for us as meeting our criteria above: it was rooted in a solid understanding of the philosophical and spiritual literature and yet reflected what both our research and our interviewees revealed. Oord is a theologian, philosopher, and scholar of multidisciplinary studies; his work covers not only philosophy and theology but also social psychology and science, particularly cosmology and biology. In particular, his pragmatism and depth of knowledge in both defining and applying love seemed to provide an excellent starting point for an exploration of leading with love in the workplace. For Oord, as a theologian, love will include the concept of God. He defines love as follows:

> To love is to act intentionally, in sympathetic response to others (including God), to promote overall well-being.
>
> *(Oord 2010: 15)*

We suspect that the most jarring element of this definition will be the reference to God. 'God' can provoke negative emotions and associations. For some, God is represented pictorially as an old white man sitting on a cloud in judgement of the human race. Or possibly God has negative associations with historical Catholicism, such as the Crusades, the Inquisition, or the destruction of indigenous cultures in South America. Other negative associations might be more recent malign aspects of world religions: conflict, terrorism, intolerance, political strife, paedophilia, and the repression of groups such as unmarried mothers or women in general. Put simply, throughout history, God has been appropriated by human beings to promote power and hate – this is undeniable. This is what we term 'God in the image of humankind' – a projection of our dark, shadow side and a tool for power, conquest, and self-enhancement.

However, in the more mystical spiritual traditions, 'love' and 'god'[1] (or the Divine, the Beloved, Great Spirit, Essence, Brahman, the void, superconsciousness) are often interchangeable. Contemporary Christian authors such as Richard Rohr, Matthew Fox, and Cynthia Bourgeault draw on many of the world's mystical and wisdom traditions to explore the notion of 'love as god' while applying it to contemporary political and social issues in a powerful, revolutionary way. For these writers to love god is to love love, to love life – human and the more than human – and to love the planet. This is the mystical (rather than religious) tradition we draw on, which accepts that there is a force (love) that resides within us, between us and beyond us; while some may call this force 'the love of god,' others may see it in terms of the interconnection of all life, the force that permeates all life forms, Great Spirit, divine consciousness, Gaia – or something more scientific such as the quantum field.

The notion that there is a transcendent force that exists to be tapped into for the wellbeing of ourselves, others, and the planet as a whole is common to spiritual and philosophical traditions throughout time and place. Even today, people who deny the existence of 'God' or gods will often say that they sense a force above and beyond what we can know materially. A recent study suggested that between 30% and 75% of people among Western populations report having had a spiritual experience (Tassell-Matamua and Frewin 2019). We will see in Chapter 4 that when people reach higher levels of human development, they become more open to mystery, more aware that there are aspects of life that are beyond the ability of human rationality to fathom. In other words, love is a mysterious force beyond understanding, but which can be experienced and expressed – and many have spoken of this experience throughout time.

Because, for some, the word 'God' represents a barrier, we have made the decision to use a different term. Firstly, we have chosen the word 'divine,' which we feel is more inclusive of a wider range of spiritualities. There are references to the divine in many mystical traditions, and it is a word that includes notions of the Beloved (Sufi), Great Spirit (Shamanism), Brahman (Hinduism), and God (Judaism, Islam, and Christianity). We hope our use of the word 'divine' from this point on will appeal to those who embrace a formal faith or religion without alienating those who do not.

For the agnostic and those without a belief in a higher power, we will add another, more accessible, term: 'the sacred.' *Sacred* means 'set apart' from the materialistic or mundane. When we approach the sacred, we do so with a different state of consciousness: one founded in mystery, majesty, awe, and wonderment – the kind of consciousness that we may experience at the birth of a child, when walking in nature, or when looking up at the night sky to ponder stars, galaxies, and the mystery of the universe.

Finally, we would like to take the liberty of adjusting Oord's definition further by adding a specific focus on individual as well as general wellbeing. This simply reflects the emphasis placed by our interviewees on responding to individual members of their teams, as well as a focus on the general wellbeing of the team and the organisation. For any leader who leads with love, the individual, the other, takes central place in the embodiment of love in action.

This means we end up with the following definition of love:

> To love is to act intentionally, in sympathetic response to others (including the sacred or the divine), to promote individual and overall well-being.

We hope that readers will find this definition acceptable as a starting point.

Perhaps the simplest way to bring this definition to life is via a live example from our research: at one level a simple, very ordinary story, yet quite extraordinary when viewed in the context of one of the most competitive, commercial businesses on the planet, one subject to all the destructive forces we have described above. It is a story that says so much about both the simplicity and the difficulty of leading with love.

> There was a person who has worked for me, I think, oh, probably, five, six, seven years, who had a degenerative disease. And I actually was his local manager. He retired earlier this year. I actually was his local manager, and he had a functional manager in the US. I found him a great coach and mentor to me, even though he worked for me. And I think we had a very good kind of two-way relationship, and it didn't matter who worked for who, we were just kind of like at this point in time you need the help, so I'm coaching you, kind of thing. And you know he came to me one day and kind of told me that he had [a degenerative disease]. And he was relatively young...
>
> So, we then worked together with Occupational Health, on what can we do, you know, to make this as easy as possible for you, and actually, frankly, I mean, keep you working as long as possible, you know, and you know there are kind of benefits to both parties for that. And, yeah, we worked with Occupational Health, who were really good, and put in place some measures. And that worked for a while.
>
> But then, as you know, it's a kind of one-way road. You don't get better. You kind of have periods where it stays flat for a while, stable, and then it kind of gets worse again. And you know, each time it got worse, it was kind of well, you know, let's do something different. And, in the end, he got signed off. And, quite frankly, and very disappointingly, you know, he was off for probably two-and-a-half, three years; his functional manager never spoke him throughout that whole period.
>
> Whereas even though he didn't really work for me, I was just doing his local cardholding stuff, so, kind of pay, salary, bonus, that kind of stuff.

You know, I had a call with him every other week. ... And we met once a quarter. Because he didn't live too far from me, so we used to meet for lunch. Talk about how things were. I'd keep him informed of what was going on at the company.

And he, he then decided to come back. After about two-and-a-half, three years out. And during that time, you know, we'd had some discussions, and he'd say, 'Yeah, I can still add value here.' So, I managed to negotiate, with his functional manager and with HR, that we would come back on a kind of part-time basis, and on a ramp-up programme, which he did very successfully. And then, he got to [the point where he could] access [his] pension pot ...

I think I really did lead with love there, because you know I didn't have to spend that amount of time with him ... but I absolutely believed, and still believe, it was the right thing to do, for everyone. We had him back, adding more value. You know he was able to work to a point where he felt ready to leave, not that he felt forced to go.

Author: **And what is it that makes you do it? You know we all have good intentions, don't we, but you actually did it.**

Yeah. You know, Karen, for me, it comes back to priorities again. If I'm the type of person that prioritises the business above all else, I probably wouldn't have done it, because I'd have been worried about my own numbers ... but again, for me, if you prioritise people and the individual, then that leads you down that path. That's, you know, to me, that was the right thing to do. And I would not have forgiven myself if I hadn't done it.

(Max)

Moving back to our definition, there are four elements to it: firstly, to act intentionally; secondly, in sympathetic response to others; thirdly, responding to the sacred or the divine; and, fourthly, to promote individual and overall wellbeing. We will now look at these one by one.

Acting intentionally

The leader who leads with love *acts* with love. Love is not simply, or even necessarily, an emotion; rather, it is a force that is embodied in action. For a person to act with love, they have to have a clear intention to do so. They also have to have a capacity to see, and in some way to resist, the negative systemic and cultural forces at play in their organisation. This is because love is rarely the instinctive or automatic choice in our behaviour, especially in competitive, pressured environments characterised by the powerful systemic forces we discussed above. If we are not consciously alert, we are very likely to get 'caught' in behaviours that have nothing to do with love, and indeed often embody the opposite. Our awareness therefore needs to be primed to choose the loving action over the predominant self-serving or system-serving one. Keeping an intention in conscious awareness then drives *attention*. This will cause us to notice that we have a choice: there is another way of doing things. At its simplest, it would cause us to ask, 'What would love have me do in this situation?'

Having a clear intention

Having a clear intention implies that the leader has a sense of what they are working towards – that this goal is always positive and, in some way beyond, but not necessarily negating, personal self-interest. Intention drives energy into action. One of the common themes across all the interviewees was some sense of higher purpose, which they held as a conscious intent in their daily leadership.

> [T]o keep returning to yourself, when you can, to your values and what is important to you and how does that fit with what I am doing now.
>
> *(Naomi)*

This is not to imply that leaders who lead with love need to be saints. People who work in leadership and management are often ambitious to further their careers and influence their organisation, and those we interviewed were no exceptions. Indeed, such leaders may be more ambitious as they can conceive a picture of the good they might be able to do in senior positions. However, those who lead with love, while not ignoring their own prospects, will commit to something beyond that: perhaps creating more employment; perhaps taking over a project with positive potential for the company; or perhaps landing a senior management position so they can shift policy in line with their own values. All our interviewees had ambition. What was noticeable was that their ambitions were positive and life-affirming for the whole community.

It is difficult to lead with love if you are fretting over your bonus, stressing over whether you will get a promotion, or being defensive and protective of your patch. Negativity generates stress, which narrows the field of vision; negative leaders become obsessed with threats. Positive, trusting leaders are more open to opportunities, more able to listen to other points of view, and are more creative and innovative because they have an underlying belief or trust that things will generally turn out for the best: our interviewees had a positive outlook on life and a belief that things would be okay regardless of what was thrown at them. They led with a positive intention to change things for the better, for their organisations, for the people who worked there, sometimes for the wider planet, and, of course, for themselves

> So, and that's kind of what drives; that's the motivator: it's what can I do to improve not only the work environment that we're in, of which we spend more time here than we do with our families, but broader than that: how

can we improve society going forward? And that's been a continual learning curve for me.

(Dan)

Minimising being 'caught' by the negative systemic and cultural forces in the organisation

All organisations have shadow sides. There are always undiscussable aspects of
the organisation and its leaders: everyone knows about them, but they usually
dare not say anything to the people responsible; if they do, they are ignored and
often side-lined (viewed as dangerous loose cannons). Many bureaucracies will
be home to a number of socially dominant leaders (we will examine this more
in Chapter 4) scattered throughout the hierarchy, protected by a raft of 'yes men
and women' with the tacit bargain of 'you do as I say without question and I
will protect your job (even promote you) as long as your performance is "good
enough".' This leaves an organisation with a lot of illogicalities, such as: why on
earth did *he* get promoted? Why does no one do anything about her bullying
behaviour? We all know the strategy is wrong: why doesn't anyone say anything?
The biggest problem in our organisation is lack of investment in X: why is this
being ignored? In most corporate scandals and failures, people in the organisation knew the answers to the problems but were ignored by senior leaders;
this is the case, for example, with Nokia, Volkswagen, and Wells Fargo.[2] Even
more worrying is that, in organisations involved in corporate scandals that led to
customers' *deaths*, people knew about problems but were ignored; this includes
Toyota, Ford, Boeing, and GM.[3]

Such illogicalities are endemic in organisations and often emerge from psy-
chodynamic processes: people's need to retain power, to defend against incon-
venient truths, and to be seen to be in charge; fear of difficult information, fear
of threats to their power base, fear of being found to be wrong, and fear of losing
control.

Those who lead with love will minimise their engagement with this negative side and find freedom from such forces – not least because otherwise they
would divert them from their original intentions. But this requires maturity: an
awareness of one's own ego defences and an ability to address them – to be able to
listen to critiques and address problems while managing feelings of vulnerability
in a way that minimises one's own defensiveness. A platform for attaining this is
a basic trust in the world – a belief in yourself and your people. Neil, one of our
interviewees, highlights this very point:

> [I]f you've got the confidence and recognise your own shortcomings and
> being able to ask for help and being able to trust other people to help
> you, and surrounding yourself by brilliant people, because that's one of

the bravest things you have to do, because they might look at you and go, 'How is this fool running the business?'

(Neil)

Secondly, those leading with love will minimise time spent on complaining, criticising, getting angry, or feeling like a victim, knowing that this kind of behaviour only serves to generate negative energy. Despite their organisation's illogicalities, they remain positive – aligned to their intentions. This is not to say they never feel down, depressed, or stressed; rather, they are aware of these feelings and have the resources to manage them or transform them into positive action.

Thirdly, those who lead with love will not get 'caught' by the behaviour of others; they know that they cannot change others, only themselves, and that by spending time blaming and criticising they are not changing anything in the external world but are simply feeding their own negativity. They will be capable of wise acceptance: that there is no point dedicating energy and attention to things they cannot, at this time, affect or change.

In sympathetic response to others

If the action of leaders flows from their clarity of intention, the next question is: what informs and infuses this intention? Our definition proposes two distinct sources: our relationship with others and our relationship with the sacred or divine.

Martin Buber in his renowned book *I and Thou* (2014) reveals an important insight in the opening pages of the first chapter. Every person can have two kinds of relationship to the world: either 'I–thou' or 'I–it.' The 'I–it' relationship is not really a relationship at all, according to Buber; it is more of a fantasy. When we view another person as part of *our* experience, that person becomes simply a phenomenon in our own subjective consciousness. She becomes an object, an 'it.' In becoming that object, the person is reduced to categories in our own minds – categories that reflect our past sense-making which are often dualistic (lazy/hard working; compliant/resistant; competent/incompetent). However, if we embrace the 'I–thou' (or 'I–you') relationship, we see that person as an amazing, unique creation with whom we have a deep shared human connection. Buber describes it thus:

> If I face a human being as my *Thou*, and say the primary word I–thou to him, he is not a thing among things, and does not consist of things … nor is he a nature able to be experienced and described, a loose bundle of named qualities. But with no neighbour, and who in himself, he is *Thou* and *fills the heavens*.
>
> *(Buber 2013, p. 5)*

Clearly, the connection we might develop from an 'I–it' perspective stands in huge contrast to the relationship we develop from an 'I–thou' perspective. For example, one manager on hearing this distinction realised that he tended to view his team members from a 'thou' perspective but viewed contractors as an 'it' – a unit of production that was costing money for every hour they were present.

However, Buber goes further and claims that the 'I' in each case is a different 'I.' The 'I' that views the world from an 'I–it' perspective is a different 'I' from the one that relates to the world and to people from an 'I–thou' perspective. And this is not simply philosophical abstraction; we intuitively know this to be true. The 'I' that we bring to work is perhaps more likely to be an 'I–it' variety, which instrumentalises work colleagues into units necessary to achieve personal objectives, whereas the 'I' that we bring to our homes and families is more likely to be of an 'I–thou' type. All Buber is saying here is something that we all know: that the self we bring to work can be very different from the self we (hopefully) allow ourselves to become among our families and/or friends. We may even go further to suggest that, if we are not careful, the self that we bring to work eventually transplants the self that we bring home and we lose the capacity for any kind of 'I–thou' relationship at all. We all know people who spend their home lives bragging about their achievements, who they know, and their status symbols. These people have very little capacity to listen sympathetically to others, and their very presence tends to trigger a climate of competition and judgement. These people have become objects to themselves – they have allowed the 'I–it' of their work personas to suppress any capacity for love and concern for others, even at home.

To lead with love is to bring the deeper 'I–thou' self to work – the self that is generous, funny, kind, compassionate, wise, and humble. This is the self that values the other, does not instrumentalise him, sees him as a unique, if flawed, human being, with a family who love him and may be dependent upon him. The leader who leads with love takes great interest in her people and, as per Buber's insight, does not diminish them into a pile of useful competencies but sees them as whole human beings – with strengths and weaknesses; hopes, dreams, and disappointments; and needs and values – and treats them fairly and with respect. Most of all, a leader who loves 'relates' to her people, responding to their needs in their various stages of life and showing kindness and compassion as well as firmness and fairness, as and when needed. We are not establishing an impossible and naïve ideal here; we know that people *do* lead like this at work and that colleagues and team members respond extremely well to this kind of leadership. We are asking rather that we challenge ourselves by questioning if our leadership style is just an expression of our egoic needs (for profit, power, pleasure, and prestige) or whether we have the courage to lead according to deeper personal values. Do we and can we lead according to humanistic principles that generate trust, commitment, loyalty, and cooperation while placing real value on our environment, our communities, and our planet? And the benefit for us in adopting this approach is that we are free from striving, fear, and self-judgement.

Responding to the sacred or the divine

In Chapter 1 we proposed that without some sense of a sacred, purpose-giving force in life – whether this is a dedication to the needs of the planet, future generations, or an openness to the divine, God or Mystery – it is more difficult to lead with love. This is because without a sense of there being a higher, sacred element to life it is easy to fall into the default position in Western, materialist society of seeing life in terms of a social Darwinist competition in which individuals are set against one another in a survival-of-the-fittest game of one-upmanship. As the car bumper sticker has it: 'He who dies with the most toys wins.' In the social Darwinist world view, everything, including rainforests, the virgin tundra of the Arctic, all non-human species, indigenous peoples, the poor and less powerful, all are 'commodities' to be exploited in the race to the top. Embracing a transcendent view of life, on the other hand, enables us to see some elements of life as 'sacred' or 'set apart.' What we regard as sacred we *set apart* from the material, mundane world that we typically instrumentalise in order to meet our needs, and we treat as holy, to be revered. If nothing is sacred in our lives, we will tend to view everything and everyone as an object to meet our own needs.

Michael Sandel, the renowned Harvard philosopher, has written a remarkable and horrifying book showing how Western capitalist society (now a global phenomenon) has lost its sense of the sacred. Everything is marketised, including human beings, and when something 'sacred' is marketised, both the object and the society or community involved in this marketisation are corrupted and instrumentalised. He shows quite clearly through both argument and example how:

> [w]hen we decide that certain goods may be bought and sold, we decide, at least implicitly, that it is appropriate to treat them as commodities, as instruments of profit and use. But not all goods are properly valued in this way.
>
> *(Sandel 2013: 9)*

He cites slavery as an example of treating human beings as commodities rather than valuing them 'as persons worthy of dignity and respect, rather than as instruments of gain and objects of use' (Sandel 2013: 10). While the institution, if not the practice, of slavery has been abolished, there are other subtle forms of enslavement to the market. For example, there is a market in human kidneys; you can Google this to find out for yourselves. In 2011, a 17-year-old boy sold one of his kidneys for just over $3,000 in order to buy an iPad. You might think that there is nothing wrong with this: a kidney is a product with a value, so why should we not be allowed to sell it? Sandel is very clear on this point. He claims that marketisation of kidneys has a corrupting influence on society and that this occurs in two ways. Firstly, those who choose to sell their kidneys are those with impoverished life choices – the poor. If all things were equal, and these people had access to a comfortable lifestyle, they would probably not choose to sell their kidneys. The 'choice' is actually forced upon them. Secondly, the very process of selling kidneys, or livers, commodifies human beings, changing how we view people. Slowly but surely, we begin to see others as potential sources of spare parts. Indeed, Sandel quotes US Judge Richard Posner as suggesting that babies available for adoption should be auctioned and sold off to the highest bidder so that younger, healthier, more beneficially genetically endowed babies would go to the rich while older, more vulnerable, less-in-demand babies would go to the poor. What is wrong with this? It seems a logical approach as the adoption agencies would be able to raise more money in order to help more people. But something tells us, some inner instinct or moral reflex, that there are certain things money should not be able to buy and that clearly includes human beings. But if we are not careful, this inner instinct or moral reflex will atrophy and marketisation will corrupt our sense of what it means to be human. We will lose our notion of the sacred.

So where do we go in search of the sacred? Different people will of course have different answers to this, but it is important to be able to access the sacred to provide some kind of access to a non-materialist consciousness. The material-istic consciousness is driven by self-interest, whereas the sacred consciousness is driven by self-transcendence. When we access the self-transcendent conscious-ness, we are more likely to know what it is to engage in life with a sense of awe, mystery, and wonder.

Some people may access the sacred through religion or through their spiritual practices. A couple of our interviewees, for example, brought their faith directly into their leadership.

For those to whom the sacred does involve God or the divine, we should note that all the major religions in the world today highlight the importance of love. In the Christian tradition the word used by Christ for love is 'agape,' which is distinguished from eros (romantic love), storge (familial love), and philia (broth-erly/sisterly love as between close friends and companions). Agape is a form of sacrificial love which Jesus refers to when communicating the two greatest commandments: 'Love the Lord your God with all your heart and with all your soul and with all your mind ... and love your neighbour as yourself.' Agape love is manifested when we act to promote the flourishing of all human beings, as well as non-human species and the planet. In Buddhism and Hinduism there is kama, or sensual love, which is distinguished from prem in Hinduism, elevated love, and the four elements of true love in Buddhism, which are *maitri*, or lov-ing kindness (the intention and capacity to offer joy and happiness); *karuna*, or compassion (the intention and capacity to relieve and transform suffering and lighten sorrows); *mudita*, or joy (bringing joy to ourselves and to the ones we love); and *upeksha*, or equanimity (non-attachment, non-discrimination, even-mindedness, or letting go) (Thich Nhat Hanh 2014). In Islam, 'compassion' is the most frequently occurring word in the Qur'an. Each of its 114 chapters, with the exception of the ninth, begins with the invocation 'In the name of God, the Compassionate, the Merciful...' (Ingram 2016); and Sufism puts the love of God ('The Beloved') as its core practice – as do contemplative Christianity and the Bhakti tradition of yoga. Christianity, Hinduism, and Sufism in fact directly equate God with love. In the Bible, 1 John 4:7 states:

Dear friends, let us love one another, for love comes from God. Everyone who loves has been born of God and knows God.

To love truly is to empty oneself of egoic neediness and to make oneself available as a channel of love in this world.

Clearly, in this book, we are not referring to romantic love nor familial love; we are turning our attention towards the 'higher' love described in these various spiritual traditions. This is love as a spiritual force capable of transforming the world for the better. In this view, love is not something we have to drum up for ourselves, but rather we seek to be a channel for it. This is love not as a warm emotion but as a higher state of consciousness, and much spiritual teaching is about developing higher states of consciousness to make us more capable of being a channel for love.

But we do not need to believe in God or a creative force to view human life as sacred, i.e. 'set apart' from the marketplace in terms of its profound spiritual value. A sense of the sacred might emanate from a profound commitment to humanist values just as much as from a belief in a creative force that seeded all life. Most of us would consider a society that treats human life as sacred to be highly developed, whereas a society that views human life as an object, to be utilised in whatever project the powerful deem necessary, would be viewed as primitive, dangerous, and evil.

For many, the sacred includes all forms of life on the planet, the planet itself, and the cosmos beyond. In researching what Americans mean by 'spirituality,' Ammerman identified four kinds of spirituality: a theistic spirituality tied to personal deities; an extra-theistic spirituality locating spirituality in various naturalistic forms of transcendence; an ethical spirituality focusing on everyday compassion; and a contested belief and belonging spirituality tied to cultural notions of religiosity (Ammerman 2013: 258). Ammerman relates how those drawing on extra-theistic spirituality

> speak of spirituality in terms of a different kind of transcendence, of experiences 'bigger than me' and beyond the ordinary. Here spirituality is located in the core of the self, in connection to community, in the sense of awe engendered by the natural world and various forms of beauty, and in the life philosophies crafted by an individual seeking life's meaning.'
> *(Ammerman 2013: 268)*

Spirituality in this view entails identifying the sacred in life, and the sacred is what is experienced in community, in awe, in the natural world and beauty, and in what engenders meaning. For example, viewing non-human species as sacred involves developing a profound relationship with nature such that every human being *wants* to prevent species extinction. This is a point argued by eco-psychologists, who see our current relationship with nature not only as damaging to our planet but also damaging to ourselves. We are meant to be in profound and loving relationship with nature; when we are not, *we* suffer – mentally, emotionally, and spiritually. This point has been embraced by poets and artists throughout human history who have shared their insights in order to stir in us a sense of wonder and awe of nature, an awe that today is increasingly rare and diminished.

Another example of how our consciousness can shift when faced with the sacred or transcendent is the 'overview effect.' Astronauts who have had the privilege of seeing Earth from the vantage point of space report a shift in consciousness. On viewing our planet remotely as a sphere suspended in the cosmos, they experience a sense of unitive connection to the whole of the human race; what was previously 'us and them' suddenly becomes just 'us.' The experience provokes a wonder and awe of the grace of human existence and the planet we inhabit – a sense of the oneness of life and the interconnectedness of all beings. Earth is seen as a tiny, fragile ball of life hanging in the cosmos, and the human race is a tiny, fragile species invested with the awesome responsibility of keeping this beautiful phenomenon alive and thriving. This shift of consciousness is not simply an interesting insight; it is transformative: friends and family of those affected have noted a profound change in behaviour. The description of the overview effect recalls descriptions of enlightenment as described by Eastern religions and the mystical union with God as described by the Christian mystics.[4] Common to all is an experience of oneness with the cosmos, with the divine and with all life: what is known as a unitive experience.

Promoting individual and overall wellbeing

The final aspect of the definition is the focus or goal of love: the promotion of individual and overall wellbeing – the human, social and planetary good that is the outcome of love's action.

It is difficult to focus on the promotion of individual and overall wellbeing when you are living a life dedicated to survival in our performative workplaces. Here are the reflections of a self-confessed workaholic American female executive after she was laid off from a job which, according to her, was the centre of her being.

> I became deeply aware of the thoughts running around in my head. I started to tune into the messages that I was telling myself, especially the ones urging me to keep going *no matter what*, that there was no slowing down, no Off switch, that saying No was for sissies or wimps or people who didn't 'get' it, that there was no space reserved for me, my needs. No time for the dentist! Damn the torpedoes! Full steam ahead with that PowerPoint!
>
> I realized that, while I had been working so feverishly on all fronts, I was actually running away from – ugh – another terrible confession: low self-worth. I had papered over feelings of not being good enough, smart enough, loveable enough, by doing more, going all out, being friendlier, more helpful-ier, competing in a fantasy game of one-upmanship of people-pleasing.
>
> *(Alexander 2019)*

Note how this successful executive, currently an editor of an online magazine, despite the seniority of her role before being laid off, admitted that she only felt good enough 'by competing in a fantasy game of one-upmanship': the hallmarks of a culture influenced by social Darwinism. The 'I–it' leader's self-esteem is always conditional on others' recognition of her performance. This is a loser's game: constantly seeking reassurance from people with whom you admit you are in competition or who give and withhold their approval in order to manipulate you in a game you will never win.

The 'I–thou' leader learns not to fall into this trap – through processes such as meditation, self-compassion, letting go of material ambition, and dedication to something much more significant. Similarly, the 'I–thou' leader learns to remain in the present (not to catastrophise about the future or to wallow in the shame and regret of the past); she learns to accept the situation as it currently stands, realising that no amount of worrying will change it; she does not pass fear and stress down and around the organisation and hence develops a loyal following; she does her best, realising that this is all that can be expected of her; she has a positive vision of the future which energises her and helps her to make good decisions. Ultimately, of course, the 'I–thou' leader works for a higher purpose – whatever that might be. It could be to provide secure jobs for employees (this is part of what motivated our entrepreneurs); it could be the belief that the work undertaken will benefit society (which is what motivated our leaders who worked for charities); it could be a desire to promote equality and fairness in the organisation (a motivator for two of our interviewees who worked in large corporates). Whatever the motivator, none of our interviewees worked solely for the money, status, power, or any other egoic needs. They all had clearly articulated values that they felt passionate about (in fact, that was the most popular theme in the interviews) and which prompted them to work for something higher than their own self-interest.

* * *

So applying our definitions to the practical day-to-day world of leading in organisations, in what way can we say that our interviewees led with love?.

Firstly, our interviewees all led within a specified organisational role. They occupied senior roles in organisations, but they exercised influence with care and concern for the people they were leading and did not treat them as objects in their own campaigns for personal success. This does not mean that they shirked the difficult conversations or avoided confronting poor performance. This will become clear as you read through the book. They led others with care and concern; they stood firm on their values and were also highly successful in delivering great performance.

> [I had] one particular boss saying 'you're too soft on the guys' ... you know, and then going through a salary increase plan, and he went, 'Oh, we're just going to like give everyone this percentage, trim everyone on this percentage.' And me going, 'No, we're not; there are some people who

do not deserve a pay rise and they're not getting a pay rise in my department, and there are some people who deserve far more than the average and they're getting it, and that's going to take some time and effort, and that's going to get some good conversations, but I'm going to have those, because that is how, that's doing it right and being fair to the people, again not necessarily equal to the people, but fair to the people.' And at the end of the day the results were delivered.

(Naomi)

Secondly, they had clear intentions that drove their leadership style. All were in tune with their values around how to treat people and could clearly articulate the people-based ideals behind what informed their leadership style. Our leaders were also ambitious and had clear intentions around achieving success in their organisations.

I had to just say to myself, 'Well I'm going to do the best I can, I'm going to stay true to my values, you know, maybe I need to be more self-aware and maybe there are some things I need to improve, maybe there're some skills I need to develop, but I can keep doing what I'm doing and performing and bringing my team along with me.'

(Ann)

Thirdly, they led in sympathetic response to others. They built relationships of trust and dedicated their efforts to understand the people they led and what motivated them. They knew the backgrounds of their people, when they were struggling and when they needed support. They were great coaches and mentors and wanted to develop their people as much as their people wanted to be developed. They knew when to challenge and when to support, and they also knew when to challenge upwards in defence of what they considered to be right.

[W]e can't be machines and simply just keep banging a drum to demand more and more from people. But maybe ultimately the outcome [is] where we do more with less. But that's no good if the individual gets lost ... the individuals aren't binary objects: they are people with beating hearts and souls, as we talked about earlier, that need love and attention.

(Dan)

Fourthly, they had some notion of the sacred, although many would not have used this word! They had clear boundaries around what was ethical and what was not, and, in many cases, they took risks to establish and hold to those boundaries. Some had a faith which they drew on when faced with difficult decisions. For these, their faith was also a source of both comfort and clarity. Others had no faith but, interestingly, were open to the mystery and awe of life. They often had a sense of something bigger in life and would refer to spiritual ideas such as karma or loving one's neighbour. Our interviewees often felt that leadership was something that was entrusted to them and they accepted this trust with great reverence and respect.

> So, you know, I guess to use a biblical analogy of Peter sort of standing in the water and as his faith goes he sinks. And I identify with that really strongly because, as you lose self-confidence, as you lose sight of your own values and then you start to chastise yourself before stepping away from your values, you know it is a self-fulfilling and discrediting action that you perform on yourself and therefore quite important to keep returning yourself, when you can, to your values and what is important to you and how does that fit with what I am doing now. But also to have others around you to challenge you and to be aware of how you behave and how this comes about.
>
> *(Matthew)*

> Because it's all about what you give back to people, you know, and what you give back is what you're going to, it's kind of like your business karma in a way.
>
> *(Ann)*

Finally, they led in order to promote individual and overall wellbeing. We hope this is clear from what has been said so far, but it will become even clearer as we go through the book. For now, we finish with a quote from Max:

> If I can make it a more diverse and inclusive environment for them, then I've done something; I've done something quite major, if you can, you know, if you can really make it successful. You can't do it on your own; it's a whole cultural thing. But you know that's a big motivator for me at the moment.
>
> *(Max)*

Notes

1 We use the lower case when referring to god in order to differentiate god as the force of love from the Western and Middle Eastern concept of God the Judge, which has been used to control, kill, exploit, and dominate.
2 For Nokia, see O'Brien (2010); for Volkswagen, see Smith and Parloff (2016); for Wells Fargo, see Wikipedia: https://en.wikipedia.org/wiki/Wells_Fargo_account_fraud_scandal.
3 For Toyota, see Taylor (2010); for Ford, see Hosken and Knowler (2017); for GM, see Foroohar (2014); for Boeing, see Yglesias (2019).
4 See, for example, *The Upanishads* by Swami Paramananda; it contains the Isa, Kena, Katha, and Mundaka Upanishads with a commentary and is freely available on the internet (for example, https://www.gutenberg.org/ebooks/3283 [accessed 21 July 2020]). A more modern and accessible description of enlightenment is by Ramana Maharshi, the great Indian saint and guru, available at: https://enlightened-people.com/ramana-maharshis-enlightenment-story_(accessed 21 July 2020). For

Christian descriptions of mystical experience, readers are directed to Teresa of Ávila, *The Interior Castle* (1577), Julian of Norwich, *Revelations of Divine Love* (fourteenth or fifteenth century) and *The Cloud of Unknowing* (unknown author, fourteenth century).

References

Alexander, A. (2019) The embarrassing truth of self-care. *Mindful*, 13 February 2019. https://www.mindful.org/the-embarrassing-truth-of-self-care (accessed 21 July 2020).

Ammerman, N.T. (2013) Spiritual but not religious? Beyond binary choices in the study of religion. *Journal for the Scientific Study of Religion*, 52(2), 258–78.

Buber, M. (2014) *I and Thou*. London: Bloomsbury Academic.

Collinson, D., Jones, O.S. and Grint, K. (2018) "No More Heroes": Critical perspectives on leadership romanticism. *Organization Studies*, 39(11), 625–47.

Foroohar, R. (2014) Here's who is really to blame for the epic GM scandal. *Time*, 2 April 2014. http://time.com/46860/gm-scandal-blame/ (accessed 12 June 2019).

Hogg, M.A., van Knippenberg, D. and Rast, D.E. (2012) The social identity theory of leadership: Theoretical origins, research findings, and conceptual developments. *European Review of Social Psychology*, 23, 258–304.

Hosken, G. and Knowler, W. (2017) Insurers confirm they had warned Ford about flammable Kugas. *Business Day*, 16 January 2017. https://www.businesslive.co.za/bd /companies/transport-and-tourism/2017-01-16-insurers-confirm-they-had-warned -ford-about-flammable-kugas/ (accessed 12 June 2019).

Ingram, P.O. (2016) *You Have Been Told What Is Good: Interreligious Dialogue and Climate Change*. Eugene, OR: Cascade Books.

Kowitt, B. (2019) Google's civil war. *Fortune*, European Edition, 6 (June 2019), 30–39.

May, S. (2012) *Love: A History*. New Haven, CT: Yale University Press.

O'Brien, K.J. (2010) Nokia's new chief faces culture of complacency. *New York Times*, 27 September 2010. http://www.nytimes.com/2010/09/27/technology/27nokia .html (accessed 24 September 2011).

Oord, T.J. (2010) *Defining Love: A Philosophical, Scientific, and Theological Engagement*. Grand Rapids, MI: Brazos Press.

Sandel, M. (2013) *What Money Can't Buy: The Moral Limits of Markets*. New York: Farrar Straus Giroux.

Shahid, S. (2014) Why the world in 2015 faces a leadership crisis. *World Economic Forum*, 7 November 2014. https://www.weforum.org/agenda/2014/11/world-2015-faces -leadership-crisis (accessed 2 April 2019).

Smith, J. and Parloff, R. (2016) HoaxWagen. *Fortune*, 7 March 2016. https://fortune.com /longform/inside-volkswagen-emissions-scandal (accessed 12 June 2019).

Tassell-Matamua, N.A. and Frewin, K.E. (2019) Psycho-spiritual transformation after an exceptional human experience. *Journal of Spirituality in Mental Health*, 21(4), 237–58.

Taylor, A. (2010) How Toyota lost its way. *Fortune*, 12 July 2010. Full version: http:// archive.fortune.com/2010/07/12/news/international/toyota_recall_crisis_full_ version.fortune.index.htm?postversion=2010071204 (accessed 12 June 2019).

Thich Nhat Hanh (2014) *How to Love*. Berkley, CA: Parallax Press.

'Wells Fargo' (2020). *Wikipedia*. https://en.wikipedia.org/wiki/Wells_Fargo_account _fraud_scandal

World Economic Forum (2015) Lack of leadership. In *Outlook on the Global Agenda*. http://reports.weforum.org/outlook-global-agenda-2015/top-10-trends-of-2015/3 -lack-of-leadership (accessed 2 April 2019).

Yglesias, M. (2019) Boeing: The emerging 737 Max scandal, explained: It's more than bad software. *Vox*, 29 March 2019. https://www.vox.com/business-and-finance /2019/3/29/18281270/737-max-faa-scandal-explained (accessed 25 January 2020).

3

HOW TO INSTRUMENTALISE A SOUL

Before we move on to explore leading with love as an important response to the challenges of our time, we will use the next two chapters to explore in more detail some of the forces that we are up against. The most fundamental of these is the tendency to instrumentalise people, a trend that reaches back into the history of capitalism but is increasingly being exacerbated by modern technology.

In 1842, a UK government investigation into the employment of children in the coal mines interviewed a manager concerning the option of using horses instead of children in the mines. He replied: 'Horses are not so handy as Christians, and we could not do with them' (East-Durham.co.uk).

Over 100 years later, F.W. Taylor, the so-called father of scientific management wrote: 'Now one of the very first requirements for a man who is fit to handle pig iron as a regular occupation is that he shall be so stupid and so phlegmatic that he more nearly resembles in his mental make-up the ox than any other type' (Taylor 1911).

Just over 100 years after this was written, the UK government investigation of employment practices at Sports Direct quoted Steve Turner, the Assistant General Secretary of the Union Unite:

> There is a contempt for employee rights. I do not think it is a lack of understanding, and I do not think it is an issue that they necessarily think is relevant. When you employ people on the sorts of contracts that they are employed on you find yourself viewing the human being as a disposable asset.
>
> *(House of Commons Business, Innovation and Skills Committee 2016)*

Business has always employed people as a means of making profit and has continuously been exploring how to do this with the most efficiency. For owners and managers within business, and latterly within the public and not-for-profit sectors, labour is a cost that must be minimised without jeopardising the productivity that can be gained from it. This chapter explores the moral implications of this process: the constant drive to pay the minimum, and in some cases a mere subsistence wage, and yet extract the maximum possible amount of labour. We will firstly look at the current ideological underpinnings of this instrumentalisation, focusing specifically on neoliberalism – a set of values and beliefs that reaches back into the very origins of capitalism. We will then explore the mechanisms of instrumentalisation: how do organisations objectify us, and why are these methods so powerful?

Neoliberalism: an ideological basis for instrumentalisation

In 2016, the UK government produced a report into working practices at Sports Direct (SD), a retail outlet offering a range of low-cost sports equipment and apparel. SD operates a number of warehouses across the United Kingdom where people are employed to service the online and high-street businesses. The report highlighted a number of poor working practices but also made a more general point:

> The way the business model at Sports Direct is operated, in both the warehouse at Shirebrook and in the shops across the country, involves treating workers as commodities rather than as human beings with rights, responsibilities and aspirations. The low-cost products for customers, and the profits generated for the shareholders, come at the cost of maintaining contractual terms and working conditions which fall way below acceptable standards in a modern, civilised economy. There is a risk that this model – which has proved successful for Mr Ashley – will become the norm.
>
> *(House of Commons Business, Innovation and*
> *Skills Committee 2016: 12)*

The business model that we will explore here has emerged from a paradigm or world view that has been so thoroughly and cleverly inculcated into us that the vast majority of us believe it simply to be 'true.' If you ask people working in business to identify the obligations management hold towards their shareholders, many will say 'to maximise shareholder value.' Should you reply that nowhere in the law does it state that it is the legal obligation of management to maximise shareholder value and that this notion is a fallacy, you will be met not just with disbelief but possibly even aggression. It is as if this mantra has become part of their identity. In fact, in the United Kingdom, the law states that managers are entrusted with the long-term success of the company. According to section 172 of the Companies Act 2006:

A director of a company must act in the way he considers, in good faith, would be most likely to promote the success of the company for the benefit of its members as a whole, and in doing so have regard (amongst other matters) to —

a)   the likely consequences of any decision in the long term
b)   the interests of the company's employees
c)   the need to foster the company's business relationships with suppliers, customers and others
d)   the impact of the company's operations on the community and the environment
e)   the desirability of the company maintaining a reputation for high standards of business conduct, and
f)   the need to act fairly as between members of the company.

So why do so many of us blithely believe that the role of business is to maximise shareholder value? How did this paradigm and its assumptions about the role of business in society, and its relations with its employees, gain such currency?

Many valid reasons can be offered to explain this recent preoccupation with maximisation of short-term profit: globalisation and hyper-competition; the process of financialisation, whereby businesses become abstractions traded on stock exchanges in microseconds by algorithms focused on share price; the exponential speed of change and technological innovation with a concomitant emphasis on short-term decision-making; even human greed (see e.g. Harvey 2007; Friedman 2006).

As we saw in the quotes that opened this chapter, the focus on profit maximisation can be traced to the very origins of capitalism. But this does not explain the recent resurgence and intensification of value extraction in the context of late-twentieth-century capitalism, sometimes referred to as neoliberalism. According to the influential political economist David Harvey, Distinguished Professor of Anthropology at the Graduate Center of the City University of New York, the current neoliberal ideology was deliberately cultivated and promoted in an effort to increase the power of business over labour and government (Harvey 2007).

As Harvey recounts, a small but highly influential group of economists, academics, intellectuals, and business leaders, among them Milton Friedman and Friedrich Hayek, came together in 1947 with an explicit agenda to increase the power of business vis-à-vis government and the trade union movement. Calling themselves the Mont Pelerin Society,[1] their purpose was to promote the values of free trade, small government, individualism, and the freedom of companies to pursue the maximisation of profit without interference from the state or from interest groups, such as trade unions, who might seek to regulate and constrain managerial prerogative. The group's long-term vision, Harvey explains, was to spread their values and ideals throughout Western society so that free trade, minimal government intervention, individualism, and free competition would become the norm. This would take at least one generation to achieve, if not two, as the post-Second World War mindset in the West was firmly rooted in welfarism, Keynesianism, and state intervention. Nevertheless, the plan to embed the neoliberal world view into the psyches of political and business leaders, as well as those of the general populace, was pursued with determination, skill, and intelligence. The Mont Pelerin Society attracted powerful support from corporate leaders and other wealthy patrons who could afford to finance think tanks such as the Institute of Economic Affairs in London and the Heritage Foundation in Washington.

It was during the 1970s, in the context of industrial decline in the West, that neoliberal ideology began to gain traction among political leaders, economists, and mainstream academia, in the latter especially after Hayek and Friedman were both awarded Nobel Prizes for economics. Friedman was particularly visible in the media; in his famous *New York Times* article of 1970, 'The Social Responsibility of Business is to Increase its Profits,' he maintained that 'there is one and only one social responsibility of business – to use its resources and engage in activities designed to increase its profits'; to do otherwise by taking on additional responsibilities in relation to the environment or social justice was 'preaching pure and unadulterated socialism' (Friedman, 1970). According to Friedman, '[b]usinessmen who talk this way are unwitting puppets of the intellectual forces that have been undermining the basis of a free society these past decades' (ibid). An outcome of the neoliberal obsession with increasing profits for shareholders – and their growing distrust of managers whose decisions might be motivated by criteria other than profit maximisation – was what is known as 'agency theory.'

In 2005, Sumantra Ghoshal, Professor of Strategic and International Management at the London Business School, wrote an article on neoliberal philosophy's influence on business practice and teaching. Here, he described how agency theory had emerged from a growing suspicion in academic and intellectual circles that corporate managers could not be trusted to pursue the interests of shareholders – interests that were invariably defined as the maximisation of shareholder value. To address this problem, agency theory proposed that managers' interests and incentives should be aligned with those of shareholders by means of stock options and bonuses that reflected increases in the share price. The attraction of this in practical terms for business managers and corporate leaders cannot be overemphasised. With agency theory – and a new language of 'golden handcuffs,' 'golden hellos,' stock options, and performance-related bonuses – came an explosion in executive pay and a new phenomenon whereby wealth became concentrated in the hands of the top 1% (with inconceivable amounts accruing to the top 0.1%). There was now a powerful, rich, global elite whose interests were firmly yoked to the neoliberal credo of maximisation of shareholder value; the further this became normalised, the richer they became, funnelling off the lion's share of corporate profit and national wealth.

It took half a century to embed the notion into the majority of minds across the world, in developed and developing nations alike, that it is the legal responsibility of businesses to maximise shareholder value. It is not.[2] Their legal responsibility is simply to look after the interests of shareholders; however, that may be viewed. Some may make the point that shareholders mainly comprise pension funds; hence, the benefits are spread among working people across the whole of society. However, private pension funding is becoming the norm, and this benefits top earners far more than those on lower incomes and in fact exacerbates inequality (Goudsward et al. 2012). Moreover, those working in the gig economy, those on low incomes, and the young (who are spending disproportionate amounts of their income on rent, mortgage, and university loans) have little or no access to pensions. Pension fund growth mostly benefits the rich: those who have really benefited from pension fund growth are the top 0.1% – corporate executives and their servants (top lawyers, accountants, professional services providers, financial advisors) and those working at the top of finance (bankers, hedge fund managers, and pension fund managers), i.e. all those who benefit from income based on share options or whose personal wealth is heavily based on the ownership of shares.

The implications of this for labour practices are clear: if it is the role of business to maximise share price, then its goal must be to maximise the productivity of its human capital or, to put it more literally, to utilise human beings so that maximum labour is extracted from them at the minimum possible cost. So exactly how is this being done?

How to instrumentalise a person

In order to maximise the productivity of human beings, you need to control them. Since the beginning of the twentieth century, with the widespread use of the assembly line and time and motion studies, we have refined the technology of worker control to such an extent that we can now control an employee's hand movements, use technology to assess the tone of their voice, and continuously monitor their brainwaves. To add to this, we have a range of psychological, social, and economic tools to control employees' lives 24/7. We will see how these methods are being applied in the twenty-first century as instrumentalising working practices by a range of organisations and governments.

We have clustered the practices into six main methods and will use examples to illustrate how these methods are used on the job to control people and maximise their productivity:

1. dehumanising targets and excessive work demands
2. fear and punishment
3. electronic surveillance
4. abuse of power to degrade and humiliate
5. generating financial insecurity
6. denying what it means to be human

1. Dehumanising targets and excessive work demands

Warehousing is big business in the internet age. The general warehousing and storage market is expected to reach a value of nearly $300 billion by 2022 (Business Research Company 2020). There is 2.1 billion square feet of warehousing in the United Kingdom alone (Pool 2017), and in 2016 more than a quarter of this was taken up by Amazon (Bury 2016).

The business of warehousing involves the receipt and storage of items for the purposes of later distribution to either retail or wholesale customers. The efficiency of a warehouse is in part measured by how quickly an item can be stored, located, and distributed to a customer once an order has been received, and warehouse staff are measured according to how many items they can 'pick' (locate and deliver to the correct distribution station) within a particular time frame. By means of wearable technology, warehouse workers' movements can be traced constantly and the time it takes to locate and deliver an order is therefore determined with precision. According to one Sports Direct employee:

> [Y]our pick was timed to the second. If your pick was late you got a strike [six strikes meant you were sacked]. But when the aisles are full of other pickers, this is impossible to meet.
>
> *(House of Commons Business, Innovation and*
> *Skills Committee 2016: 8)*

Alan Selby, an undercover reporter, worked at Amazon's Tilbury warehouse in the United Kingdom and was tasked with picking 300 items per hour. He wrote:

> Whatever the hour thousands of workers are racing to hit goals set by computers monitoring their every move. In my five weeks I saw staff struggling to meet impossible targets, in constant fear of the sack.
>
> *(Selby 2017)*

Picking rates are constantly monitored, and workers receive real-time feedback via their wearable devices. According to the author James Bloodworth, who also worked undercover at an Amazon warehouse, a worker would soon be made aware that his or her picking rates were not meeting the target. At the end of each day, all workers were ranked from highest to lowest and the worst performers were either sacked or warned of imminent sacking should their performance not improve. This cultivated a climate of fear and constant anxiety (Bloodworth 2019: 16). Workers walk around ten miles a day on average to pick their items, and the warehouses are so large that to access a water dispenser or a toilet is to risk a penalty for missing targets.

According to Selby, Amazon treats its workers as 'expendable commodities':

> At every turn it felt like the human staff were reduced to livestock, existing only to service the machines. The repetitive, monotonous work at its

ironically named 'fulfilment centre' did me no favours mentally, either. In the early weeks I was depressed, until my brain switched off.

(Selby 2017)

The increase in work intensification affects many other sections of society too. Carter and his colleagues studied clerical workers in a UK government processing centre; they described how skilled workers

> had that knowledge appropriated, codified and transformed by management into fragmented measurable tasks. ... The outcome was a production environment dominated by hourly targets for each task, ranging from six items an hour for tax letters to 80 for opening cases. Compounding the loss of professional judgement was the prominent display on whiteboards of team and individual progress against hourly targets, with demonstrative underperformance likely to lead to corrective and even disciplinary action in cases of recidivism.
>
> *(Carter et al. 2013: 752)*

Research conducted in the United Kingdom in 2017 showed how doctors in general practice were

> under intense and historically unprecedented pressures. ... Many reported that being a full-time GP was too stressful: work-related stress led to mood changes, sleep disruption, increases in anxiety, and tensions with loved ones. Some had subsequently sought ways to downsize their clinical workload. Workplace change resulted in little time for the things that helped GP resilience: a good work–life balance and better contact with colleagues.
>
> *(Cheshire et al. 2017: 428)*

Jeffrey Pfeffer, in his fascinating but horrifying book *Dying for a Paycheck* (2018), shows how the workplace is a major cause of stress. Workplace stress has been shown to cause employee illness and even death. His research directly linked job stress to 120,000 unnecessary deaths per year in the United States, a figure he believes to be an underestimate. According to an article in *China Daily* (2016), over 600,000 Chinese workers die from overwork a year; in 2006, the *China Labour Bulletin* (CLB) set that figure at over 1 million. The *CLB* site (*China Labour Bulletin* 2006) lists some of the tragic cases of young people (aged 23–35) dying of overwork, many simply collapsing from exhaustion after working 14–15 hours a day and never regaining consciousness. Chinese companies' view of workers as expendable commodities for the maximisation of profit is evidenced by the fact that China has now overtaken Japan for the number of people dying of overwork.

The issue of excessive work demands is explored in depth by Pfeffer, who offers comprehensive statistics, coupled with the human stories that underlie them, that reveal how excessive targets combine with constant measurement to form a powerful source of stress in the workplace. According to Pfeffer, 'People feel that they are always being assessed and evaluated, and if they even temporarily don't perform as well as expected, they will be dismissed' (Pfeffer 2018: 68). The constant measurement and assessment causes people to objectify themselves. Pfeffer's human stories tell of people working excessive hours in response to a feeling that they are only as good as their last measurement: mothers returning to work two days after giving birth; lawyers engaging in drug and alcohol abuse to fuel a punishing work schedule; and highly paid executives being glued to their devices at night, at weekends, and on holiday just to ensure they do not fall behind. One of the causes of such self-objectifying behaviour is fear.

2. Fear and punishment

Fear seems to be a constant companion for those working in highly monitored, target-driven environments. This is the case for skilled white-collar workers as much as the unskilled. A famous *New York Times* article (Kantor and Streitfield 2015) interviewed Amazon white-collar employees, some who had left and some still working for the company. It is a fascinating and shocking read and raised a deal of controversy, with Amazon CEO Jeff Bezos coming forward to defend his workplace culture and leadership principles. According to the article, Bezos created a culture that deliberately uses fear, competition, and Darwinian survivalist principles to cause workers to push themselves to the extreme in terms of dedication to their work. The article describes an 80-hour week as an expected norm; systems and processes that encourage workers to give anonymous, critical feedback on each other (data that is monitored and used by their managers); and tournament-style end-of-year culls, where every employee is ranked according to performance, and the lowest-ranking employees are automatically fired. In response to this 'river of intrigue' (a term used by Amazon staff), employees, driven by fear and competition, would make pacts with colleagues to bury individuals in negative criticism, thereby protecting their own jobs. Such behaviour particularly impacted those dealing with life challenges – illness, sick parents, and even motherhood – who were targeted because they could not put in the requisite amount of hours. There were reports of employees working without sleep for many days, working continuously during weekends and bank holidays, as well as throughout their holidays in order to ensure that their work got done. While some employees found this an exciting work environment, many found it stressful, anxiety-provoking with an unsustainable workload, often ending up with stress-related illnesses. The article goes on to point out that such a culture has a disproportionately negative impact on women; this might go some way to explain the lack of female executives in companies in which such norms prevail.

Amazon is a well-known case, of course, so perhaps an extreme and relatively rare example? Yet other Silicon Valley companies have been criticised for thriving from a culture of fear, including Netflix (*Daily Mail* 2018), Tesla (Levin 2017), and Uber (Isaac 2017).

Fear is increasingly being deployed in other white-collar, skilled and professional environments. Teachers, for example, are evaluated according to the results achieved by their pupils; this, especially under the leadership of a controlling, punitive headteacher, creates a fear-based culture in which pupils are 'taught to the test,' required to learn by rote and reproduce 'correct' answers in exams – nineteenth-century teaching principles in a twenty-first-century world (Counsell and Wright 2018; Seith 2018). Other research shows how marketisation and competition has led to fear-based cultures in academia, veterinary practice, and hospitals. Researchers examining conditions in academia argue:

> Close and constant scrutiny and judgment, competition and preoccupation with winning 'in a game of academic prestige' (Adler and Harzing 2009: 74) expose academics 'to deep insecurities regarding their worth, their identity and their standing' (Gabriel, 2010).
>
> *(Knights and Clarke 2018: 138)*

Pfeffer reported a Chinese study that showed 70% of China's intellectuals, mostly university professors, were at risk of premature death from exhaustion. The *CLB* website reported that the average lifespan of Shanghai's intellectuals in 1996 was 58–59 years; by 2006 it had fallen to only 53–54 years. From 2001 to 2006, 134 professors and academics from the Beijing Academy of Social Sciences and various local universities died from overwork (*China Labour Bulletin* 2006).

Hospitals in the United Kingdom have been shown to have developed fear-based cultures that have led to the deaths of patients, including children. In a 2018 *British Medical Journal* article, Navjoyt Ladher, the journal's Clinical Editor, calls for an ending of a culture of fear in healthcare. Referring to a recent example of 600 unnecessary deaths in a hospital in the south of England, Ladher argues: 'Subservience and deference, endemic in health systems, are harming patients, they say, with professionals fearing retribution, disapproval, career-limiting consequences, and worse if they dare to question or challenge colleagues' (Ladher 2018: 1). This is not a new issue. In the period leading up to 2001, 30 young children died unnecessarily at the Bristol Royal Infirmary due to a 'club culture,' in which there was an 'imbalance of power, with too much control in the hands of a few individuals' (HM Government 2001: 2). This style of management 'had a punitive element to it,' which meant that 'it was difficult to raise what were considered to be legitimate concerns.' Indeed, to bring concerns into the open was not seen as either 'safe or acceptable' (HM Government 2001: 165). In 2013, the official report into the UK Mid-Staffordshire hospital scandal suggested that large numbers of patients died as a result of poor care, exacerbated by staff's reluctance to raise concerns due to 'fear and bullying' (Campbell 2013). In the *BMJ* editorial mentioned above, Ladher reinforces a point made by colleagues

Philip Darbyshire and David Thompson: that no further research is needed on this issue; rather, 'we need more leaders with the courage and creativity to implement what we already know.' This has been the case for over 20 years, yet such leaders apparently are not emerging.

Even senior executives fail to thrive in these kinds of cultures. Pfeffer notes the suicide in 2016 of an Uber software engineer on $170,000 a year. According to his parents, he was under immense pressure at work, scared he would lose his job, and had completely lost confidence in himself. Pfeffer cites numerous other examples where stress and excessive hours contributed to suicides. We know that workers from lower socio-economic strata are more at risk of suicide than those from higher levels, but even these latter souls are not immune. Pfeffer also reports the suicides of Swisscom CEO Carsten Scholter, at the age of 49, and Zurich Insurance Group CFO Pierre Wauthier, at the age of 53 – both because of work-related pressures, including, in the latter case, conflict with the CEO.

A 2018 *Forbes* report (Sturt and Nordstrom 2018) reveals that 53% of Americans are currently unhappy at work. US workers forfeited nearly 50% of their paid vacation in 2017, with nearly 10% taking no vacation days at all – all of which can be attributed, according to the research, to a fear of falling behind.

We could go on. Suffice it to say that fear at work, in part due to increasing targets, in part due to increasing levels of job insecurity, is widely used as a tool in employee control. It is easier to implement a fear-based culture than it is to instil a culture of respect, encouragement, and kindness.

3. Electronic surveillance

A recent article by Angela Martin and her colleagues (2016) at the Tasmanian School of Business and Economics in Australia summarised the extensive research on surveillance in the workplace. It shows that surveillance has a range of detrimental effects on employees, such as high levels of stress, reduced levels of trust in management, negative work attitudes, and poorer social interaction in the workplace. The research shows how increased levels of electronic surveillance trigger counterproductive work behaviours such as reduced effort at work, less cooperation, absenteeism, lateness, and working around the monitoring systems, sometimes by sabotaging them. Not only does the existence of such monitoring trigger stress and resistance in employees, but it is perceived as a violation of their rights, an intrusion into their privacy, an insult to their character (implying they are untrustworthy), and a threat to their personal freedom. The authors show that despite these negative effects, monitoring of employee behaviour is increasing significantly: through the use of video cameras (both remote and attached to computers), listening devices (e.g. as used in call centres to monitor length and effectiveness of calls), electronic location sensing, and computer monitoring.

This extended use of organisational surveillance has led, according to researchers Sewell, Barker, and Nyberg (2011: 190), to assumptions that organisations have the right to measure 'everything that moves' and to punish any deviance from performance norms and expectations that are routinely high and sometimes excessive. The issue of electronic surveillance raises interesting ethical and practical questions. What precisely does an organisation buy when it pays for an employee's labour? Does it buy the right to determine every movement, every word uttered, every expression of emotion or belief? Does it buy the right to control every expression of an employee's behaviour? Does it buy the right to prevent an employee from talking to a work colleague or spending some time booking a dental appointment? In fact, does it buy the right to prevent an employee from attending the dental or hospital appointment? Does it buy the right to prevent a mother from picking up her sick son or from talking to the child's teacher during the work day? What does an organisation buy exactly? Does it buy us all – behaviour, emotion, beliefs, even spirit or soul? These questions are rarely raised in public, but the time has urgently come to address them. The authors of the above-mentioned study referred to employees who resisted the assumption that an organisation has the right to buy us lock stock and barrel as 'deviant.' As far as the researchers were concerned, given the increasing use of surveillance in the workplace, the problem was framed as how the negative consequences could be avoided; specifically, how can attitudes of workers be changed so that they are more accepting of the practice?

This is another example of how practices that involve a shift of power in favour of the organisation are becoming normalised to the extent that it appears impossible or naïve to challenge them. A recent survey showed that nearly a third of its 1,000 respondents said their employer tracked them via GPS, and 15% said they were tracked 24 hours a day – which is in fact illegal in the United States where the survey took place (TSheets n.d.); 22% claimed that they were not informed about the tracking when they first took the job. The survey, paid for by a company selling worker surveillance technology, showed that employees who were tracked were more positive towards such technology than those who were not tracked. This clearly contradicts the article by Martin and her colleagues (2016), although an article in *The Guardian* (Saner 2018) might explain this anomaly. It reports on a US company, Three Square Market, which microchipped its employees at a 'chip party.' Out of 90 employees, 72 volunteered to have a small device implanted under the skin between their thumb and forefinger, which would enable them to open security doors, log on to computers, and even make payments at company vending machines. The CEO of the company was surprised by the number of volunteers but attributed it to a generational difference: the millennials and digital natives are less averse to the idea of being monitored than older employees. So varying reported levels of acceptance of surveillance might be attributable to young people's more positive attitudes towards technology.

However, the same *Guardian* article revealed that there is now technology on the market to monitor employees' emotions, stress levels, brainwaves, tone of voice (e.g. when selling over the phone), hand movements (used to monitor the movements of pickers in warehouses), and to track how often employees speak in meetings, who they speak to, and for how long. While millennials are blithely signing up to be monitored 24 hours a day, it is not difficult to see how companies will be using this information to control our every move – including our emotions, our tone, and our behaviour in meetings. This technology is predictably being used especially within the gig economy and for unskilled labour. The same article quotes Jamie Woodcock, a sociologist who spent six months working in a call centre:

> You get a sense of the monitoring, he says, 'from the moment you walk in. You have TV screens that have everyone's relative performance to each other displayed. Managers collect data on almost every single part of what you do. Every single phone call I ever made was digitally recorded and stored. In terms of monitoring, it's like being able to call back every single thing somebody has made on an assembly line and retrospectively judge it for quality. We all make mistakes and we all have bad days, but this kind of monitoring can be made retrospectively to sack people and is used to give people a sense that they could lose their jobs at any moment.'
>
> *(Saner 2018)*

The ability to monitor the minutest of actions, even aspects that the employee themselves are not aware of (brainwaves, stress, emotions), raises important questions about the status of employees in the eyes of society and in the eyes of the companies they work for. There are positive aspects, of course: truck and bus drivers' hours are monitored for health and safety compliance, and technology measuring employees' brainwaves is being used to assess fatigue and alertness levels in drivers of high-speed trains.

The danger is that, given the employment precarity of the Fourth Industrial Revolution, the accelerating instrumentalisation of workers will reach a point where employers will be able to choose only the healthiest, most dedicated, hard-working, ambitious, and compliant employees – i.e. the young, uncritical digital natives, who in turn will be discarded when they are no longer able to comply with the demanding work ethic.

The technology itself is not the issue; the issue is how it is used. Are leaders using technology to support their people? Or do they use it to control them in order to maximise the amount of labour that they can extract at the minimum cost?

4. Abuse of power to degrade and humiliate

We have already observed a variety of methods used to instil fear in the workplace. But workplace bullying is a distinct category with a long research history of its own. Heinz Leymann, a German psychiatrist, founded the international anti-bullying movement and established the world's first Work Trauma clinic in the 1980s (Namie 2003). It may be no coincidence that the majority of workplace bullying research has taken place over the last four decades (De Cieri 2019), since the establishment of the neoliberal agenda in the 1980s and its emphasis on performativity.

In a 2020 survey of UK workers, 15% had experienced workplace bullying whilst 24% believed workplace bullying was ignored (CIPD 2020). Bullying is worse in the public sector. Amongst doctors, 39% claimed bullying was a problem in their workplace (NHS 2017) and, according to the NASUWT union, 80% of teachers experience bullying at work (NASUWT 2019). Bullying has been linked to certain kinds of workplaces with regard to their systems, processes, and culture; for example, research has shown bullying to be more prevalent in bureaucratic organisations that emphasise compliance with rules (De Cieri 2019). A study by Power and colleagues (2013) found that a strong emphasis on performance increased workplace bullying, whereas a culture characterised by a 'humane orientation' decreased it. High-performance expectations linked to pay, stressful workplaces, limited resources, and competitive cultures are all more likely to generate workplace bullying (Valentine et al. 2017). A leading US expert on workplace bullying, Gary Namie (2003), has identified the organisational characteristics most associated with bullying:

- 'making the numbers' – an obsession with outcomes – is uncritically adopted
- recruitment, promotion, and reward systems focus on individuals' 'strength of personality' or interpersonal aggressiveness while ignoring emotional intelligence
- short-term planning, e.g. to meet quarterly investor projections, governs operations
- internal codes of conduct limit prohibitions to narrowly defined illegal incidents
- executives give higher priority to personal friendships than to legitimate business interests
- fear is a dominant, desired workplace emotion, whether deliberately engineered or inadvertently created
- misuse of performance appraisal processes occur with impunity

Although most bullying is perpetrated by bosses, once established in a workplace, according to Valentine and his colleagues, bullying often spirals out of control and can lead to peer bullying. According to one piece of research, 20% of workers in the United Kingdom have been bullied by peers via messaging apps (Total Jobs 2018).

While all these statistics make interesting reading, more compelling are the personal stories of how people in the workplace are regularly humiliated, degraded, and demeaned. The UK government's report on employment practices at Sports Direct contains many such examples:

Working for Sports Direct is a very love/hate relationship. I think you could call it a form of brainwashing. My area manager would send out an email on Monday mornings with a list of total hours worked by each of his store managers the week before. Whoever did the least would get a lecture – not dedicated, not showing commitment etc. This wouldn't be a one to one lecture, but a full blown rant with everyone else copied into the email to see. If you weren't doing at least 55 hours a week then you weren't doing enough.

A female member of staff being forced to talk about her periods publicly (she had been off sick, due to period pains, having regularly worked 12-hour days).

(House of Commons Business, Innovation and
Skills Committee 2016: 11)

In other sectors, examples include bullying of nurses, banking staff, and teachers. One of many examples is the following, cited by Hutchinson and her colleagues (2009), concerning a nurse, Helen, who had had time off work on account of surgery. She was told to see an individual in the hospital who is renowned for sacking people:

Helen: Yes. That's right. You're paid out. You were paid out ... [Helen has been in tears] This is hard. Oh my God. Ok. I can see, that's right, I had been off sick and I was still in pain [following minor surgery] and I had one day off, and the manager said, 'You are to see this particular person this afternoon.' I said, 'Look, really, I don't feel well. I feel quite ill.' I said, 'Can we make it another day'? And she said ... 'No, if it is necessary for you to go to Casualty then you will interviewed on the bed.' ... I was so scared.
(Hutchinson et al. 2009: 220)

The article continues with an array of testimonies from nurses in a range of hospitals in Australia, detailing how an in-group of managers took control of the hospital and promoted and even rewarded hospital managers' bullying; this is a common theme in the literature.

An example from the banking sector comes from the personal experience of a member of staff writing in the online journal *Money Marketing*:

How can you do 15 appointments in a week – I remember having one manager he said I should have 10 booked fact-finding meetings, seven booked presentations and at least five sales (allowing for two cancelled appointments) and if I didn't I would be on an audio explaining the reasons why I didn't. It's okay if your performance on sales is above target but as soon as it slips this performance management style comes into force. It didn't matter if you were up to your eyeballs in paperwork you are expected to do that as well as the appointments.

When I was working for a building society I took paperwork home and worked till midnight to make sure I was up to date as I just didn't have enough time during the day, as my diary was so booked full of appointments. ... I remember having one manager that stated 'you always give people a hard time on Fridays so they have all weekend to worry about it so they come back on Monday, work harder and make sure they are not on an audio on Friday.'

(McMillan 2012)

A recent 2019 survey by NASUWT (the second-largest union representing the teaching professions in the United Kingdom) revealed that 80% of teachers said that they had been bullied in the previous year; 69% were bullied by their headteacher or senior manager; 38% were bullied by their line manager. Some of the quotes from the report are as follows:

Being isolated from supportive colleagues. Given unreasonable workload and no support with violent pupils and extreme behaviour issues. Given no support with abusive parents.

Talking about my weight and making humour of it.

Told to deliver an unworkable timetable which constantly changed without consultation.

I was isolated, ignored and openly ostracised. I had voiced my concerns over the way the school was being led and governed, which was leading to more and more children leaving the school. One quarter of the school population left over a three-month period.

I contemplated suicide on at least 10 occasions.

Stress, pain in muscles from stress, tearful all the time over nothing. Avoiding going to meetings first, so they can't have a go at you without witnesses.

Nervous breakdown with PTSD.

When asked what forms the bullying took, the top five responses were being undermined or belittled (84%), being ignored or ostracised (51%), having their work criticised in front of others (44%), being threatened with capability procedures (42%), and having rumours or allegations spread about them (28%).

A Google search for bullying in the workplace generated over 300 million hits. It is clear that this is an epidemic that seems mostly to have come to light since the 1980s, which involves all sectors and professions, and which leads to severe health consequences for those on the receiving end. It appears to be related to an increasing emphasis on performance, measurement, and abuse of power by senior executives.

5. Generating financial insecurity

Underpinning all the above practices is financial insecurity and the fear of losing one's job. The introduction of zero-hour contracts and agency working are probably the most powerful tools that employers have for controlling workers and generating fear. The government's report on Sports Direct illustrates how work contracts guarantee very few hours yet in return expect the worker to accept any suitable assignment offered by the company. If she or he refuses, that worker will be deemed not available for work, which may be regarded as gross misconduct. This can result in the 'termination of employment without notice and without payment in lieu of notice' (House of Commons Business, Innovation and Skills Committee 2016: 7).

This kind of restrictive contract is now common, and it requires a worker to be on call throughout the day, without guaranteeing any amount of working hours yet prohibiting a worker from taking employment elsewhere. The imbalance of power here is breathtaking. If you find this perfectly reasonable, ask yourself: would you want your children to be working under these conditions? Here is what Steve Turner, Assistant General Secretary of Unite, stated in the report on Sports Direct:

> It is not just about insecurity. It is also about no guarantee on hours, giving absolute control to the employer. … There is no process; there is no access to justice. Even though on paper you may be regarded as an employee and able to access, if indeed you can afford it, the employment tribunal system, the reality is, for most zero-hour workers and short-hour workers, you are simply denied work if you raise a grievance or raise a concern with your employer.
> *(House of Commons Business, Innovation and*
> *Skills Committee 2016: 7)*

This kind of working practice often goes under the name of 'flexibility,' and, of course, 'flexibility' sounds efficient and desirable. But desirable for whom? The Taylor Report of modern working practices in the United Kingdom (Taylor 2017) keenly promotes the idea of flexibility, claiming that it makes the UK economy one of the most efficient in the world. However, this can be contested. A recent study into work–life balance showed that the United Kingdom came 16th out of 20 industrialised nations, beating only Greece, the United States, Japan, and South Korea (Martin 2018). Yet, while UK staff spend a disproportionate amount of time at work, they have one of the lowest productivity levels. The UK Office for National Statistics (ONS 2018) has shown, for example, that the French produce more in four days than the United Kingdom produces in five. Zero-hour contracts are a cheap way for employers to increase the maximum amount of work they can from their employees without having to invest in large sums in order to increase productivity. This suggests that the people who benefit from this practice are those who gain from the returns on short-term investments in these companies.

The Taylor report outlines a range of working practices which, despite promoting 'flexibility,' have negative effects on the most vulnerable workers. Agency work involves employees working for large companies via employment agencies. Through this means, companies can employ staff for many years without those staff acquiring employment rights – such as sick pay, holiday pay, pensions, or legal rights to challenge wrongful dismissal. According to the report, agency workers fear that if they insist on even those few rights they do have (e.g. in the United Kingdom, they have rights to holiday time), this will count against them in terms of gaining access to future work. The report also showed how these agencies unilaterally deducted fees for administering tax and national insurance payments. The UK government Sports Direct report, too, described how agencies often underpaid workers, taking months to rectify their mistakes once they had been noticed. The two agencies involved in the case of Sports Direct were paid a total of $30 million a year.

The Taylor report commends flexible working for its suitability for students and the retired. However, it is not these groups that need work in order to buy a house, raise families, and provide for their future security. These functions are the foundations of a civilised society; in the midst of our working lives we all need the security of a regular income, a secure home in which to raise a family, and a pension to provide for ourselves in retirement.

The prevalence of zero-hour contracts, insecure jobs, agency work, and the lack of access for many people to a pension or basic employment rights are the background to the climate of fear that organisations exploit. As the Taylor report points out, many employers were simply using flexible working models to reduce costs and withhold employment rights (Taylor 2017: 42).

But it is not only the lowest-paid workers that suffer from job insecurity. Academics, for example, are more likely today not to be offered secure contracts but instead work as hourly paid lecturers, with no guarantee of work from one semester to another. More and more work has been outsourced to contractors – whether in IT, human resources, or management. And the culture of 'hire and fire' even affects senior executives who, if they fail to perform satisfactorily within a very short span of time (a huge expectation in today's large, complex organisations), are simply asked to leave. In our own personal experience, many senior managers suffer from stress and the ever-present feeling that if they don't perform they will be fired. This is an economic model which at its heart regards all workers – skilled and unskilled – as units of production, and the laws and culture that underpin the model encourage the disposal of such units whenever necessary. It is interesting to contrast this culture with that of Germany, where there is a 'long-term loyalty between employers and workers' (Marsh and Bischof 2012) and a raft of laws and norms to sustain that loyalty.

In sum, in all of our examples, we have seen that the threat of losing one's job – whether one is an agency worker, a teacher, or a manager – underpins the success of these instrumentalising methods. This leads us to our last item.

6. Denying what it means to be human

What unites all the factors above is a denial of what it means to be human. Organisations control when (and if) we go to the toilet; whether we can build relationships and chat with our work colleagues; and whether we can be ill, give birth, or raise a family. They are denying us the right to a secure income, a rest from work, and a secure old age. They are instilling fear and encouraging bullying. They are pressurising us to work long hours, with little rest, poor work–life balance, and little time to devote to our families and our communities. They are claiming the right to monitor us – our voices, our brainwaves, our health, our movements – 24/7 and undermining our right to privacy. We are losing our right to have a bad day or to be ill, tired, or fed up. The feelings of insecurity we have around work are enabling organisations to pay us far less than we contribute towards their profitability – with those at the top benefiting disproportionately from soaring profits while the rest are surviving on wages that in real terms have declined over the past four decades.

Is this what we want?
Is this what we want for our children?
Who is really benefiting from these arrangements?

We ask you to ponder these questions rather than answer them straight away. Reflect on them during your day. Do we really want to live in a social Darwinist society that treats people like instruments, assets, or units of production? Do we want to bring up our children in a society characterised by fear, insecurity, excessive competition, workaholism, and abandonment of family and community? Do we want to be responsible for the deterioration of the planet and of the quality of life for the many, or would we prefer to live a good life, one well spent in promoting a flourishing, healthy economic, social, political, and environmental system?

When you have thought about these questions, we would like to pose another. Is it still possible that we can use our organisations to serve humanity rather than humanity serving our organisations? And how do we cultivate the leaders with the courage, humanity, and creativity to implement what we know is right?

* * *

We know that these are complex questions involving aspects of power and control, economics and politics, values, meaning, and identity. But these questions are *really* important at a time when technology is delivering more and more power to those who lie at the top of our organisations.

On a more positive note, it was encouraging to hear coming from some of the senior managers we interviewed a very explicit recognition of this issue, including one from a leading technology company:

> I think we're going through a massive corporate cultural change, and it isn't just us. … I think it's the world is going through it.
>
> The more AI comes into play the more that we are looking for autonomy I think the more need there is for more empathetic, transparent, genuine

leadership. ... I think we can't be a reflection, we can't be machines and simply just keep banging a drum to demand more and more from people. But maybe ultimately the outcome is just evolution, we do more with less. But that's no good if the individual gets lost ... individuals aren't binary objects, they are people with beating hearts and souls, as we talked about earlier, that need love and attention.

It doesn't mean to pander to everything or to wrap them in cotton wool, but it does mean to show them the genuine side of compassion and that you care about, not only what they're doing, but where do they want to go.

(Dan)

We do not claim in any way to provide the answers, but we believe passionately that, even to have a constructive, generative, honest, and heartfelt debate on these issues, we need more people to lead with love. But there are significant obstacles to this; for example, how do we get the right people to assume leadership? It is to this question we now turn.

Notes

1 You can visit their website at: https://www.montpelerin.org. According to the site, members of this society (which is an elite group) 'see danger in the expansion of government, not least in state welfare, in the power of trade unions and business monopoly, and in the continuing threat and reality of inflation.' Despite mentioning the dangers of business monopoly, they are not known for pursuing this part of their agenda, which could be seen to run counter to their main aim of free trade. The history of the society is available on the site as a pdf, and it does not materially contradict Harvey's account.
2 Thank you to Richard Tudway for pointing this out and explaining it to me.

References

Adler, N. and Harzing, A.W. (2009) When knowledge wins: Transcending the sense and nonsense of academic rankings. *Academy of Management Learning & Education*, 8(1), 72–95.

Bloodworth, J. (2019) *Hired: Undercover in Low Wage Britain*. London: Atlantic Books.

Bury, R. (2016) More than a quarter of UK warehousing let this year was taken by Amazon. *The Telegraph*, 29 November 2016. https://www.telegraph.co.uk/business/2016/11/29/quarter-uk-warehousing-let-year-taken-amazon (accessed 20 February 2020).

Business Research Company (2020) *General Warehousing and Storage Global Market Report 2020*. https://www.thebusinessresearchcompany.com/report/general-warehousing-and-storage-global-market-report (accessed 20 February 2020).

Campbell, D. (2013) Mid Staffs hospital scandal: The essential guide. *The Guardian*, 6 February 2013. https://www.theguardian.com/society/2013/feb/06/mid-staffs-hospital-scandal-guide (accessed 12 July 2019).

Carter, B., Danford, A., Howcroft, D., Richardson, H., Smith, A. and Taylor, P. (2013) "Stressed out of my box": Employee experience of lean working and occupational ill-health in clerical work in the UK public sector. *Work, Employment and Society*, 27(5), 747–67.

Cheshire, A., Ridge, D., Hughes, J., Peters, D., Panagioti, M., Simon, C. and Lewith, G. (2017) Influences on GP coping and resilience: A qualitative study in primary care. *British Journal of General Practice*, 67(659), e428–e436.

China Daily (2016) 600,000 Chinese die from overworking each year. *China Daily*, 11 December 2016. https://www.chinadaily.com.cn/china/2016-12/11/content _27635578.htm (accessed 19 June 2019).

China Labour Bulletin (CLB) (2006) Death from overwork in China. *CLB*, 11 August 2006. https://clb.org.hk/content/death-overwork-china (accessed 19 June 2019).

CIPD (2020) Quarter of employees believe bullying and harassment are overlooked, 21 January 2020. https://www.cipd.co.uk/about/media/press/bullying-harassment -overlooked#gref (accessed: 12 March 2020)

Counsell, S.L. and Wright, B.L. (2018) High-stakes accountability systems: Creating cultures of fear. *Global Education Review*, 5(2), 189–202.

Daily Mail (2018) Netflix no chill: Employees describe climate of fear at streaming service where peers are encouraged to rate each other, emails are sent slamming former workers and managers feel under constant "pressure to fire people". *Daily Mail*, 26 October 2018. https://www.dailymail.co.uk/news/article-6318259/Netflix -employees-reveal-companys-culture-fear.html (accessed 4 June 2019).

De Cieri, H. (2019) Workplace bullying: An examination of power and perpetrators. *Personnel Review*, 48(2), 204–19.

East-Durham.co.uk (n.d.) *Children in the Mines*. http://east-durham.co.uk/wp/children -in-the-mines/ (accessed 6 December 2018).

Friedman, M. (1970) The social responsibility of business is to increase its profits. *New York Times*, 13 September 1970.

Friedman, T.L. (2006) *The World is Flat: The Globalized World in the Twenty-First Century*. London: Penguin.

Gabriel Y. (2010) Organization studies: A space for ideas, identities and agonies. *Organization Studies*, 31, 757–75.

Goudsward, K., Van Vliet, O., Been, J. and Caminada, K. (2012) Pension and income inequality in old age. *CESifo DICE Report* 4. https://www.ifo.de/DocDL/ dicereport412-forum4.pdf (accessed 2 April 2020).

Harvey, D. (2007) *A Brief History of Neo-Liberalism*. Oxford: Oxford University Press.

HM Government (2001) *Bristol Royal Infirmary Inquiry*. Norwich: Stationery Office Limited, July 2001.

House of Commons Business, Innovation and Skills Committee (2016) Employment practices at sports direct: Third report of session 2016–17. *HC 219*, 22 July 2016. https://publications.parliament.uk/pa/cm201617/cmselect/cmbis/219/219.pdf (accessed 14 July 2020).

Hutchinson, M., Vickers, M.H., Wilkes, L and Jacks, D. (2009) "The worse you behave, the more you seem to be rewarded": Bullying in nursing as organizational corruption. *Employee Responsibilities and Rights Journal*, 21(3), 213–29.

Isaac, M. (2017) Inside Uber's aggressive, unrestrained workplace culture. *New York Times*, 22 February 2017. https://www.nytimes.com/2017/02/22/technology/uber -workplace-culture.html (accessed 4 June 2019).

Kantor, J. and Streitfield, D. (2015) Inside Amazon: Wrestling big ideas in a bruising workplace. *New York Times*, 15 August 2015. https://www.nytimes.com/2015/08 /16/technology/inside-amazon-wrestling-big-ideas-in-a-bruising-workplace.html (accessed 12 June 2019).

Knights, D. and Clarke, C. (2018) Living on the edge? Professional anxieties at work in academia and veterinary practice. *Culture and Organization*, 24(2), 134–53.

Ladher, N. (2018) End the culture of fear in healthcare. *BMJ*, 363:k4467 (25 October 2018).

Levin, S. (2017) Tesla workers claim anti-LGBT threats, taunts, and racial abuse in lawsuits. *The Guardian*, 19 October 2017. https://www.theguardian.com/technology /2017/oct/19/tesla-factory-workers-discrimination-claim-race-lgbt-elon-musk (accessed 4 June 2019).

Marsh, D. and Bischof, R. (2012) 'Hire and fire' has destroyed Britain's jobs economy. *The Guardian*, 26 January 2012. https://www.theguardian.com/commentisfree/2012 /jan/26/hire-and-fire-destroyed-uk-jobs (accessed 19 June 2019).

Martin, A.J., Wellen, J.M. and Grimmer, J.R. (2016) An eye on your work: How empowerment affects the relationship between electronic surveillance and counterproductive work behaviours. *International Journal of Human Resource Management*, 27(21), 635–51.

Martin, D. (2018) Britain is revealed to have the WORST work–life balance in western Europe (and we toil an hour a day longer than the Germans). *Daily Mail*, 2 November 2018. https://www.dailymail.co.uk/news/article-6344357/UK-worst-work-life -balance-western-Europe-best-Scandinavia.html (accessed 19 June 2019).

McMillan, P. (2012) Editor's comment of the week: Bank advice problems come from the top. *Money Marketing*, 13 September 2012. https://www.moneymarketing.co.uk/ opinion/editors-comment-of-the-week-bank-advice-problems-come-from-the-top (accessed 28 June 2019).

Namie, G. (2003) Workplace bullying: Escalated incivility. *Ivey Business Journal*, November/December 2003. https://iveybusinessjournal.com/publication/workplace -bullying-escalated-incivility (accessed 19 June 2020).

NASUWT (2019) *Bullying and Harassment Survey*. https://www.nasuwt.org.uk/article -listing/bullying-and-harassment-survey-april-2019.html (accessed 28 December 2019).

NHS (2018) NHS Staff Survey. March 2018. https://www.nhsstaffsurveys.com/Caches/ Files/P3088_ST17_National%20briefing_v5.0.pdf (accessed: 12 March 2020).

ONS (Office for National Statistics) (2018) *International Comparisons of UK Productivity (ICP), Final Estimates: 2016*. https://www.ons.gov.uk/economy/economicoutputa ndproductivity/productivitymeasures/bulletins/internationalcomparisonsofprodu ctivityfinalestimates/2016 (accessed: 20 February 2019).

Pfeffer, J. (2018) *Dying for a Paycheck*. New York: HarperCollins.

Pool, C. (2017) *Mapping the UK warehouse Market*. https://www.stowga.com/blog/ mapping-the-uk-warehouse-market (accessed 20 February 2020).

Power, J.L., Brotheridge, C.M., Blenkinsopp, J., Bowes-Sperry, L., Bozionelos, N., Buzády, Z., Chuang, A., Drnevich, D., Garzon-Vico, A., Leighton, C., Madero, S.M., Mak,W.-M., Mathew, R., Monserrat, S.I., Mujtaba, B.G., Olivas-Lujan, M.R., Polycroniou, P., Sprigg, C.A., Axtell, C., Holman, D., Ruiz-Gutiérrez, J.A. and Nnedumm, A.U.O. (2013) Acceptability of workplace bullying: A comparative study on six continents. *Journal of Business Research*, 66(3), 374–80.

Saner, E. (2018) Employers are monitoring computers, toilet breaks – Even emotions. Is your boss watching you? *The Guardian*, 14 May 2018. https://www.theguardian .com/world/2018/may/14/is-your-boss-secretly-or-not-so-secretly-watching-you (accessed 29 July 2020).

Seith, E. (2018) "Culture of fear" is driving teacher workload, admits Swinney. *Times Educational Supplement*, 17 May 2019. https://www.tes.com/news/culture-fear -driving-teacher-workload-admits-swinney (accessed 8 April 2020).

Selby, A. (2017) Timed toilet breaks, impossible targets and workers falling asleep on feet: Brutal life working in Amazon warehouse. *The Mirror*, 25 September 2017. https://www.mirror.co.uk/news/uk-news/timed-toilet-breaks-impossible-targets-11587888 (accessed 20 February 2020).

Sewell, G., Barker, J.R. and Nyberg, D. (2011) Working under intensive surveillance: When does 'measuring everything that moves' become intolerable? *Human Relations*, 65(2), 189–215.

Sturt, D. and Nordstrom, T. (2018) 10 shocking workplace stats you need to know. *Forbes*, 8 March 2018. https://www.forbes.com/sites/davidsturt/2018/03/08/10-shocking-workplace-stats-you-need-to-know (accessed 19 June 2019).

Taylor, F.W. (1911) *The Principles of Scientific Management*. Harper & Brothers. http://www.ibiblio.org/eldritch/fwt/t2.html (accessed 20 June 2019).

Taylor, M. (2017) *Good Work: The Taylor Review of Modern Working Practices*. UK Department for Business, Energy & Industrial Strategy, 11 July 2017. https://www.gov.uk/government/publications/good-work-the-taylor-review-of-modern-working-practices (accessed 29 July 2020).

Total Jobs (2018) *The Apps and Downs of Messaging at Work*. https://www.totaljobs.com/insidejob/messaging-apps (accessed 19 June 2019).

Valentine, S.R., Hanson, S.K. and Fleischman, G.M. (2017) The spiraling and spillover of misconduct: Perceived workplace bullying, subclinical psychopathy, and businesspersons' recognition of an ethical issue. *Employee Responsibilities and Rights Journal*, 29, 221–44.

4

LEADING WITH LOVE AS THE HALLMARK OF HIGHER MATURITY

In the previous chapter, we adopted a social perspective, exploring how forces in our society pull us inexorably in the direction of the instrumentalisation of people at work. In this chapter, the focus is on the individual, with a perspective on the forces at play within us as leaders. One of the challenges of leading with love is that it requires a level of maturity normally associated with higher levels of human development: wisdom, self-awareness, self-control, self-sacrifice, and emotional balance, coupled with a commitment to the beneficial flourishing of all life on the planet. Unfortunately, in the West at least, adults who achieve such levels of development may be few and far between.

Because of this, when we actually become aware of someone who is leading with love, we stop, admire, and recognise the power. Paul Polman, former CEO of Unilever, is an example. According to the *Financial Times* (and many other commentators), he was a standout CEO who worked with passion to bring together fellow business leaders in a campaign for social and environmental justice while at the same time delivering outstanding returns to his shareholders (Skapinker 2018). Polman, in one of his many interviews, said, 'True leadership is putting yourself to the service of others and, if you can, marry that with a very noble cause, to make this a better place for all' (Skapinker 2018). Leading with love can be done in a commercial environment; Paul Polman provides a role model for this at the highest of levels of business.

In these uncertain times, we desperately need leaders with this kind of wisdom and self-awareness. The question is: how do we find and develop these leaders? We suggest that this kind of wise leadership is a sign of advanced human development. In contrast, egotistical, intimidating, and manipulative leaders represent the other end of the scale: they are developmentally immature and clearly detrimental to the healthy functioning of our societies and the planet. It is an obvious point, really – we should expect people in positions of leadership to be capable of functioning at a psychological and emotional level commensurate with their responsibility and impact.

So what does advanced, mature human functioning look like?

What is psychological maturity?

Developmental psychology is a branch of psychology that examines human development from childhood to the final stages of adulthood. Piaget was the seminal thinker in the field of childhood development, and a number of researchers have contributed to adult developmental theories, among them Erik Erikson, Abraham Maslow, Robert Kegan, and Lawrence Kohlberg. Their seminal works have more recently been augmented by Lars Tornstam's theory of gerotranscendence and Michael Levenson's theory of self-transcendence and wisdom development. All these theories show a process of development that involves, firstly, an increasing independence of thought – the ability to think, judge and act according to inner directed values as opposed to basic impulses or the need for approval by significant others or society in general; secondly, an increasing interest in leaving a beneficial legacy for the flourishing of others; and, thirdly, a decreasing attachment to ego needs for status, wealth, or power.

We will briefly touch on these theories and focus on their descriptions of the higher levels of adult development before linking these to leading with love.

Erik Erikson

Erik Erikson was one of the first researchers and writers to systematically study the phases of adult development and to suggest that adults can and do develop throughout their lives (Allen and Wergin 2009).[1] He proposed eight stages of development from birth to death, all of which involve the reconciliation of tension, the success of this reconciliation resulting in the emergence of a particular virtue. There are three adult stages, according to Erikson, beginning with stage 6, which tends to take place between the ages of 18 and 40, and in which adults develop loving relationships and intimacy with others. If adults can overcome the tension between intimacy and isolation, they achieve the virtue of love. Stage 7 is the stage of generativity (ages 30–65), in which adults devote themselves to the development and guidance of the next generation and of their community and society. Generative adults are creative and generous and care about people beyond their immediate circle. The virtue of 'care' results from the successful resolution of the forces of generativity versus stagnation. Adults who do not achieve this become self-centred and uninterested in contributing to others or to society as a whole. They tend to hoard their possessions, become selfish and mean, finding little meaning or purpose in life beyond meeting their own needs. Erikson proposed a final stage 8 affecting those of 65 plus. He suggested that the virtue of wisdom resulted from the tension between ego integrity and despair. It is characterised by a sense of satisfaction and an acceptance of one's life, including its failures or less than ideal outcomes. There is a sense of dignity and wholeness about those who have achieved wisdom – whereas those who fail to achieve this virtue look back at their lives with self-contempt, bitterness, and despair (Yount 2008). In later life, Joan Erikson, who had worked closely with her husband, proposed a ninth level, which she called 'gerotranscendence,' Her ideas were taken up by Tornstam, whose research into gerotranscendence we will look at later.

Abraham Maslow

Maslow's famous hierarchy of needs has often been reduced to a mere shadow of its original brilliance. Maslow proposed a hierarchy of developmental stages, whereby, having achieved love and acceptance, a person pursues self and social esteem needs until progressing onto the last stage: self-actualisation. Self-actualised people accept themselves and others; they are spontaneous, creative, independent, and open; they have a positive sense of humour and develop relationships of mutual respect and trust (Yount 2008). They appreciate nature more intensely and experience 'peak moments': times when the self seems to blend with the cosmos, in a spiritual connection to others and the universe. Later in life, Maslow proposed a final, eighth stage of development which he called 'transcendence.' People in this stage regularly experience times where they transcend themselves and peak experiences become a central part of their lives. They are both loving and lovable as they inspire awe and deep respect from others. These are likely to be the Nelson Mandelas, Mahatma Gandhis, Mother Teresas, and Martin Luther Kings of our time – those whom we consider extraordinary and who manifest the apex of what it is possible for human beings to achieve.

Robert Kegan

Robert Kegan's theory of adult development is less well known but has been influential in professional and academic circles. He proposes five stages of development through which adults progress by means of a process of transformation. Transformation involves a profound shift in the way we make sense of the world such that we are able to handle greater complexity and uncertainty. One way of looking at this is that our paradigm changes such that what we pay attention to, how we make sense, and how we feel and act are more complex, subtle, and nuanced. Hence, adult development is in part viewed as the capacity to incorporate increasing complexity. Another important concept central to Kegan's stage development is what the adult views as subject or object. 'Subject' is what one is, and it involves taken-for-granted assumptions about the self and the world; 'object,' on the other hand, can be reflected upon and changed, as it is viewed as something outside the self. For example, at one stage in our lives we might conceive of our gender as 'subject' – a component of just who we are and not open to challenge. At another, later stage, however, we might view our gender as 'object': something that has been imposed on us by society and hence more fluid and subject to change. The more an adult transforms what they once viewed as 'subject' into 'object,' the more they are able to change, critique, evaluate, and separate themselves from phenomena previously taken as given, making their world views more complex and rich. The third in Kegan's developmental stages is the 'socialising' stage, in which we act in relation to the expectations that others hold of us: in other words, a predominantly conforming mode of being. In this stage, we believe that others make us feel certain emotions and we defend ourselves by attributing our feelings to the actions of others. In his fourth stage, called 'self-authoring,' Kegan argues that adults become more self-determining and can see how their roles, relationships, expectations, and demands are all contingent and hence can be negotiated and made sense of in more subtle and nuanced ways. Such adults have their own meaning-making systems, which afford them an independence that is lacking in stage 3. They take responsibility for their own emotions and actions and, rather than blaming others for their reactions, are able to self-reflect and realise that how they react is due in part to how they themselves have interpreted a situation. The fifth and final stage of development, 'self-transforming,' is achieved by very few and comprises the rare ability to see one's sense-making processes as fully 'object,' i.e. a product of a particular culture, place, time, and relationship. Everything is contingent, and contradiction and paradox are fully embraced. An adult in the fifth stage is more likely to be able to see similarities in differences, less likely to be drawn into the dichotomies of 'either/or' thinking, and more able to embrace the paradoxes of 'both/and' thinking.

Lawrence Kohlberg

Lawrence Kohlberg is famous for his theory of moral development, which describes six stages of moral reasoning, each of which influences sense-making in order to reach an understanding of what the morally correct decision should be in any one situation. The later stages of development comprise what he terms 'post-conventional morality.' Most people only attain 'conventional morality,' however, in which the adult reaches conclusions based on the norms and values of society, i.e. what society deems acceptable. In post-conventional morality (stages 5 and 6), adults begin to question social norms and are prepared to make decisions based on personal values. In stage 6, the adult develops a set of overarching higher principles such as human rights, social justice, equality, and sustainability, and will be prepared to fight for such principles even if that means social exclusion and disapproval or even punishment such as imprisonment.

Like both Erikson and Maslow (indeed, being influenced by them), in later life, Kohlberg posited a further stage of development, which he termed 'transcendental morality.' It is worth quoting a significant passage from Kohlberg and Power's article:

We term this new perspective 'cosmic' and 'infinite,' although of course the attainment of such a perspective is only an aspiration rather than a complete possibility. The attainment of this perspective results from a new insight. Using Gestalt psychology language for describing insight, we term it a shift from figure to ground, from a centering on the self's activity and that of others to a centering on the wholeness or unity of nature or the cosmos. ... This act of insight is, however, not purely cognitive. One cannot see the whole or the infinite ground of being unless one loves it and aspires to love it. Such love, Spinoza tells us, arises first out of despair about more limited, finite, and perishable loves. Knowing and loving God or Nature as the ground of a system of laws knowable by reason is a support to our acceptance of human rational moral laws of justice, which are part of the whole. Furthermore, our love of the whole or the ultimate supports us through experiences of suffering, injustice, and death.

(Kohlberg and Power 1981)

Kohlberg came to see the final stage of human moral development as non-egoic, non-dualistic, and unitive – a sense that one is part of 'life-as-a-whole,' and hence the ethicality of one's actions can only be understood insofar as they beneficially affect that 'life-as-a-whole.'

Michael Levenson

Michael Levenson criticises these kinds of life stage models for downplaying the role of individual differences and in particular the role of volition. According to Levenson, we are conscious beings with the capacity for choice, discrimination, judgement, and, ultimately, wisdom. While our agency is limited by culture, structure, age, time, and place, elements of choice and personal differences do, according to Levenson, play some role in our personal development. The pinnacle of his personal development theory is self-transcendence, which involves the development of a capacity to achieve goals while at the same time decreasing one's attachment to those goals. However, here, the 'self' that needs to be transcended is not the 'self' that is often described in typical Western psychological theory. Levenson's 'self' consists of patterns of reaction that derive from attachment to material goods and desired outcomes, which arise from greed, anger, and ignorance. Levenson describes a 'liberative' model which draws on developmental methods of older, spiritual traditions of adult development, such as Buddhism, Taoism, Sufism, Yoga, and contemplative Christianity.

The goal of such a liberative model of adult development is the reduction of social conditioning in order to attain relative freedom. But this does not mean liberation from an obligation to others; on the contrary, it is linked to an increasing concern for others. This is developed through the conduct of certain practices, such as generosity, to detach oneself from material possessions; patience, to counter anger and hostility; humility, to counter pride; and self-discipline, to counter lust and gluttony. Ultimately, wisdom is the result of our losing or transcending the egoic self whose attachments lead to suffering, 'egocentrism, fear, arrogance, and aggression, to name a few of the more important impediments to development' (Levenson, Aldin and Cupertino 2001: 100). In the Christian tradition, this may be framed as 'dying to self.'

The liberative model differs from previous developmental models in many respects: for example, adult development here entails increasing *simplicity or honing* of perspective rather than increasing complexity. Another area in which it differs is its emphasis on the conscious development of maturity or 'ego transcendence.' This is acquired by engaging in regular contemplative practices which include meditation, focused self-observation, and various practices to cultivate self-awareness and self-transcendence. In other words, it is possible to influence proactively one's psychological development, which makes Levenson's model perhaps more proactive and empowering than those theories that tend to leave the development of maturity to sometimes little more than chance.

Lars Tornstam

Tornstam's theory of gerotranscendence is based on both quantitative and qualitative data collected from a number of surveys, the first one of which took place in 1985. Tornstam shows how individuals manifesting gerotranscendence

> described how they had become less self-occupied and at the same time more selective in their choice of social and other activities. A transpersonal sense of affinity with others and with earlier generations had developed, as well as a sense of being part of a whole. Informants also talked about a kind of redefinition of time, space, life and death, and an increased need for positive contemplative solitude.
>
> *(Tornstam 2011: 168)*

Tornstam notes three distinct dimensions apparent in the construct of gerotranscendence, which he calls the 'Cosmic,' the 'Self' and 'Social and Personal Relationships.' The Cosmic dimension is described as a growing sense of how unimportant an individual life is in comparison with the continuation of life in general. It is characterised by less fear of death and a greater acceptance of 'Mystery,' recognising that not everything in life can be explained through the medium of the human intellect and the logical, rational sciences. 'Cosmic' also includes a greater experience of joy and a greater affinity with nature – including the ability to have transcendent experiences when communing with nature.

In the 'Self' dimension, individuals experiencing gerotranscendence are able to reconcile themselves to their 'shadow' sides. Tornstam shows how they can identify previously hidden parts of themselves, both good and bad, and reconcile themselves to these while reducing the more egoic aspects of their personality. According to Tornstam:

The individual experiences a new awareness of the fact that he or she is not the centre of the universe. In an illustrative interview, one male informant admitted with a laugh that during his working life he really thought he was the most important person on earth and more or less the centre of the universe. Now he admits with relief that he is not. His overly elevated self-esteem had taken on more realistic proportions.

(Tornstam 2011: 171)

In the Social and Personal Relationships dimension, the individual focuses more on the needs of others, in particular the following generations. Interest in superficial socialising declines at this stage to be replaced by greater interest in the depth of relationships and in spending time alone in contemplation. Individuals are more desirous of transcending roles, conventions, and norms in pursuit of coming closer to the genuine self. Those experiencing gerotranscendence discover a new innocence, a new joy in flouting convention and seeing the world through a child's eyes. With this comes a new wisdom and tolerance, a reluctance to judge, and a forbearance from giving unwanted advice. Finally, individuals in this stage are less materialistic and focused more on relationships and spiritual transcendence.

Tornstam estimates that only 20% of the population reach a high level of gerotranscendence, partly due to the fact that Western society does not expect maturation in the second half of life and can view these kinds of changes in a negative light, i.e. as signs of loneliness, depression, or dementia. He quotes Carl Jung, who:

> maintained that, in our part of the world, it is a tragedy that many of us live our entire lives with the erroneous idea that it is only during the first half of life that we develop and mature. Practicing such a way of life ends up in our dying as only half-matured individuals. Then, according to Jung, we develop psychiatric symptoms including depression, anxiety, fear of death, disgust and a feeling that life has been stolen from us.
>
> *(Tornstam 2011: 177)*

Eco-psychology – Bill Plotkin

This point leads to the final contribution to our overview of adult developmental theory: the perspective of eco-psychology. Eco-psychologists have introduced new, more critical narratives of adult development which are based on inherited wisdom rather than theory, principles rather than empiricism, and poetry rather than social science. We use the term 'narrative' rather than 'theory,' as much of this work is drawn from world views embedded within indigenous cultures, particularly North American Shamanism. These ways of understanding and relating to our planet, and the human and non-human life that inhabits it, can be seen as 'mytho-poetic' and are designed not to be scientifically evaluated but rather to be embodied, entered into, experienced, and fused into the psyche. Eco-psychology is as much a practice as it is a world view; it is more embodied and enacted than theorised and investigated, and hence it can be more transformative and personally challenging than a neat and tidy theory.

Perhaps the most comprehensive eco-psychological narrative or model of adult development comes from Bill Plotkin, in particular in his book *Nature and the Human Soul*. It is illustrative to see how Plotkin describes his work:

> A model of human development that is both ecocentric and soulcentric – that is, a nature-based model that fully honors the deeply imaginative potentials of the human psyche ... a new natural history of the soul, a description of the organic, indigenous process by which a human child grows into a soul-initiated adult ... a field guide for growing a genuine elder.
>
> *(Plotkin 2008: 5)*

We can see from this that the model is being described from a 'transcendent' perspective. Plotkin sees the development of true 'elders' (akin to the highest levels of human development) as relying on the unfolding of the soul both by tapping into the human imagination/psyche and by developing a deep and intimate relationship with nature (our planet, its ecosystems, and all non-human life). The introduction of nature, and our relationship with her, as a central element of human development is the unique contribution of Plotkin's work and reflects an expanded awareness of the unity and interdependence of all life. Each stage of Plotkin's model includes a developmental task (similar to Erikson's) which involves not only a culture-oriented dimension but also a nature-oriented one. He argues that in the twentieth and twenty-first centuries, human development has been arrested – both culturally and ecologically – leading to the vast majority of adults stuck in an adolescent, egocentric stage of development. He describes eight stages of development, which are superimposed upon the wheel of life, reflecting the interdependence of human development with the cycles, rhythms, and patterns of nature. Each stage is worth quoting simply for the beauty of the language: The Innocent in the Nest (early childhood); The Explorer in the Garden (middle childhood); The Thespian at the Oasis (early adolescence); The Wanderer in the Cocoon (late adolescence); The Apprentice at the Wellspring (early adulthood); The Artisan in the Wild Orchard (late adulthood); The Master in the Grove of Trees (Early Elderhood), and The Sage in the Mountain Cave (late elderhood).

The Wanderer in the Cocoon involves perhaps the most important, difficult, and painful transition in the development wheel. The previous stage, The Thespian at the Oasis, involved the developmental task of 'fashioning a social presence that is both authentic (the nature task) and socially acceptable (the cultural task)' (Plotkin 2008: 166), but, as the Wanderer in the Cocoon emerges, a deep encounter with the soul occurs – an encounter that reveals the individual's unique place in nature and society. This involves the 'death' of the adolescent personality that has been painstakingly constructed in the previous stage and the dissolution of the conventional ties that previously anchored the individual in their culture. Plotkin describes the nature of this transition:

> Where once you thought life was primarily about social, academic, economic, or religious projects, now you recognize it for the spiritual adventure it truly is. Now you begin to search for the shape of that greater story you're destined to live, the larger conversation you might have with the world, a conversation that is not only the ego's. Your foremost quest becomes your own soul, that unique psycho-ecological niche that only you can inhabit.
>
> *(Plotkin 2008: 233)*

Unfortunately, many people in modern Western society lack the courage, the depth, the support, the understanding, the imagination, and the spiritual insight to do this. The challenge of the Cocoon involves leaving 'the home of your former identity ... [and] explor[ing] the mysteries of nature and psyche in preparation for Soul Initiation' (Plotkin 2008: 255). This is a task that must be accomplished alone, independent of the norms, values, and authority figures of the past (although new mentors and guides may turn up). It is ultimately about choosing authenticity over social acceptance. Sadly, most people in the West never progress beyond the Thespian stage with its focus on the approval of peer groups and society. Stuck in arrested development, the egocentric self is an isolated, competitive, independent entity focused only on its own survival and the approval of others. It has little notion of responsibility to others, to the community, to society, to future generations, or, tragically, to nature or the planet. The egocentric self is an 'I–it' self, focused in every sphere of its small existence on 'personal possessions, a job, a few amusements, their own body, and a small band of acquaintances and loved ones' (Plotkin 2008: 46). A society that cultivates egocentric identities is characterised by egocentric leaders and egocentric, destructive, planet- and community-destroying behaviours. And such leaders are victims, too, since they never encounter their true souls, they never realise their unique contribution, their purpose for being here, and end up living hollow lives.

* * *

The foregoing by no means exhausts the huge wealth of available work on developmental psychology, but what is remarkable about the work as a whole is its coherence, regardless of who is writing and within which paradigm. By way of a brief summary, the signs of a mature adult appear to be:

- attaining a more transcendent, spiritual, interconnected, responsive, and responsible sense of self

- liberation from the socialised self, which is constructed to conform to social norms or to please and impress others in order to pursue a higher purpose or deeper calling
- an ability to connect with others from an 'I–thou' perspective, developing empathic, loving, respectful and democratic relationships with all others
- a desire to leave a legacy, to support the next generation in order to promote the beneficial flourishing of all life and the planet
- non-attachment to material goods or to other socio-psychological sources of ego-identity (status, power, popularity, fame, pride, achievement)

Linking psychological maturity to leading with love

For the coherence of our framework in this book, we have mapped these indicators against the definition of 'leading with love' that we outlined in Chapter 2 (see Table 4.1).

What this implies, for us, is that those who lead with love are developmentally more mature than those who do not; those whose leadership is shaped primarily by personal egoic needs are developmentally less mature adults and should therefore not be in positions of senior organisational or institutional leadership.

A valid critique of developmental psychology is its age-related, linear 'stage-driven' framing. The reality is much more complex. Certainly, age is no predictor

TABLE 4.1 Mapping indicators of 'transcendence' from developmental psychology paradigms with our definitions of 'leading with love'

	Leading with love	Developmentally mature
1 (i)	Acting intentionally – *Having a clear intention*	Liberation from the socialised self, which is constructed to conform to social norms or please and impress others, in order to pursue a higher purpose, or deeper calling.
(ii)	*Minimising being 'caught' by the negative systemic and cultural forces in the organisation*	Non-attachment to material goods or to other socio-psychological sources of ego-identity
2	*In sympathetic response to others*	An ability to connect with others from an 'I–thou' perspective, developing empathic, loving, respectful, and democratic relationships with others
3	*Responding to the sacred or divine*	Attaining a more transcendent, spiritual, interconnected, more responsive, and responsible sense of self
4	*Promoting individual and overall wellbeing*	A desire to leave a legacy, to support the next generation in order to promote the beneficial flourishing of all life and the planet

of wisdom, and many younger people operate at high levels of self-actualisation. More importantly, the stages are much more fluid than the theories might suggest. People can operate at the highest stages of functioning in one minute/context and then at the lowest in another. It is not so much that each of us is a single 'self'; it is more a question of which 'self' shows up and when. Ken Wilber's (2016) notion of 'states' and 'stages' is very helpful here. While we are all capable of higher or lower 'states' at any time, the real matter is our ability to sustain these states consistently – what Wilber calls a 'stage.' Developmental theory might therefore be best viewed as a scattergram of behaviour: as we mature over time, the critical mass of our behaviour starts to shift towards the higher states. There may be significant transformational moments in our lives, when we break through to new ways of seeing and experiencing ourselves and the world. But, even in such cases, it takes time for our old habits and conditioned patterns of responses to adapt. This is important for our theme of leading with love. It is not something that can ever be 'achieved.' No one can be expected to lead with love all the time. It is a percentage game; the nominated subjects in our research stood out because their scattergram had more love in it, including with regard to the non-obvious things where there was no other motive for their behaviour than love itself.

So far in this chapter, we have concentrated on the 'higher' developmental states; our proposition is that if we accept the validity of this framing, we should therefore expect our leaders to be drawn from people operating at these more mature stages. Clearly, this does not hold true in a large number of cases. When seeking nominations for the research, it was noticeable how many people we approached were unable to think of anyone who led with love – and many laughed when we raised the idea. Why is it that so many people without these qualities attain positions of high influence and authority? Or is it a question of what goes wrong – what happens to people when they find themselves in positions of power?

The answer may lie in the nature of power itself. In an ideal world, people would be selected into positions of power on the basis of their maturity. In the real world, they are often selected for such positions because of their ability to wield and manipulate power.

This takes us into research on the opposite end of the developmental scale, interrogating the nature of leaders who evidence hubris and a social dominance orientation (i.e. a delight derived from wielding power for its own sake). It is not our purpose to go into great detail here; much has already been written about the problems caused by power attracting inappropriate people and about how power affects the psychology of those who exercise it for long periods. Below we will touch briefly on research into the hubris syndrome and social dominance orientation to show how it is easier for the more egocentric to access, maintain and abuse power in organisations. We do so simply as a reminder of how crucial it is to monitor the culture of leadership within large organisations and institutions.

Signs of psychological immaturity: hubris and social dominance

As a member of Tony Blair's Cabinet in the UK Labour government of the late 1990s and early 2000s, Lord David Owen had first-hand experience of power at the highest levels. To document his experience, he wrote a short book titled *The Hubris Syndrome: Bush, Blair and the Intoxication of Power*. His thesis was that, over time, he noticed behavioural changes in Blair which included increased arrogance, contempt for the opinions of others, exaggerated self-belief, recklessness, incompetence, messianic tendencies, and social isolation, all of which significantly impaired his judgement and led directly to the disastrous decision to go to war in Iraq, which cost Blair his premiership.

Later, Owen was involved in supporting research into the hubris syndrome, defined as an "'acquired personality change' ... sparked by a specific trigger – exercising power.'[2] Research into the syndrome is now extensive and has shown that to hold power for an extensive period of time generates hormonal changes in the brain – specifically, testosterone levels rise while oxytocin levels fall (Robertson 2012). This is of great relevance to our current thesis. Oxytocin is known as the 'love hormone'; for example, when a mother gives birth, her oxytocin levels soar, facilitating the bonding process between mother and child.[3] From one perspective, therefore, a conscious focus on leading with love is a matter of priority for anyone in a position of power – as an antidote to prevent the hubris effect from taking hold and the capacity for love diminishing, with potentially disastrous consequences.

Eugene Sadler-Smith at Surrey University recently conducted a review of the research on hubris. It is worth quoting from his article:

> Hubris is a potentially dangerous cocktail of over-confidence, over-ambition, arrogance and pride. ... It is a malaise of the powerful and successful which, when allied to contempt for the advice and criticism of others, causes leaders to over-reach themselves significantly. ... As a consequence, hubris has the potential to destroy careers, wreck organisations and wreak havoc on entire industries; if left unchecked, hubristic leadership can undermine institutions, threaten societal well-being and destabilise global security.
>
> *(Sadler-Smith 2017: 525–26)*

The extensive research available on this topic is subtle and complex, and there is no space to go into detail here. However, it is important to raise the issue because of its relevance to a discussion of access to power in organisations. Sadler-Smith and his colleagues note that hubris is not simply the outcome of one person being in a position of power and abusing that power; rather, it reflects the structures, norms, systems, and processes that enable those less likely to lead with love to occupy positions of power.

Social dominance orientation

Jim Sidanius is the John Lindsley Professor of Psychology at Harvard University. He has devoted his professional career to elaborating the theory of social dominance orientation (SDO). It is a complex theory which examines the tendency for societies, groups, and organisations to develop structures and norms that promote social hierarchies. According to Sidanius, at the individual level – which is the focus of this chapter – people differ in terms of how much they view the world through the notion of hierarchy. Those high in SDO tend to sort people into superior and inferior and to discriminate against those who are lower in their subjectively constructed, but often socially reinforced, hierarchies.

People high in SDO see the world as a zero-sum game whereby people compete for goods such as wealth, education, health services, status, and influence. High social dominants are more competitive and less empathetic and regard those low in SDO as inferior (Sidanius *et al.* 2013). Regarding themselves as naturally superior to others, they believe they are entitled to greater access to valued resources than those lower in the hierarchy.

If you were to meet an individual with a high SDO, she/he would immediately and instinctively classify you in terms of your power in the system: 'Are you a player? Do I need to take you into account? Are you for me or against me? Are you useful?' Such an assessment is usually quick but sophisticated and (in the logic of self-fulfilling prophecies) accurate, and will determine the level of listening and engagement this individual will accord you. It is a functional assessment and surprisingly capable of adaptation if the power balance changes and you become, or cease to be, a power player.

Sidanius's research demonstrates that powerful, hierarchical organisations attract those who are high in SDO (Pratto et al. 2006) and that, once in place, social dominants are more likely to reach the highest levels of seniority than those who are more competent or more effective leaders (Anderson and Brown 2010). Having attained senior positions, they are motivated to acquire even more power and will use reward, fear, and punishment to control others. They value and promote those high in SDO at the expense of women (predominantly lower in SDO than men) and other groups viewed as lower status (Sidanius et al. 2013). They instinctively distrust (though may wish to be seen to espouse) egalitarian principles and are far more likely to be climate change deniers and to reject ideas around corporate responsibility (Jylha and Akrami 2015). Their greatest fear is loss of power and control, so they demand obedience and are susceptible to flattery and deference. They expect a disproportionate share of any financial or status-based rewards and see this as entirely legitimate and natural.

Leaders who appear to have SDO characteristics include those responsible for hugely damaging corporate scandals: Bernie Ebbers of WorldCom, Tony Haywood of BP, Didier Lombard of French Telecom, Bob Diamond of Barclays, and Ferdinand Piëch of Volkswagen; the latter, according to a *Fortune* article on the emissions scandal, was 'a brilliant engineer and a ruthless, terrifying manager who dominated VW for more than two decades' (Smith and Parloff 2016: 103).

The difference between SDO and the hubris syndrome is that the former is a personal preference (maybe even a personality trait), while the latter develops over time as a result of wielding power. Nevertheless, the two are similar in their effects.

Psychological maturity: implications for leadership

If we accept these conclusions about the negative psychological characteristics of many who attain power, then three important questions emerge:

1. How can we help those who are likely to take control of our organisations and institutions so that they mature into these important positions and lead us wisely?
2. How can we help those who are more developmentally mature get into positions of power in order to lead us wisely?
3. How can we prevent those too high in social dominance orientation from gaining access to power and also manage our leaders' susceptibility to the hubris syndrome?

It is clear that the aspiration to lead with love has to take into account, and overcome, the reality and distortions of power. So how, in the real world, do people go about this? Is it even possible to lead with love, or is it a recipe for career suicide? To address this question and the many more that we have raised earlier in the book, the next chapter moves on to look at leading with love as it is being manifested today by real people in real organisations.

We can leave the last words in this chapter to Martin Luther King:

> Power without love is reckless and abusive, and love without power is sentimental and anaemic. Power at its best is love implementing the demands of justice, and justice at its best is power correcting everything that stands against love.
>
> *(Kahane 2000: vi)*

Notes

1 Although Jung was a pioneer in this field before Erikson, Jung's ideas are strongly influenced by spiritual concerns and generally not incorporated within mainstream developmental psychology.
2 See http://www.daedalustrust.com/about-hubris/how-hubris-syndrome-arises/ (accessed 13 September 2020).
3 A high level of oxytocin can have drawbacks, too. It has been shown to lead to in-group preference over out-groups, or 'parochial altruism' (Carsten et al. 2010).

References

Allen, S.J. and Wergin, J.F. (2009) Leadership and adult development theories: Overviews and overlaps. *Leadership Review*, 9, 3–19.

Anderson, C. and Brown, C.E. (2010) The functions and dysfunctions of hierarchy. *Research in Organizational Behavior*, 30, 55–89.

Carsten, K.W.D., Greer, L.L., Handgraaf, M.J.J., Shalvi, S., Van Kleef, G.A., Baas, M., Ten Velden, F.S., Van Dijk, E. and Feith, S.W.W. (2010) The neuropeptide oxytocin regulates parochial altruism in intergroup conflict among humans. *Science*, 328(1), 408–11.

Jylha, K.M. and Akrami, N. (2015) Social dominance orientation and climate change denial: The role of dominance and system justification. *Personality and Individual Differences*, 86, 108–11.

Kahane, A. (2000) *Power and Love: A Theory and Practice of Social Change.* San Francisco, CA: Berrett-Koehler Publishers.

Kohlberg, L. and Power, C. (1981) Moral development, religious thinking, and the question of a seventh stage. *Zygon*, 16(3), 203–58.

Levenson, M.R., Aldin, C.M. and Cupertino, A.P. (2001) Transcending the self: Toward a liberative model of adult development. In Neri, A. L (ed.), *Maturidad e Velhice: Um enfoque multidisciplinary* (pp. 99–115). São Paulo: Papirus.

Plotkin, B. (2008) *Nature and the Human Soul: Cultivating Wholeness in a Fragmented World.* Novato, CA: New World Library.

Pratto, F., Sidanius, J. and Levin, S. (2006) Social dominance theory and the dynamics of intergroup relations: Taking stock and looking forward. *European Review of Social Psychology*, 17(8), 271–320.

Robertson, I.H. (2012) *The Winner Effect: How Power Affects Your Brain.* London: Bloomsbury.

Sadler-Smith, E., Akstinanaite, V., Robinson, G. and Wray, T. (2017) Hubristic leadership: A review. *Leadership*, 13(5), 525–48.

Sidanius, J., Ketily, N. Sheehy-Skeffington, J., Ho, A.K., Sibley, C. and Duriez, B. (2013) You're inferior and not worth our concern: The interface between empathy and social dominance orientation. *Journal of Personality*, 81(3), 313–23.

Skapinker, M. (2018) Unilever's Paul Polman was a standout CEO of the past decade. *Financial Times*, 11 December 2018. https://www.ft.com/content/e7040df4-fa19-11e8-8b7c-6fa24bd5409c (accessed 3 February 2019).

Smith, J. and Parloff, R. (2016) HoaxWagen. *Fortune*, 7 March 2016. https://fortune.com/longform/inside-volkswagen-emissions-scandal (accessed 12 June 2019).

Tornstam, L. (2011) Maturing into gerotranscendence. *Journal of Transpersonal Psychology*, 43(2), 166–80.

Wilber, K. (2016, September). States and stages and the three kinds of self. https://integrallife.com/states-stages-and-3-kinds-self/ (accessed 16 January 2019).

Yount, W.R. (2008) Transcendence and aging: The secular insights of Erikson and Maslow. *Journal of Religion, Spirituality & Aging*, 21(12), 73–87.

5

LEADING WITH LOVE IN PRACTICE

The research

This chapter presents the findings of research we conducted in order to address the very question that inspired this book: how do people, operating in highly complex and pressured environments, lead with love? There is a lot of material here, and some readers may prefer to use this chapter as a reference point rather than read it through from start to finish.

We started with the assumption that those being led with love are the best placed to recognise it and identify what it looks and feels like in practice. So we asked people in our networks to nominate leaders from their own experience whom, they felt, in some way 'led with love.' Most of our interviewees were nominated by someone who had worked for them or, occasionally, a peer who had worked alongside them.[1]

Both authors had access to people leading in organisations: Chris through his highly successful leadership development consultancy Waverley Learning, and Karen through her roles as Head of the Centre for Responsible Leadership, Programme Leader for the Doctorate of Business Administration, and teacher on the MBA programme, all at University of Winchester Business School. When we asked for nominations, we were surprised by how seriously people took the challenge. Try asking people around your own organisation to nominate leaders who lead with love: you will get some interesting reactions. After a conversation about what the notion means – although people often know instinctively what you are getting at, mentioning qualities such as empathy, kindness, compassion, care, and emotional intelligence – we found that people were rarely able to identify managers and leaders in their organisations who seemed to fit. However, occasionally, someone said that they knew a leader who fitted that descriptor perfectly; often they were quite excited to talk about the leader concerned because they had many happy memories of working for them. After some months of asking, we ended up with nine nominees (Table 5.1).

Table 5.1 List of nominees

Interviewee (not real name)	Role and sector	Age bracket
Charles	National director, global charity	60–65
Neil	Business owner and entrepreneur, medium-sized tech company	50–55
Matthew	Chief executive, global financial services organisation	45–50
Peter	Business owner and entrepreneur, medium-sized tech company	50–55
Ann	Director, transport industry	50–55
Naomi	Director, IT company	45–50
Susan	Founder and leader of national social action charity	30–35
Max	Director, global IT services company	50–55
Dan	Senior manager, global IT services company	35–40

It is obvious that this is by no means a representative sample of the UK organisational landscape, nor was it intended to be. If that was the goal, there would have been too many people in the high-tech industry, too few women, and little ethnic diversity. Instead, our first aim in interviewing our nominees was to gain an insight into how practising managers in hard-headed, target-driven environments (which includes the charity sector) manage to put loving leadership into practice and to explore some of the tensions and dilemmas they encountered in the process. The interviews, despite the narrowness of the sample, generated useful data both to inform our own understanding and to provide our readers with solid examples of how leaders put these ideas into practice. Our second aim was to analyse the interviews and to apply the analysis both to inform a framework for leading with love and to test it. We did not rely exclusively on the interviews when putting our framework together but we did use them to inform, shape, and test the rigour of the final version.

Before the interviews took place, we sent the questions to the leaders in advance to allow them to prepare their answers, as some questions needed deep reflection and thought. We were wary that spontaneous responses during the interviews could lead to superficial answers. We also felt that having the questions in advance would prepare them emotionally and psychologically for the kinds of areas we were going to probe: childhood, blind spots, mistakes, and failures, as well as motivations, successes, and achievements. Interestingly, the leaders took this process very seriously and often sought feedback from spouses and teams in order to gain deeper insights into their answers.

The completed interviews were transcribed, and a thematic analysis was conducted, using NVivo software, to identify the main themes.

In this chapter you will find the results of our analysis of the interviews. The thematic analysis generated a list of 104 open codes constructed using the language of our interviewees. We clustered similar codes together and identified the most popular codes, which are listed in Table 5.2 under 'sub-themes.' These were then formed into six broad themes (axial codes), which were then clustered into three areas which we called 'motivations,' 'character formation,' and 'expressing love in action,' as shown in Table 5.2.

The themes

We describe each of these broad themes below and explain how they emerge from the interviews. We will present the themes in a 'raw' form and not say too much about them until the next chapter, where we will combine them into an interpretative framework.

At this point we should note that we considered sharing all the stories we encountered of leading with love as 'exemplars,' thereby demonstrating ways in which those who would like to embody this kind of leadership might behave. However, we were deterred from this approach by two of the interviewee stories, which highlight the extremely personal and situational nature of this process.

Neil had decided to handover the CEO role in order to take a step back from the business and operate as chairman. As he observed the new CEO operate, he noticed something important:

> But it was interesting watching somebody almost mimic your style of management but not mean it, so for example he would walk through the office … he would say to one of the guys, 'Oh, how was your weekend this weekend?' They would start telling him and he would walk off. And I … and I did say to him one day, I said … 'You would be better off not asking [about their weekend], but to ask then not show interest is really quite insulting.'
>
> *(Neil)*

What Neil is getting at here is that leading with love is not a behavioural trick or technique; it comes from within and from a genuine interest in the people you are leading. This point appeared frequently in the interviews. Matthew put it like this:

> Whilst this very senior leader would say that investing in people is really important and would pronounce that he was committed to principles of mentoring and developing others and helping them to make the most of their potential, his actions didn't bear that out, and in fact he was more willing to make decisions to impress the owners than to make decisions that would enrich, inspire and motivate the staff to bring the very best they can to the office every day.
>
> *(Matthew)*

Matthew also made the point that a leader's underlying motives will 'leak' through their language. Hence, the senior leader he referred to above would say

TABLE 5.2 Thematic analysis of the interviews

	Broad theme (axial codes)	Sub-themes (open codes)	Meanings
1. Motivation	1.1 Deep motivators	1.1.a Staying true to values	Personal values as guides to leading others and making key decisions
		1.1.b Personal motivations	Personal goals, needs, and desires as drivers of action
		1.1.c Guiding philosophy or faith	Identifying normative beliefs that inform decision-making and action
2. Character formation	2.1 Character	2.1.a Childhood influences	An ability to stay open and connected to experience without losing touch with the felt sense of a true self and without getting too driven by ego needs. Referring to personal authenticity as a guide to decision-making Drawing on important childhood influences when developing a management style
		2.1.b Self-awareness and self-regulation	
		2.1.c Authenticity	
	2.2 Leadership learning and reflection	2.2.a Learning and reflexivity	Reflecting on the drivers of your behaviour and working on aspects of the self, including blind spots, in order to align behaviour with values, motivations, and beliefs. Reflecting on what works and what does not work in practice and changing behaviour in response Openly sharing mistakes in order to facilitate learning and encourage risk taking
		2.2.b Openness about mistakes and blind spots	
	2.3 Self-acceptance	2.3.a Developing self-confidence and self-respect	Developing self-respect based on a healthy acceptance of one's strengths while also cultivating kindness and compassion towards oneself and acceptance of one's imperfections
		2.3.b Self-compassion	

(Continued)

TABLE 5.2 (Continued)

	Broad theme (axial codes)	Sub-themes (open codes)	Meanings
3. Expressing love in action	3.1 Leading people	3.1.a Leading and managing 3.1.b Developing people 3.1c Building trust 3.1.d Managing power	Building trust to motivate, develop, and guide others towards a business aim. Managing power confidently and sensitively
	3.2 Building caring relationships	3.2.a Taking a genuine interest in people 3.2.b Expressing empathy and kindness to others	Building genuine relationships with your people, knowing them, understanding their lives outside work, and authentically taking an interest in them. Expressing love, empathy, kindness, respect, care, and compassion to others

things like 'We need to axe jobs' or 'We need to cut head count.' The images conjured by the word 'axing' and the use of 'head count' indicated an instrumental perspective in relation to people and a distancing of his decisions from the personal and often traumatic implications for those involved.

Both interviewees pointed out, either directly or indirectly, that leading with love is an emanation of deeply held values and beliefs and cannot be learned by simply mimicking behaviour. We identify this here as a potential trap for those interested in learning from our examples before further sharing the details of our research.

There follows a brief description of each code and some short quotes to illustrate the meanings. In a few cases we used the same quote in two different sections as it provided an illustration of more than one theme.

Section 1. Motivation

1.1 Deep motivators

All of our interviewees were outstandingly successful leaders inhabiting senior positions in their organisations, with many exerting influence over their own organisational policy and culture, and beyond into wider society. They did not attain these positions without having a focus on performance and achievement. All mentioned motivations such as achievement, success, ambition, perfectionism, performance, and status. Clearly, such motivations are necessary to survive and thrive in most organisations; however, while they are important, what was much more energising for all our interviewees was *how* they achieved success, with virtually all of them stating that they would not seek success at the cost of their underlying principles and values. A few conveyed the sense that they had perhaps not progressed as far as they could have because of their values, but they remained content with their decisions and would not have done otherwise: they would not have sacrificed their authenticity and principles for the sake of personal ambition.

1.1.a Staying true to your values

I had to just say to myself, 'Well, I'm going to do the best I can, I'm going to stay true to my values. You know, maybe I need to be more self-aware and maybe there are some things I need to improve, maybe there are some skills I need to develop, but I can keep doing what I'm doing and performing and bringing my team along with me.'

(Ann)

To use the biblical reference of Peter standing on the surface of the water looking at Jesus, but in a moment, as his faith weakens, he begins to sink and, as he sinks, he panics and rapidly his faith goes out of the window. I identify with that really strongly, because when I lose self-confidence, when I lose sight of what really matters to me, then I feel self-critical and, before I know it, I am stepping away from my values. This kind of downward spiral is driven by a self-fulfilling and discrediting action that you perform on yourself, and it is so important for me to keep returning, when I can, to my values and what is important to me.

(Matthew)

Honesty was the other thing from my parents, because lies will catch you up, nothing extraordinary but it's quite amazing. … I meet other people and sometimes think, 'Crikey, your values are really not there, are they?' Values are important – if someone is prepared to lie to you, then they are just prepared to lie and therefore probably best not to get involved.

(Peter)

An important element of this was *taking risks for your values.*

And I don't want to say too much, but I had an example last year, of where I was asked to carry out some, let's say, personnel action, which, to me would have completely undermined my credibility, and went against everything I believe in, and I refused to do it … if something feels morally wrong, it generally is, and don't do it.

(Max)

Matthew talked about a time when he challenged the decisions of the most senior people in the organisation:

It feels risky. Risky because you fear that you will be seen to be weak, or not a team player, or in some way trying to undermine somebody and their decision-making. But fundamentally, I know it would not sit well with me to not say something … and once the moment has passed I would lose the right forever more to say how I felt about it after the decision is taken. It is important for me to take that risk and to say 'This is how I feel' in that moment and not to let it pass.

(Matthew)

1.1.b Personal motivations

As stated above, all our leaders were motivated by some kind of task-oriented values such as career success, competence, or achievement, just as any other leader would be. However, these values were balanced by people-oriented motivations such as the desire to develop people and see them achieve their full potential. This balance between focusing on the needs of people and getting the task achieved has been a feature of all leadership models since Kurt Lewin first wrote about leadership styles in the 1930s and 1940s. It was also a central feature of leadership models coming out of the humanist movement in the 1960s and later with the famous Blake and Mouton grid (Blake and Mouton 1969). It was interesting to see how all our leaders instinctively referenced the need to balance the needs of people and task. It means that while being people-focused, they were fully aware of the need to make tough decisions that were right for the business. Therefore, the question was often: how can we make the tough decisions in a way that is as fair and as humane as possible for the people affected? This can perhaps be described as 'tough love.' And, while it is common to refer to people-oriented leadership styles as 'soft,' none of our leaders here could ever be described in such a way. They faced decisions in a clear-headed manner and were prepared to have the tough conversations that went with them. Remaining fair, honest, and transparent, they maintained the trust of their people, despite having to make difficult, bottom-line-focused decisions. In this respect, because they did not avoid the challenging conversations but faced them with compassion, respect, fairness, and honesty, they could be said to be courageous, strong, and 'tough-minded' leaders.

The quotes below show how, in their different ways, our leaders embodied this 'tough love,' combining people- and task-related motivations.

[S]uccess and status are important to me, but not at any cost …
… being known as someone that acts in the way I do, that's approachable, that's a good coach, that will take the time to care, love people.

(Max)

I really love difficult challenges, love solving problems and if something is challenging and difficult and on some level rewarding, either because I succeed or maybe because I learn why I didn't and I can improve for next time around, then I become energised. I would have to say I am very ambitious but I think I am 'challenge ambitious.' I'm not 'competitively ambitious.' ... I like to work to my standards not those of others.

... [F]rom a very young age I've always enjoyed coaching and supporting others and was often found at school leaning over to the person next to me and teaching them what we were doing to help them understand it. ... [I]t was less of a leadership activity and more from an interpersonal relationship perspective, I really enjoyed sharing freely what I understood and seeing other people learn and flourish.

(Matthew)

I really reflected on that, and it's win, win, win, win. Because he asked me one day, he said, 'What drives you? What's your motivator?' And I said, 'It's fear of failure.' Total fear of failure is, I'm the kind of guy I have nightmares of being out in the middle of the street with no clothes on. You know fear of failure to me is, and it drives me, I just never want to fail ...

... Because I think the majority of people are good ... I look for the good in people all the time. I try to look, I have a very empathetic view to life in general, so, one of the things I teach people when they join, is in their induction programme, is the, not only the rule of reciprocation and being nice to people is: you get kindness back, but also there's no such thing as bad dogs, there's bad owners, and a no-blame culture.

(Neil)

Max had to sit on a management board to decide on a significant number of redundancies:

We had a board of representatives from employee representatives and management representatives. ... I had the 'joy' of chairing that ... I remember the first meeting, and I said, 'Right, you know, none of us want to do this, but you know here are the reasons that this is happening, the way I'm going to run this, I'm going to be completely open and honest with you, and we're going to work on it together ... as a team, you know: this is not management versus employees. We will work on this together to make this as painless as possible for the people in the teams.' And that's what we did. And it was really interesting, because you know at the end of the day, I'm ... representing senior management [and] at the end of the process, which I think was a couple of months, the employee reps on the council insisted on taking me out for dinner.

(Max)

1.1.c Guiding philosophy or faith

For most of our leaders there was also something 'bigger,' behind or beyond these motivations – what we categorised in the research as a *guiding philosophy or faith*. This varied considerably, from deeply embedded principles often stemming from childhood to personally derived ethical standards or a spiritual faith. These seemed to provide an alternative reference point that helped them bring love to bear in their leadership.

> It set me thinking, on hearing I would be appointed to the role of chief executive … my first thought, my gut reaction, was that I wanted to embody a certain leadership. … I wanted to be the right kind of leader, I wanted to lead with authenticity, lead with honesty, and I was reminded of teaching and experiences at Harvard Business School about moral issues that we can face as leaders, of the challenges that power and decision-making can bring, where people throughout history have fallen over, were caught in the wrong place or doing the wrong things, in a secular or spiritual context. … There has to be an awareness of common good, I need to understand the role and purpose of the company from a societal perspective, despite working with people and in a system which has lost sight of this and which is focused on making money as its primary objective …
>
> *(Matthew)*

> So, and that's kind of what drives; that's the motivator, is: What can I do to improve not only the work environment that we're in, of which we spend more time here than we do with our families, but, broader than that, how can we improve society going forward?
>
> *(Dan)*

> What gets me up in the morning is knowing that campaigning can work, seeing how it's changed history for the better, and truly, like the cliché, truly believing that if we do it in a loving way, it can be even more effective. I think if loving activism wasn't as effective as hateful activism, I might not get up in the morning.
>
> *(Susan)*

> So, a lot of my whole leadership issue is to do with the fact that God chose me to be a leader, called me into leadership. So, therefore my foundation, the thing I stand on, has to be that calling. It has to be my connection to the God who calls. So, that's very important to me, that I'm connected to the God who calls … I think it's when, when I'm out there in the world and I'm meeting people and I'm listening to their stories, I get excited. I get inspired. If you see my Facebook page, on a Monday morning, often it's to do with the people that I met on the Sunday, people who are engaged or transformed.
>
> *(Charles)*

> I don't have a particular kind of religious philosophy, but I do believe that you have to do the right thing. … And that's grown stronger in me as I've got older … so, I think that there is that sense of doing, you have to do

the right thing, and that often is the right thing by yourself and by other people.

(Naomi)

So I have a natural sort of guilt that I don't want to do bad things, I don't want to have bad thoughts, I just don't ... but do you know I wrote down when I was going through the questions, I think I am quite a spiritual person ... I am absolutely 100% signed up to being agnostic but I've got buddhas on my desk and I'm fascinated by religion. But I'm not religious but I would say I'm spiritual ... I don't believe there's a God. I believe, spiritually, we go on ... something's got to go somewhere, so, that's why I feel spiritual, that I feel there's, we've got a soul; I really believe in the soul. You've got something inside you that's magical, that's something, you can't bottle it, you can't see it, but it has to be there.

(Neil)

I'm trying to think what other way I can express that. Just doing right by others because actually things come around. ... Do you know what I mean? Karma? ... not sure whether there is any mathematics around that.

(Peter)

Section 2. Character formation

2.1 Character

This is one of the most complex threads in the research because there are so many variables that contribute to it. By 'character' we mean a certain inner stability or emotional maturity, formed from life experience, which seems to underpin the capability to reconcile the often competing imperatives of leadership and love. It is beyond the scope of this book to attempt any thorough analysis of these factors, but we can pick out some common themes from the analysis of the interviews that seem to describe it.

One very noticeable factor was how people referenced their childhood as a source of the qualities they were embodying. Alongside this was self-awareness and self-regulation of their ego-drives which enabled them to keep enough perspective in leadership situations to allow love to come through. These seem to be quite deep foundational structures. Another key aspect of character was the commitment to authenticity, similar in many respects to staying true to values. Whereas the deep drivers that we highlighted above seem to relate to the 'source' of loving action, these attributes of character seem to relate to people's ability to manage themselves in the day to day and to stay connected to their true selves.

2.1.a Childhood influences

It is certainly not the contention of this book that the quality of upbringing in one's early years determines the capacity to lead with love, but what was noticeable among our interviewees was how 'fresh' and accessible were principles learned from childhood and how these principles influenced their leadership styles as adults. Many of them referred to lessons learned from childhood as being one of the main foundations of their ability to lead with love. It was also interesting to notice that most of our leaders appeared to have been brought up in stable, loving households.

> But I still come back to the sport piece; so, that was at about, yeah, eleven/twelve years old. I was in a football team. And I was the centre back for that team, so I could see the entire field. It was my job to adjust how we were playing through the course of a game and, again, just being given that responsibility early, to say: this isn't about you anymore; this is about the other ten players on the pitch – that was something I took to heart I think, and that's where it kind of formed the self-awareness aspect.
>
> *(Dan)*

> If asked, I think I would typically most often say that my father had the strongest influence on me as a child, because he had a very strong idea of how I should be raised, of the importance of education and good qualifications, of dedication and hard work. And so, no surprise, he was quite clear and quick to correct me about what was expected and was precise about how to go about things. But, actually, I think a much softer, but perhaps more impactful, influence came from my mother. She is terrifically forgiving, caring, a superbly humble person – too humble in my opinion, to a fault, almost – but she puts others first always and I learned from watching her ability to see a bigger picture, to see what is really happening outside of an immediate situation and to think about the longer term, the bigger impact. To me she's a very, very Christ-led person in her outlook on life as if in deciding how she conducts herself she first considers Christ's character and how he would see the situation.
>
> *(Matthew)*

> I was a trusted child, with boundaries; in that sense, I was, you know, I was able to try new things, to do things, but also there was a firm set of 'these are the rules and these are the boundaries that you have to stay within' as part of that, so, I think I felt trusted. I never felt distrusted as a child. It was always a case of: well, I could have a go at whatever. But also, I think I, there's an element of individuality about this; to be empathetic and to trust people you have to treat everyone as an individual. Both of those are dependent on that. And so, therefore, it's, and I was very much brought up with this sense of, you know: everyone is equal; they're not all the same. So, I think it's, when I first joined XXX actually, one of their values was respect for the individual. And that's the thing that certainly my parents very much taught me: it's respect for the individual, which I think comes

therefore out of this believing that every individual is worth looking into, is actually trying to do their best.

(Naomi)

I think it's being brought up in that loving environment, without being, not wrapped in cotton wool at all and I think it was the phrase – and I wrote down the phrase, you know – 'if you leave the cage door open the bird will return,' and they let me do what I wanted to do, and we discussed this the other day, the freedom they gave me was remarkable and I was a bit of a problem child. ... I played around, I played around and got in trouble ... so my parents gave me a bit of 'tough love,' I think the word would be ... they trusted me and it was amazing. The more that they trusted me with, I guess with love, rather than discipline, the better I got.

(Neil)

I think my mum and dad, they were very, I wouldn't say they were religious particularly, but they were very humane, I guess: you know the impact of your decisions and what you do to others comes around. ... Trusting, you know, the value of trust, gosh so many things, it is almost difficult to think, to put the words around them. ... I just remember them working really hard, me going into work with mum when she worked down the front road for a finance company and she's, yeah, an amazing lady: everybody loves her; she's a real gentle soul.

(Peter)

Whatever doesn't kill you makes you stronger, but it was, it was tough. But my mum and dad were amazing, just drip-fed us about constantly, where if you ever said that person's a 'bleep,' from any age, my mum would be really shocked; be like 'No, they're not, but what they've done is "bleep", you know. ... So, it was always an air of 'we don't label people and what they've done is awful, but we also need to try and understand where it's come from.' So, I always knew growing up that people were hurting other people because of their own hurt, and I was really lucky to have a stable, two-parent family, who both could work.

(Susan)

2.1.b Self-awareness and self-regulation

Alongside this ability to reference their own core principles, our interviewees also exhibited a level of self-awareness that enabled them to sense when they were being captured by their egoic concerns – and therefore to make decisions from a different reference point rather than just trying to meet the needs of their own egos. This seems to be crucial in maintaining enough independence of thought and action to be able to lead with love.

[S]o, I can choose in this moment how I'm going to react, and is it going to be a way that I'm going to be proud of, or is it a way that I'm going to be disappointed in myself, disappointed in my reaction, disappointed in the way that I had a choice, and I chose to go one way rather than the other. So, I think that's always kind of part of my decision-making, I have a choice

(Ann)

And because I am a bit of a perfectionist, I used to get really, really stressed if anything went wrong. I felt I'd made a mistake, hadn't done it perfectly, and she has, over the years, taught me and said to me, 'Did anyone die?!' … and it's stuck with me over the years now. When I get wound up about, I'm like, 'Did anyone actually die because I didn't do this or I did this wrong …?' Right, no, okay, right.

(Max)

… it's interesting, I think I have moved, I have moved from initially what I wanted was to be accepted, and for things to be completed and kind of tidy; that's where I started from. Now, I am more in the, I want to be respected and to do the right thing.

(Naomi)

I think it's that belief, not being in love with yourself but being able to be happy with yourself, be at one with yourself, being, I think, not worrying about stuff outside of your influence, worrying about the people directly involved around you and looking after yourself and just getting that balance there.

… If you've got it in you and you've got, I think, if you've got the confidence and you've got the – what's the word called? – recognising your own shortcomings and being able to ask for help and being able to trust other people to help you, and surrounding yourself by brilliant people, because one of the bravest things you have to do, because they might look at you and go, 'How is this fool running the business?'

(Neil)

Authenticity

Closely linked to the above is the theme of authenticity: the capacity to stay true to one's felt sense of self and express this openly in one's leadership – to allow oneself to be seen for who one really is.

And I think if you feel like you've done that, and you've really been true to yourself, then it makes it easier to make that decision. Because we're going to be faced as leaders with lots of tough decisions. It's about being sure when you're making that direct, difficult, decisive decision, that you know you're not going to second-guess yourself…

(Ann)

I'm just an employee, with a set of responsibilities; I'm no better than you; I don't know more than you; I'm exposed to things that you may not be, and I'll share all of those as much as I can, but it's to make the human side come out. And I think it's very easy for people in leadership positions to be abstracted away from who they are as a person, to feel they have to put a front on. Perfectly frank, that takes up too much energy.

(Dan)

Yeah, be yourself. I think you have to be true to who you are, because you get caught out very quickly if you're not. Be open and honest; and you know I think that's easier to say than to do sometimes, particularly when you're in management positions in a company when you know there are certain things I guess that are difficult for people to accept and understand. But I've always found if you try and hide that stuff, and it will come out in another way, and it's so much worse than if you'd just been open and honest in the first place, said, 'Hey, you know, here's the situation, this is what's going on,' and go with a plan.

(Max)

It is important to me to talk about how I feel about decisions because I can't always influence every decision being made in the way that I might like to, and sometimes all I can do is make sure that I have explained what I think is important and how I feel about something.

> **Author: To whom?**

Ultimately to the team, the main decision-makers or the ultimate decision-maker if it doesn't rest with me.

> **Author: Right, and what were the repercussions of that?**

Very few actually … it can be difficult to overcome fear, the natural instinct to keep quiet when I am against the majority view and to disagree with something, to go mutter to somebody else about it. But if I explain what I think is important, why I think it is important and how I think it should influence our decision, then even if the consensus doesn't go my way, I have done all I can to share the values I carry and colleagues understand where I am coming from.

(Matthew)

2.2 Leadership learning and reflection

All the characteristics we have described so far are deep-rooted in the values that guide the behaviour of our leaders. These deeper qualities run the risk of being 'buried' in the day-to-day practicalities of leading large and complex organisations. There was another cluster of attributes that emerged from the research, and these seemed quite different, being expressed almost as a deep, heartfelt appreciation of the need for space to pause, reflect, and learn; this was a discipline – something they had to be conscious of. Without this discipline, they may have struggled to integrate and align their outer world of decisions, communications, plans, and activities with their inner world of values, care, trust, and respect.

2.2.a Learning and reflexivity

[A]nd I think, today, reflection is so important … and I haven't had much time lately for reflection, personally, because we get so busy, you know, just like we've talked about: you know, Christmas and the run-up to it. And, I mean, I think people have to make that time; that's so important, but I think people underestimate how much they need to do that, and they undervalue it …

… And being reflective … And if you look at yourself in the mirror and you feel like 'Oh, gosh, I really sucked'… you know, go back and tell somebody, say, 'You know what? That wasn't the right thing for me to do.' … Don't be afraid to go back, you know, 'On reflection, I've thought about this, and I'm not sure that was the best decision'…

(Ann)

***Author*: And what do you think is the differentiating factor that enables people to lead with love?**

Calm … I think it is, you have to … the remaining relatively even and relatively calm, is important, because, yes, there will come times when you, like everyone else, just wants to explode or just wants to say, 'Please, get the hell on with it,' but if you do that, you break the consistency, and so that ability to sort of be able to see that coming, and remain calm, or even to step away. There are times when I have said, 'I can't talk to you about this at the moment, because I am not in the right headspace to do so.' Because, and I know if I have that conversation at that time, it's going to go wrong, because, you know, I'm tired and I know, therefore my fuse is short and this is going to be a challenging conversation.

(Naomi)

And, weirdly, yes, being angry about injustice, but probably being more angry that our campaigning was crap; it was clicktivism, it was slacktivism, it was shouting at people thinking they were going listen, when it's like this is completely illogical, and common sense tells us if we scream at people, people close up or they fight back. It just felt immature and stupid, not loving, not respectful, you know, and I just thought 'Oh,' and I still, to this day, it gets me out of bed, to be 'Oh, bloody hell, you know, we're intelligent human beings, we can do this in a better way … this isn't effective, there're other ways we can do it.' And knowing what Martin Luther King had done, what Desmond Tutu had done, what Mandela had done with conflict resolution, learning a lot from history as well …

(Susan)

So, I'm sitting there, and whenever I'm in a conversation where there's a difference of opinion, it's important for me, in my being, to be right; to know that I'm right. So, I'm sitting there; initially, she's shouting and going on, and her behaviour tells me she's wrong and I'm right. I don't even have to dig deep; her behaviour tells me I'm right, she's wrong. And then, as she calms down and she starts talking, I'm having to dig deeper about whether I'm right … you see, in the beginning I was confused that she didn't get this because she's bright, she's an intelligent woman…

Then I'm starting to feel insecure about my position.

Because my position is, it cannot be maintained here. This girl will never be better by the way I'm working with her … and eventually I'm beginning to feel sorrow and shame, because I'm feeling 'You never bothered to get to know this girl; if you'd just thought that because you knew what was right and wrong about her presentation that you could impose that knowledge on her; you'd never bothered to learn how to guide her.' So, by the end, I'm feeling very sorry. And, so, it was a very important catharsis moment for me; you started this conversation being right, but you were actually wrong, and you have to deal with that. So, I had to deal with all of those things while talking to her.

(Charles)

And it was like an arrow between the eyes, it was like 'Oh, okay, I need to catch myself from saying that.' And I just said it this morning … and I stopped to say 'I'm really sorry, I didn't mean it that that may have been received.' … And you know he said, 'It's absolutely fine.' But it's a constant now, right, catch yourself and learn and change your language. So, again, a key characteristic is knowing when you need to learn and evolve, and learning and evolving and being passionate about that is hugely important.

(Dan)

2.2.b Openness about mistakes and blind spots

One aspect of this spaciousness and learning is a vigorous commitment to overcoming blind spots and giving others permission to speak into their leadership. Our leaders were conscious of how admitting mistakes and being open about their own limitations made them more human and more approachable. It also built tremendous levels of trust. Openness about making mistakes, according to Dan, 'builds all of the trust that you need.'

> So, I think it's about being really open and being really honest and sharing not only your successes, but sharing your failures or when it hasn't gone your way too. ... And if you look at yourself in the mirror and you feel like 'Oh, gosh, I really sucked' that, you know, go back and tell somebody, say, 'You know what? That wasn't the right thing for me to do.' Don't be afraid to go back [and say], you know, 'On reflection, I've thought about this, and I'm not sure that was the best decision.'
>
> *(Ann)*

> And an element of what is important ... is that accepting that if ... you're not failing you're not pushing hard enough. And I tell my teams that. But what's important is that you learn from that. So, I think ... 'Okay, I've messed up; how [do] I fix that?' And sometimes ... 'Oh dear, I've really messed up, you know, I mean I've really messed up, I've really got this wrong, I need some help sorting it out' ... and that ... brings the integrity back into it that says ... 'If I've messed up, I should admit that I've messed up, and try and put it right, as best I can,' but then, also, to try and work out 'Okay, well, how I make sure that doesn't happen again. Where did it go wrong? Where was the bad decision? Where is the bad road that I took?'
>
> *(Naomi)*

> I do talk very openly to my assistant, and if dark thoughts come into my mind or I start getting negative, either about myself or about others, I'll often ask her 'Am I going down the wrong road here?' I also feel very lucky to have two male friends outside of work who challenge and encourage me. We are all of different ages and different stages in life and have different backgrounds and we meet regularly as a 'three' and we advocate for each other and listen to each other's life situations and challenge each other. Over the years, we have been able create a space where no subject is off the table, and so the dialogue can be hard-going and tough, but it really feels like iron sharpens iron and we have grown together.
>
> *(Matthew)*

> Because, unless you meet somebody, you don't, it's very hard, in black and white, to pick up on it. ... And it's that constant challenging of yourself around your own biases, and, and questioning your viewpoint all the time, so that you get to the better conclusion...
>
> *(Dan)*

> So, you know, that is always something I say to new managers, is, you know, 'Look around the team and what are the strengths and weaknesses?

What are you missing?' you know, 'Bring in the oddballs ... the maver-
icks, the people that think differently, that are going to challenge you,'
because, you know, it will add a whole other dimension.

(Max)

Our leaders were also aware of how admitting to their own mistakes encouraged
others to admit to theirs while also encouraging others to take risks in their own
learning and growth.

Yeah, so, you know, if things do go wrong, and sometimes they will, or if
they don't go as well as you would have hoped they went, then, you know,
you made the decision to give them that independence, to give them that
opportunity, then you've got to be prepared to stick with it, and support
them through that. And, you know, they'll learn from it and, you know,
most of the time people don't make the same mistake again. That it's just
part of the learning process. And that's key, and I think if people see that
they know you've got their backs.

(Max)

2.3 Self-acceptance

2.3.a Developing self-confidence and self-respect

Another factor that emerged consistently among our leaders was a quiet but pervasive love and respect for themselves; they took themselves seriously but not too
seriously. A better word to capture this might be 'humility,' but it is a paradoxi-
cal humility which enabled them to value their strengths and be bold when they
needed to be. It also seemed to strengthen their ability to love, respect, and be
tolerant and understanding of others. This was a subtle dimension in the research,
which emerged 'between the lines' – often in how people spoke about themselves rather than what they said. This self-respect was consciously cultivated by
some (Charles); in others, it developed gradually through the maturation process
(Naomi); while some seemed to emerge from childhood with a natural self-love,
such as Neil, Peter, Dan, and Ann. Regardless of how it developed, all of our
leaders demonstrated what we referred to in Chapter 4 as 'self-acceptance': a sign
of entry into a mature and wise adulthood.

Here are some illustrative quotes that cover the three sub-themes of developing self-confidence, self-respect, and self-compassion.

I think respecting myself is very important, and I think that's partly what
drives the 'do the right thing,' and the reason that it's got stronger over
time is because if I am not doing the right thing, then I don't have respect
for myself.

(Naomi)

And I definitely, I'm in a place now where, you know, I do like who I am as a person. I know I have core strengths that are valuable to people, and to the business.

(Dan)

So, I grew up thinking I'm inferior to White people and I'm superior to Black people. And on top of this, I had, I understood when I was about eleven, twelve years of age, I came to understand I had a self-image problem. I had an inferiority complex, which was exacerbated by the Apartheid system. And I had to address that, I had to address the fact that I walk into a room and was tense about it … I think, I think I'm more at ease about who I am … when I first started looking at my inferiority complex years ago, I saw that the thing to do is to look at your successes; what works. And I've taught myself to feel more confident about myself by my successes. And it's the same now.

(Charles)

And I don't know whether that's kind of deliberate, but … in my own mind, I've equated love to respect. It's about yourself, being yourself. It's about self-respect. It's about just caring for people.

(Max)

If you've got it in you and you've got the confidence and you've got the – what's the word called? – recognising your own shortcomings and being able to ask for help and being able to trust other people to help you, and surrounding yourself by brilliant people, because one of the bravest things you have to do, because they might look at you and go 'How is this fool running the business?'

(Neil)

We'll leave the final note on this sub-theme to Peter, who seems to have demonstrated a healthy self-respect from childhood.

I'm comfortable with the way the business runs and the way that I interact with people…

So 'loving yourself'? That's not a question I have ever been asked before. Do you love yourself? I really ought to lose weight, you know, I'm short fat and ginger! So I'm not in the best position to answer that question! I've never been asked that question before, actually; that's interesting.

(Peter)

Self-compassion

'Self-compassion' refers to how we look after ourselves, how we forgive ourselves when we make mistakes, and how we retain our self-respect through the ups and downs of life. While our leaders tended to have high levels of self-acceptance, nearly all of them spoke of periods when they struggled with self-doubt. What distinguished our leaders, however, was their self-awareness in this process and their strategies for regaining equilibrium. We can see evidence of this in the examples below.

> And because I used to get, and because I am a bit of a perfectionist, I used to get really, really stressed if anything went wrong. I felt I'd made a mistake, hadn't done it perfectly, and she has, over the years, taught me and said to me, 'Did anyone die?' And if the answer is no, put it behind you and move on. Now, I can say that in my environment. If you're a consultant in a hospital, you wouldn't be able to say that, to be fair. But it works for me. And it's stuck with me over the years now. When I get wound up about, I'm like, 'Did anyone actually die because I didn't do this or I did this wrong?' Right, no, okay, right.
>
> *(Max)*

Matthew talks about how he frees himself from the condemnatory voice of his 'inner critic.'

> I'm very aware of the importance of self and self-awareness. I am prone to feeling that I'm not good enough at whatever it is I'm doing. I often feel that I struggle because of high empathy, that I waste a lot of time worrying about what people think. I am naturally oriented to what others think of me and that can lead me into quite a difficult cycle. I know for sure at the times when I am feeling less good about myself, I love myself less, my confidence wains and then I behave worse.
>
> **Author: And so how do you sustain that ... self-acceptance?**
>
> I think I just try to focus on self-awareness, I think the self-awareness of my own condition, of understanding what makes me weak to and talking to others about it.
>
> *(Matthew)*

For others it was how they turn to family and friends at times of self-doubt.

> And I definitely, I'm in a place now where you know I do like who I am as a person. I know I have core strengths that are valuable to people, and to the business. The missing link is, is a hundred per cent belief in that, which may hinder my progress. I don't think it will, but it has the potential to. So, I do, I do need that, again that positive confirmation of my family loving and supporting me, which they do, absolutely, and that your value is felt. Because the minute your value isn't felt, then you need to go and do something different.
>
> *(Dan)*

I spend time with family and friends, I do some yoga, but it's not all-encompassing ... and gardening is a, for me, a great stress-breaker, because I find that it's, I guess it's what really we'd now call mindfulness, which says that it's you have to concentrate enough on it that other things aren't going on in your head, but not so hard that it's taking a lot of brain power.

(Naomi)

[Y]ou know we all wake sometimes and don't want to be there, we have got a headache or things are bothering you, whatever it might be, and I've always found that ... when I can [play] my music, lift my spirits or calm me down and get me ... refocused. And [then] I get very excited about life because opportunity is everywhere, if you are in 'receive' mode. So my way of being in receive mode and get the benefits of everything is to give out, so my doors are open all the time and people on the outside perceive that as love, care and it is one hundred per cent but actually if my doors are open, I get it back.

(Neil)

[B]ut God put [my wife] in my life to help me to understand that I must connect. And she helps me. And tells me when she feels that I'm forgetting and I'm reverting to the goal is more important than the people around us.

(Charles)

Section 3. Expressing love in action

It is this section that really gets to the nub of what leading with love is: how our leaders made things happen, leading people in pursuit of tangible, challenging missions and goals while still maintaining the climate of love, respect, trust, and authenticity that we have been seeing in the sections above.

The first thing to notice, already mentioned above, is the 'tough love' category: the willingness to step into difficult and challenging conversations, usually the result of a baseline of respect built on strong relationships. What is clear is that our leaders did not shirk the use of their power; rather, they employed it with a reflexivity and awareness that did not erode the foundation of love.

3.1 Leading people

3.1.a Leading and managing

You know, it's not an individual journey. I mean, sometimes I've had to make individual decisions about a path I might take, but it's, I think, the ability to go back to as a leader, and really saying, 'Okay, well what's in it for me?' But also 'I've got to have the team, so what's in it for them?' and being able to look at being able to balance your self-needs with the team, with others. … And that doesn't mean that you can't be directive or clear in your vision, it just means that people are going to be really open and honest with you too. Hopefully, I'm bringing them along for the journey, for, you know, and they're engaged in that journey, and you know they want to do things because they believe in you as a leader and they believe in the organisation.

And deliver, and delivery is all.

(Max)

I decided to really invest in my business and my people as equally as I do with my customers. The first thing you will notice in the office is it's really light, and in fact we have just invested in full-spectrum LED lighting to make it an even better environment. We make sure when everybody comes in we water them, we [provide] food … we look after them, we check the temperature's right, real baseline stuff on the hierarchy of needs. And when you have done the baseline, then you put the philanthropy on top. It all builds and I think that's where we have done so well, not grown to be the biggest company in our sector, but you know twenty-four years consistently safely giving a good place to work and believing in what we believe in and, of course, then customers believe in you, so it is much easier to win customers, so we have effectively no sales force.

(Neil)

So being inclusive … for me, I don't understand why companies don't do it. For me, it is that black and white. If you don't create an environment where people are in for the long-term journey, then they will leave earlier and they will leave for the wrong reasons! If they can see that they are part of the plan, an important part of that plan … then they get better job satisfaction. As long as you don't abuse that … life becomes easier, you know, so you don't have to permanently motivate everybody, which can be quite tiring too, trying to keep everyone going in the same direction I guess. I don't think you have to think about that if everyone is rewarded by success … we have created an employee benefit trust which is a relatively expensive thing to do but it means people have got real participation in the output value of this business.

(Peter)

3.1.b Developing people

So, I think there is a little bit there about taking personal responsibility, and then it's about really understanding how your employees connect to your business journey. And I think people, you know, I've heard people say, 'I just don't have time to develop my employees,' and I was like, 'Well then, you're not going to be very successful.' ... Because it's all about what you give back to people, you know, and what you give back is what you're going to get ... it's kind of like that servant-leadership style.

(Ann)

Just to fast-forward, you know, thirty years to today, somebody in the team here has just been made a manager, and they're twenty-seven; I was twenty-eight when I was made a manager, so, that's, you know, it's a great age to become a manager. So, when they came around to me and shared the exciting news, I'm normally very animated with, when that sort of thing happens, but I was quite muted, and they could tell.

And we sat down and had a conversation about it, and they said, 'Why are you not really, really excited?' I said, 'I am, I'm really thrilled for you, but I wanted to have just five minutes to talk about, this isn't about you anymore, you've got a team of people now who are going to look to you. ... Now it's time for reflection, you've got huge responsibility now – delivery, revenue, people – this isn't about you.' And I think that, again, is born from all of those years of experience leading teams from a very, very young age. And, again, it didn't matter whether it was successful or not, you know, that was, that was the learning curve I needed and the challenge that I needed to get me to where I am today.

(Dan)

It's like anything: the more effort you put in the better it tends to be, which also means I find it really difficult to let go and not micromanage people, and to see people who've done stuff [thinking] that it could be better. I'm trying to find a way to say 'That's really interesting; tell me a bit more about who you're trying to target and how' in a loving way, that doesn't dismiss what they've done, but also doesn't say 'Yeah, that's great,' because my worry is by saying 'Yeah, it's all great ...' they're not going to grow in what they do, you're actually stunting their growth. You know, if it's too easy, then engagement isn't there, it's not thoughtfully done, and that's a struggle, and that's something that my friends are like 'Just let it go, and say, 'That's great,' retweet it,' which is all what they want, and I'm like 'No, I want them to learn more; I want them to do it better.'

(Susan)

Building trust

So, you know, respect, developing their careers, I think giving them independence. I'm not, never have been, a micromanager. I've worked for micromanagers and I hate it. I think you have to start from a position where you trust people. You trust them to get done what they need to get done, and I think especially in a professional environment like this.

(Max)

With the business I sold to [a large multinational corporation] there was no question the team we put together were working together really beautifully because there was a fantastic sense of community in the business. Everybody knew everyone's good points, their misgivings, it was all very open and honest …

(Peter)

And I think pulling out two the key pieces for me are: trust and empathy. So, therefore, actually, just caring about someone is not enough.

Because trust is two-way, and so, therefore, you have to explain why and how you got to where you're asking them to do, and so on and so on; leading with trust is part of the 'why.' Put yourself in their shoes, whoever they happen to be, and the more you know them the better, you know that is for you, and you will do it better the more you know them. So, spend a bit of time getting to know people. I'm not a great social chit-chatter and whatever, and I can't always remember the names of the kids of my, you know, people that work for me and things like that, but I try to get an overall sense of them: their humour and what's important to them, and that type of thing. Leadership is hard, and it's a responsibility, and you'll not always be popular or comfortable in the moment, but get used to that. There is no other way, in my view, to lead well …

(Naomi)

You can do them and the organisation harm if you're not prepared to do some of the hard things, to set the boundaries, to have the hard conversations and so on; but it's how you do those that are the key elements of it. So, one thing I think I worked out a long time ago, which was, I think, part of my first management role, I actually worked alongside, very closely with another manager, who, and we were almost the polar opposite in the fact that he was tough on the outside and soft in the middle. And as a result of that, watching his style, seeing some of the pickles he got into, made me realise that, for me, my definition of a good manager/leader is someone who is fluffy on the outside with a spine of steel.

(Naomi)

3.1.d Managing power

Our leaders were acutely aware of how their position in the hierarchy affected how people interacted with them. Many of them worked hard to be seen as approachable and trustworthy in order to alleviate others' natural wariness of those in senior positions. Some talked about using their power to confront their own managers, which was often to defend or protect their staff from intimidation, unfairness, or bullying. All were quite aware of their own power and its impact on those around them, and they all used that power consciously and with integrity.

> But I think, for me, it's more, came from there and understanding if you want to be able to do this and if you want to be able to influence this and if you want to be able to make a difference, then you have to have and assert your power. So, therefore, you've got to find a way of doing that that's within your values.
>
> ... [S]o, I kind of would sit there and go, 'I want to change that,' but to do that I have to get that job. Because I don't want that job by running over someone else, because then I don't respect myself ... but it was about seeing that to be able to make a difference, to be able to do this, I need to get there, I need more power, and I need more influence, so, how, and how do I get that? And, in a hierarchy, you have to demonstrate power and influence, and impact.
>
> *(Naomi)*

> So ... I started modelling caring leadership. Sitting down with people, refusing to have a special table ... refusing to go first in the queue. You know, just trying to see, make them see, that we are normal people. I went on Facebook and I accepted everybody as my friend on Facebook. I showed them that I enjoyed sport, that I, you know, I tried to be a normal person. And I think that, in the five years we were there, we changed the way that leadership is done in the UK. Because there were a lot of younger leaders, who wanted this leadership.
>
> *(Charles)*

> And I think it's really interesting, because I don't think there's a lot of people that would say I'm a very direct communicator, but I think in my experience, as I have grown in my leadership, I've become more of an influential communicator. So, I can communicate directly, but I also know that, you know, in a role like this, you have to influence people. You can't just be directive all time, and I think leaders get confused about that.
>
> *(Ann)*

> I am impatient, one of my worst traits, and I always explain to the guys out there that when I talk about things it's with the greater good in mind, and if I am being impatient and unreasonable then I expect them to tell me. I would have failed if I bit their heads off when they did it ... if you are not free to express your opinion. I know I'm not right all the time, by no means ... I like to think most of the time I'm quite considered.
>
> *(Peter)*

Dan challenged how his manager behaved in a team meeting.

> And that style of behaviour was only going to lead to one thing, and people would leave … So, the course of action was essentially to confront the topic, and that's exactly what I did.
>
> *Author*: **So, you confronted the topic of [your manager's] behaviour?**
>
> Yeah, with him, directly … But after the call had ended, I put my thoughts down on paper, in an email, and then said, 'We need to have a call about this,' which many people wouldn't do, because there's a risk to doing that, huge risk … But we had a phone call the next day, and I put my position across again, firmly …
>
> *(Dan)*

Finally, Max made the interesting point that, in his organisation, it was easier to get to the top by manifesting a more macho and less empathic leadership style. This supports the work done by Jim Sidanius, which we examined in Chapter 4: those with higher levels of social dominance orientation are more likely to get to the top in powerful, hierarchical organisations.

> I think we, we have quite a macho environment. … But there's a certain set of behaviours I think that are, for whatever reason, seen to be required to get to the higher levels. And I have an issue with that, because I don't like working for people that behave in that way, and it's not something I'm even really capable of doing. So, yeah, I think it does stick out, and I'm by no means the only one. You know, there are a lot of caring managers in the organisation, as you'd expect. But I think we do have a problem with getting those people to senior levels.
>
> *Author*: **So, you, did you ever feel a pressure to adapt your leadership style in order to get on in the company?**
>
> Yes, absolutely.
>
> *(Max)*

3.2 Building caring relationships

The final theme is the importance of taking a *genuine interest in people* – in their lives outside of work, in their hopes and ambitions, in their skills and their potential to develop: what we referred to earlier as an 'I–thou' perspective, from the work of Martin Buber. Just as people's core values seem to underpin their leading with love at a personal level, so this quality underpins their ability to get things done collectively, with the kind of trust and efficacy that we highlighted in the previous section.

In addition to praising their staff, our leaders were often able to respond to their people in a manner that was finely tuned to their needs. They could do this because they knew their people and were often entrusted with information about what was going on in their employees' lives outside of work. This is not a by-product of working closely with teams day after day. It is a conscious strategy of getting to know one's people in depth.

3.2.a Taking a genuine interest in people

> Be inquisitive; know your employees. So, I think it's a little bit about, you know, a little bit about that personal connection; it's not all just business. It's like how, you know, our teams spend more time in the workplace than they do at home, and how do we make this workplace that they can be successful, that they feel comfortable coming into every day, that they have great management and great tools to develop themselves, personally and professionally, and I think, for me, that's kind of been 'How do we create that?'
>
> *(Ann)*

> [D]o you know what I mean, but I'm intrigued, I'm always intrigued by people, I'm nosey!
>
> *(Peter)*

> [I]f all we are ever doing is engaging at a professional level – 'I need this from you,' 'Why have you broken my code?,' 'Where are you on these test cases?' – that's not a relationship. I want to know who the people are, and you can't force that.
>
> *(Dan)*

> And also an element of watching people's lives, you know, they have lives outside of work, and they impact significantly. And one of the ways that you can make a real positive influence on somebody's life, and on their overall business performance, is just having that awareness of where they are in life, and the fact that, while their intrinsic motivation may not have changed, there is something else going on for them at that time, and you may even not know what it is, but put that, trying to put yourself in their shoes, that to me is the, you know: sympathy is the sort of observance of something; empathy is that, without getting too emotionally involved, trying to think 'How might they be feeling about this? How might they view this? How might...?' and that piece of it, and, again, that sort of comes back from the always assuming you know people come to work to do a good job.
>
> *(Naomi)*

3.2.b Expressing empathy and kindness to others

Work is a place where judgement is everywhere. It is often shocking to listen to both casual and formal workplace discussions and note how often they are imbued with judgement and/or blame of others. This is so ingrained in many workplaces that we often fail to notice we are being judgemental, and, of course, much of the time it is a defensive strategy: we often judge others in order to deflect attention from ourselves. But, as the famous biblical quote warns us, in judging others we normalise judgement and it will surely be wielded against us: 'Do not judge or you too will be judged' (Matthew 7:1–2). This calls to mind the *New York Times* article about Amazon, cited in Chapter 3, where colleagues are encouraged to judge each other's performance and report on them anonymously. According to the article, this culture of judgement led to groups of workers making pacts and ganging up on their more vulnerable co-workers (parents with young children or those with long-term illnesses), filing negative reports on their performance while safeguarding their own jobs. This is the opposite of leading with love. Leading with love involves catching people doing well and finding opportunities to praise. Praise from a senior colleague is a blessing: it makes the heart smile, it is remembered, it reassures and calms, it brings peace.

> And that's when you realise you've got to be there for people, because, you know, you never know what's going on in the background. So, when it's physical, like you can see it, but mentally, you know … one of my guys got into [great difficulty] …
>
> … [B]ecause people confide in me in what's going on in their lives, so, now I really don't mind being Uncle Neil, I really don't mind. Some of the other managers, oh, you know: 'You waste so much time with these people time coming and talking to you,' but they want to talk, and actually if they talk I understand them, and if I understand them, I can work with them.
>
> *(Neil)*

> So, I actually, you know, I guess I've quite a simplistic approach to management generally, and it really is about, you know, showing people respect, caring about them. So, you know, I am someone that, I do try to take account of the fact that people have a life outside of work, and they may have stuff going on in that life outside of work, you know, that's really important to them. You know, and I think you have to kind of factor that into your interactions with people, kind of knowing what they've got going on. It's about, you know, I think, allowing people to develop, or, and helping them to develop.
>
> *(Max)*

Matthew talked about the reaction he received when people learned he had been made CEO.

> A lot of people said to me, 'We are so pleased that you are our CEO because people like you rarely get these kinds of jobs' … and I would immediately think that this meant I didn't deserve it or somehow I wasn't the right sort of person. But when I probed further, these people told me that they saw me as somebody who cares about people, someone who is 'human,' someone who is connected with people and has relationships with people all across the company, and someone who talks openly and honestly about problems. This emboldened me to set my sights ever stronger on servant leadership.
>
> *(Matthew)*

> So, the Senior Leadership team, it's very important that I'm speaking into their lives, not only with my mouth, but with my actions; they feel that I'm open to them, that I'm transparent, that I care about them beyond their work … and I suppose, really, I just, I focused on solving problems and on doing that through relationships and on through understanding people and trying to explain, well, what we were doing at all levels. It was probably, you know, less a leadership perspective but more of an interpersonal relationship perspective … that people could see that was important to me.
>
> *(Charles)*

Peter talked about a time when he sold another business and wanted to both incentivise and reward the people who worked in it.

> I went back to the new owners of the business. … I actually got to take the whole company on holiday, actually, to Center Parcs: we went for a week with all our families.
>
> *(Peter)*

> [B]ut it's much better to love people than to hate people. So it's much more exhausting to be really angry with people, than to say, 'I don't know their background, I don't know where they're coming from, I don't know what's going on in their family life or their work or the other pressures they've got on them, so I'm going to have to presume they're trying their best, and work from that' … and I've learnt these habits over years, where now I feel much more sustainable.
>
> *(Susan)*

* * *

In light of the interview excerpts in this chapter, we hope it is clear how we derived the themes that form the backbone of our 'leading with love' framework. In the second half of the book we will look at *how* to build our capacity to lead with love. But, first, we ask: do you really *want* to lead with love?

Note

1 The only exception to this was a leader whom one of the authors heard being interviewed on BBC Radio 4 on the subject of leading with love – she had in fact established her organisation based on these principles. Karen contacted this leader personally.

Reference

Blake, R.R. and Mouton, J.S. (1969) *Building a Dynamic Corporation through Grid Organization Development*. Reading, MA: Addison-Wesley.

6

IS LEADING WITH LOVE
REALLY FOR ME?

We have argued in previous chapters why love is so necessary in our leaders today, and we have demonstrated how love characterises the more mature levels of human functioning. We have proposed that it is not unreasonable to expect those in leadership positions to demonstrate this kind of maturity. We have acknowledged the powerful systemic forces that act to pull us away from love. But we have also seen from the research that there are people in leadership positions exposed to these forces who are known and valued for their capacity to lead with love. We have discerned from these interviews some common themes that characterise these people.

Our book now moves from analysis to development. If, as a result of your reading and reflections so far, you believe that you, too, could lead with love, you are primarily confronted with two questions: why should you? And, if you decide to commit to this, how do you go about it? This is a decision that faces many leaders, and it is a very personal one. Here is Martin Luther King on the subject:

> And I say to you, I have also decided to stick to love. For I know that love is ultimately the only answer to mankind's problems. And I'm going to talk about it everywhere I go. I know it isn't popular to talk about it in some circles today. I'm not talking about emotional bosh when I talk about love, I'm talking about a strong, demanding love. And I have seen too much hate.
> *(Martin Luther King, Jr., 1967)*

Why should I lead with love?

So to the perennial question: *is this for me?* The first, self-evident, point is that leading with love is not something that organisations and communities can require of their leaders. It has to come from within. Love is not something that can be mandated or measured, else it becomes compliance and falls into the same performativity issues that we were speaking of earlier. We lead with love because we *want* to lead with love, and the people around us will lead with love if we create the conditions in which they *want* to. That then becomes the key question: *do I really want to?*

So far, we have made the logical case for why to lead with love and why it is more necessary nowadays than ever. To restate it in brief:

1. Our current ways of working are dysfunctional, and we all have a growing sense, we cannot carry on like this. Our patterns of consumption, exploitation, and instrumentalism are choking the life out of ourselves, each other and our planet. The balance of power is out of kilter in our society, with the few benefiting disproportionately at the expense of the many. The power of technology to control and influence behaviour is growing exponentially, making it increasingly easier to 'instrumentalise' people. Even those at the top are sensing that the 'system,' the machine, is running us; it is not us running the machine.
2. We need a new kind of leadership to reset some of the forces that are driving us in our organisational life today. The 'lower' part of our nature is the one that is being called forth, and this in turn is reinforcing the patterns described above. We find ourselves in an overwhelming state of reactivity: too much fear, greed, insecurity, overwork, exploitation, and exhaustion. Not only is this oppressive, it is also inefficient and inimical to progress in the longer term.
3. All the key studies of human development indicate that conscious love is the highest stage of human attainment. It is also the foundation point of most of the major spiritual and wisdom traditions. Surely we can expect the people entrusted with leadership to be operating at these higher levels of human functioning? Why would anyone not aspire, as a trusted and responsible leader, to embody this in their leadership practice?

These are all eminently sensible reasons why we should be leading with love. *But do they really move us to action?*

Beyond these functional reasons, we can set forth more personal reasons why it is good for our own emotional and spiritual wellbeing to lead with love.

Leading with love will give you a different foundation point for your being, leaving you less vulnerable to the vagaries of life/the system/performativity. It brings you in touch with your true self and weakens the holds that others and the system exercise over your emotions, thoughts, and actions. You find yourself able to demonstrate more authenticity and less conformity to others' expectations, which in turn can generate an increased sense of freedom and happiness (Joseph 2016; Brown 2010). Secondly, research in the field of positive psychology shows that the experience of positive relationships at home and at work is an important source of personal happiness (Seligman 2004). A third reason is that love is the source of true leadership and adventure – a life worth living. You find the courage to speak and act from your core; you bring the undiscussables into the light, and good people will trust you (though others may not). When you decide to travel this path, it is a call to adventure and you never quite know what will happen. You move beyond the reactive self, where your past determines your future, to an open terrain, where you make the road by walking.[1]

Finally, there is the spiritual perspective, expressed in most of the world's major religions. Human beings are made for love – capable of giving it and receiving it. To love is to be fully alive and fully present to the divine, the sacred, the transcendent in nature and art and culture. It is the source of our greatest joy in life, and our lives have little meaning without it. Love is therefore the most profound force in the human heart. All we have to do is to tap into this force and let it infuse our action.

Again, these are all potentially compelling reasons why we should be leading with love. *But do they really move us to action?*

Heart-knowing and head-knowing

This question takes us to the heart of what we will be exploring in the second half of the book. Love is not something we simply make a decision about and then work out how to do. It has an energy of its own, and this energy needs to infuse our being at a deep level for us to move into loving thought and action. We can't just *think* our way into love, however much we try: we have to *feel* our way in. This involves a different human faculty: the heart. Love is a 'heart-knowing,' which operates differently from our evaluative and predictive reasoning processes. How do I know I love my children, my friend, or my partner? I just do. I can try to explain why, but I just know it absolutely in my heart; it is a truth that precedes the classifications of the mind, although the 'thinking' mind has to be involved, too, as it must be prepared to let go and trust this different kind of knowing.

Recent developments in neuroscience posit that we in fact have three 'brains': in the head, in the heart, and in the gut (Soosalu and Oka 2012). The heart and the gut contain neurons that process information, which is then sent to the brain to be further – consciously – processed. One of the greatest challenges we face as leaders is integrating these three processing areas, particularly the head and the heart. By and large, we use our heads as the dominant mechanism in leadership decision-making: to anticipate, predict, inform, and control – all essential aspects of the leadership task. It is what Senge and Scharmer (2000) refer to as 'cognition': drawing on past learning in order to control the present and predict the future.

This is reinforced by the dominant managerial ideology, which prioritises logic, evaluation, statistics, and apparently objective argument over values, emotion, relationships, and intuition. When we are in this mode, we might be wary of accessing our heart's insights for fear of ridicule or having our arguments used against us. As we learn to suppress the heart's wisdom, we become accustomed to living with a vague sense of discomfort or a nagging feeling that something is not quite right. Over time, we can find ourselves consciously hardening or silencing the heart because we do not want to face the discomfort or impracticality of what it is saying to us.

One of our interviewees described this balance between the head and heart explicitly:

> We lost our 'why' and we were all about what we do, not the way we do it, and so I wrote down my 'why's' and it is from the heart because I believe in it, I enjoy it. …
>
> I've been trained and trained and trained to let the head take over from the heart and I can't: it's hand in hand, hand in hand, one hundred per cent. My heart and my head have got to agree with each other and I will do whichever one leads, but I can't do one without the other.
>
> The head says, 'When you make a decision, will we make money at this; if we are not going to make money we don't do it.' The heart says, 'Are we going to enjoy this? And can we make money at it?' So I tend to lead with the heart; I will try whenever I can to not to do anything I don't want to do. That's why, when I go and do speeches, I struggle because I don't enjoy it but I know the outcome is beneficial to others, and also I feel afterwards very good about it, and especially when you get a reaction from people. So I feel, if the heart says, 'You will do this because actually it will touch the parts that make you feel like yourself,' it is worth going through a bit of pain to do it.
>
> *(Neil)*

Our conscious work, therefore, can include keeping the heart 'online' and available to us in our day-to-day awareness and decision-making as leaders. The heart knows in a different way to the head. It 'apprehends,' whereas the head 'comprehends.' Just as the head is our honing beacon for truth – 'I trust this because it has been proven to me' – the heart is our honing beacon for love: 'I trust this because it is loving and kind.' Whereas the head works by observation, classification, and evaluation, the heart works by connection – opening to allow things/people we trust/value into the core of our being to become part of our lived experience, or shutting them out if they are perceived as a threat. It is therefore also the most tender, vulnerable, and well-guarded part of us.

And it is this vulnerability that gives rise to the other great force in the human heart: fear. This fear is in turn driven by how the mind has learned, consciously or unconsciously, to construe threat; and, in the modern world, much of what we perceive as threat is in relation to our ego: our need to look good, to be in control/successful/liked/clever/strong/'good,' etc.

The heart is therefore extremely powerful and visceral, shaping our thoughts and our responses, and operating subconsciously much of the time. But despite the dangers of opening the heart, we cannot lead with love without consciously bringing heart into our leadership; and this involves risk. That is why the first question we have to ask is not whether we *should* lead with love but whether we really *want* to. *Is our heart in it?* And when, even at the heart level, we look at it honestly, there are many reasons why we might not want to take on the risks of leading with love. Let us acknowledge a few of those risks.

Why shouldn't we lead with love?

- One problem is the word 'love' itself, which has been colonised, exploited, and distorted in popular culture towards the kind of soppy sentimentalism that Martin Luther King was referring to in the quote above. 'Love' in popular usage is equated with romance, and it can therefore feel embarrassing or sentimental to refer to it. Yet some leaders are able to talk about it and model it – our interviewees being just a few examples. The language can be found if the confidence is there. But are we really that confident?

- Love is also seen as 'soft.' In a tough world, where tough decisions need to be made, leaders can think themselves weak, or fear being thought of as weak, by speaking of love. It smacks of vulnerability, a way in which the world can get at you. Or leaders may fear that, when they have to make hard decisions, or balance conflicting needs, they may be accused of hypocrisy and 'lack of love.' It is interesting to note that in arenas where love is openly spoken of as a leadership practice – religious institutions and charities – accusations of hypocrisy abound. Why would anyone expose themselves to that risk?

- Leadership takes ambition, drive, and focus; and love seems to dilute these, inviting sacrifice and patience. If we lead with love, will we lose our drive, our edge? Everything will take longer, everyone wants different things, and to be sympathetic to these will leave us incapable of decisive action. Of course, this may be a false dichotomy: it is not power *or* love; it is power *and* love. All the leaders from the interviews demonstrated this capacity: 'if you want to be able to make a difference, then you have to have and assert your power. So, therefore you've got to find a way of doing that that's within your values' (Naomi). Leaders self-evidently have to *balance* power and love – they are not irreconcilable. But this can be hard; it is much easier, especially in demanding systems, to play safe and use power.

- Then there is the performativity aspect. How do you measure love? How do you quantify it, give it out, pay it back? How do you define success and punish failure to love? How do you train and develop it? This, of course, is the whole point. You can't. Love is a different kind of knowing. It is mysterious, located in the heart, not measurable like knowledge and skill. Yet we still know it. We know it mainly in the quality of connection we find with those around us, and we know it in the little unbidden, unconditional acts of kindness, patience, forgiveness, and self-sacrifice that we offer and receive. And we know subliminally when it is there and when it is not – its presence or absence affects us deeply and the health of our enterprise, as the interviews indicate. Most obviously, where you have love, you have trust – the glue of organisational life.

- Then there is the systemic perspective, which the earlier chapters of this book have been highlighting. We are not leaders in isolation; we are exercising leadership in a network of power relationships, the purposes and motives of which may be far from loving. Most investors in our businesses today do so for money, not for love. We all find ourselves competing for limited resources. Pressures abound: to 'deliver,' to measure, to comply, to do more with less, to 'extract surplus value from our resources,' to be popular, competitive, visibly successful. What space is left for love? And, if we act with love, what value will the system place on this? And people around us may well misinterpret our motives and view us as either deceitful or 'soft.'

- Perhaps the greatest problem with the notion of leading with love is how easily prone to manipulation and abuse it can be. The nature of love is to accept others for who they are, to relate to the very best in them, and to forgive their shortcomings. Love implies a level of trust and acceptance that may seem almost impossible in organisational life. So love cannot be the only tool in a leader's box. It needs to be balanced with wise judgement. Again, our interviewees demonstrated this:

> I don't mind making tough decisions, difficult decisions, because I think all decisions can be made in the right frame. Even difficult decisions with negative consequences for people can be made within the right framework, the key question being 'Are you being actually fair in the main to the majority of individuals?'
>
> *(Matthew).*

- If you do decide to lead with love, you are inevitably going to be hurt and let down by (and hurt and let down) others. The challenge is learning to handle the hurt and to forgive others (and yourself).

- Finally, love also speaks of the deepest, most intimate, and precious relationships in our lives: the love of our family and friends, the love of the planet, its flora and fauna, the love of life, art, and culture, love and awe of the universe, and, for some, the love of God. There is a natural desire to keep it pure and not to devalue its currency by bringing it into organisational arenas where human motives may be more mixed. The reality of pure love is its vulnerability. It is the same vulnerability that we saw in Chapter 1 in the photograph of the baby. Vulnerability is one of the few things that seems able to open us to the fullness of love inside us. It is interesting how, in the research, love was often redesignated as something less exposing, such as 'care,' 'kindness,' or 'respect' – as if to make the idea more respectable and admissible in a performance-driven, individualistic business culture. Many will oppose the introduction of love into an organisational context, on the basis that it demeans and, even worse, exploits, the most pure and intimate part of our lives for the purpose of organisational gain.[2] Yet, as we have suggested in earlier chapters, what is the cost to us and the planet if we exclude love from our organisational and managerial consciousness?

Love, then, may be something that many of us choose to keep at arm's length in the world of work. It is just not 'safe.' Judge me on my results, on my performance, but please don't judge me on my love! Even people who work for charities or caring professions quickly encounter the reality of 'compassion fatigue' and find themselves 'hardening up' to survive in a world that will otherwise suck them dry with its bottomless demands.

Perhaps the greatest challenge in leading with love is simply this. It sets the bar so high. We all know we will fall short, and we just don't need another reason to be down on ourselves. We are not Christs, prophets, saints, or gurus. Great leaders such as Martin Luther King or Nelson Mandela in politics or, in business, Body Shop founder Anita Roddick, former Unilever CEO Paul Polman, or John Timpson, owner of the UK Timpsons chain, may have the confidence to find the language to talk about leading with love. But we don't. We just want to get on with our lives, to feel we are doing a reasonable leadership job. Why would anyone add the additional burden of leading with love to a life that is already full of more than enough demands?

So leading with love does not come without potential costs and risks. We can weigh up rationally the pros and cons of these, but ultimately it will be what is present in our hearts that will persuade us. All we can do is leave the question out there for you to consider as you read on. Do *you* really want to aspire to lead with love? Is your heart in it?

We need to be kind to ourselves where this question is concerned. The forces described above that make us wary of the risks are considerable, and we will succumb to them. We need to allow the legitimacy of self-protection in a tough world. And it is not a one-off question. It is something we can ask again and answer again at any given moment. Maybe it is simply a case of keeping the question present in our consciousness. If you do look within yourself and find a 'yes' response to this question, then read on, as the rest of this book will examine the *how*.

Notes

1 This phrase comes from a poem by Antonio Machado, 'Traveller, There is no Road.'
2 A similar criticism has been made of 'spiritual leadership': that it legitimises organisational incursion into the most private and intimate spaces of our lives.

References

Brown, B. (2010) *The Gifts of Imperfection: Let Go of Who You Think You're Supposed to Be and Embrace Who You Are.* Center City, MN: Hazelden Publishing.

Joseph, S. (2016) *Authentic. How to Be Yourself and Why It Matters.* London: Piatkus.

King, M.L. Jr. (1967) Where do we go from here? *Annual Report delivered at the 11th Convention of the Southern Christian Leadership Conference,* August 16, Atlanta, GA. https://kinginstitute.stanford.edu/king-papers/documents/where-do-we-go-here -address-delivered-eleventh-annual-sclc-convention (accessed 12 June 2020).

Seligman, M. (2004) *Authentic Happiness: Using the New Positive Psychology to Realize Your Potential for Lasting Fulfilment.* New York: Simon & Schuster.

Senge, P. and Scharmer, O. (2000) *Presencing.* MIT Sloan School of Management, OSG, 20 October 2000.

Soosalu, G. and Oka, M. (2012) *mBraining: Using Your Multiple Brains to Do Cool Stuff.* Scotts Valley, CA: mBIT International Pty Ltd, CreateSpace Independent Publishing Platform.

7

HOW TO LEAD WITH LOVE

Leading with love should be the simplest thing in the world. We all have it; we all feel it. Love is present within us; we don't have to work to develop or expand it: we just have to let it flow and find expression within us and between us. Eknath Easwaren, in his introduction to the *Bhagavad Gita*, explains: '[s]ince the Self is the core of every personality, no one needs to acquire goodness or compassion; they are already there. All that is necessary is to remove the selfish habits that hide them' (Easwaran 2007: 61).

We all know what love is and many of us know what it is to give it and to receive it. It is also the basis of family life and values, most religious teaching, much secular teaching, and is everywhere in the arts and entertainment.

But leading with love also seems to be one of the most difficult things in the world! Indeed, this is probably the foundational paradox of the many paradoxes we encounter in this work. St Paul famously captured this in his vexed outburst in his letter to the Romans:

> I do not understand what I do. For what I want to do, I do not do; but what I hate, I do. ... For I have the desire to do what is good, but I cannot carry it out. For I do not do the good I want to do, but the evil I do not want to do – this I keep on doing.
>
> *(Romans 7:15–19)*

In the *Mahabharata*, one of the most sacred texts of Hinduism, Duryodhana (the leader who represents the most selfish aspects of human nature) says to Krishna (the god of compassion, tenderness, and love): 'I know what is right but I am not able to practise it; I know what is wrong and I am not able to keep away from it. I act as I am directed to by some mysterious power that is seated in my heart' (verse 56, Pandava Gita). However, Arjuna, who represents wise leadership, says exactly the same thing! But there is one important difference: Arjuna asks Krishna what he can do to address it. He wants to learn to master this 'mysterious power' that is seated in the heart.[1]

The complexity arises because, however well-intentioned, we are not masters of our own will. There are huge systemic forces that drive us 'not to do the good I want to do, but do the evil that I do not want to do' – an example being the increasing tendency to instrumentalise human beings in the pursuit of profit, as discussed in earlier chapters. These forces are often construed as 'the way reality is' and are therefore almost invisible to our consciousness. Or, more significantly, they tap into the pervasive fears and insecurities that 'hook us' subconsciously and cause us to operate with a survival/scarcity rather than a loving mindset.

At the simplest level, we *forget* to love, because so many other concerns overwhelm us; and not only do we forget to love, we also forget the latent power and presence of love as a force within us. As we shut off from it, the first thing we lose (usually in very early childhood) is the capacity to love ourselves, leaving us at the mercy of the inner critic or the harsh judgments of the world. Instead of being a boundless resource that we intrinsically possess, love becomes something we long for, which we try to meet in all sorts of distorted ways, particularly in how we engage with others and the world.

A central premise of this book, therefore, is that learning to lead with love is primarily a work of *remembering* who we truly are at the deepest level of our psyche (or, perhaps, 're-membering': putting ourselves back together as we are made to be!). We all contain the living presence of love within us but most of us have forgotten this important fact. We have forgotten it because we spend most of our youngest years constructing a 'personality' (a set of beliefs around who we are), and the rest of our years identifying with it and defending it. This is why loving one's true self is so foundational. Without this self-acceptance, there is no psychic space to love others.

Once we identify with the 'personality,' which needs constant building up and defending, we are confronted with many forces in our lives below the level of our conscious control that impede our capacity to love. Perceived threats in our environment instantly trigger primal survival responses and, despite our best intentions, make us react in the heat of the moment in ways that we may not have consciously chosen and may well regret. We get 'caught' by events, people, and powerful systemic forces. We see them as obstructions or even threats to our perceived needs: what we have referred to as 'I–it' (as opposed to 'I–thou'). Therefore, besides loving one's self, the second central element in leading with love is finding the inner 'space,' freedom, and wisdom to manage our reactions to these triggers, ultimately to develop the capacity *not to react but to 'respond,'* and, ultimately, to choose the loving response. Again, this is an act of remembering: that we are conscious beings and free to choose.

Much of leading with love comes down to what we call 'leadership moments.' Are we able, in situations of personal vulnerability, where we may feel threatened by what is happening around us, to exercise conscious choice to find the wise and loving response? To what extent are we truly free to behave in the manner we desire and know is right? Stepping into such 'leadership moments' was a recurrent theme in the interviews. Matthew, for example, felt he had to challenge his manager's decision in order to stay true to his values but acknowledged that 'It feels risky. Risky because you fear that you will be seen to be weak, or not a team player, or in some way trying to undermine somebody and their decision-making, but fundamentally I know it would not sit well with me to not say something.'

What was it that enabled our leaders to find the loving response when so many forces were acting to propel them in a 'safer' direction? And how could they do this in a consistent manner to the extent that they became noticed, known, and nominated for this book as 'people who lead with love'?

In moving from theory and observation to practice and development, we need to build on the findings presented in Chapter 5, which, taken as they stand, could potentially be construed as simply a list of competencies. As we have made clear, such a reductive approach is antithetical to the whole idea of leading with love. In further developing our ideas, we first offer a deeper lens through which to view the dynamics of leading with love and explore some of the underlying spiritual and emotional dynamics underpinning these behaviours and practices. Secondly, we want to simplify the framework in order to create something practical for busy and pressured leaders. We do not claim that such a simple model contains all you need to know; rather, we offer it as a means for leaders to engage thoughtfully with the processes involved. Once you have embarked on the journey of leading with love, you will no longer need a model but, for now, it is a useful way of getting from theory to practice.

To help achieve these outcomes, it is now time to change the language of our model. Most management practitioners and academics will be very familiar with the language we have used up to this point. We have mentioned motivation, self-awareness, authenticity, values, learning, reflexivity, building character, trust, leading others, developing people, and building genuine relationships. These are all staples of management development, and, as a result, we often relate to these terms simply as skills that need to be developed. However, as we have mentioned before, despite the skills being explicit, rarely do leaders adopt them. Leading with love is no different. If we view leading with love as just another set of skills that leaders need to develop, little or no change will take place. We want to be clear about this: leading with love requires a shift in consciousness rather than the development of a set of skills. In order to signify this, we want to move away from 'management speak' to a language that provokes – a more poetic language capable of conveying the idea that leading with love entails a new transformational perspective on the self, on others, and on the world. Typical management speak does not accomplish this; rather, it tends to imply that the same old ideas are being presented in a different wrapping.

So we are now making a number of changes to signify that the ideas we present here are different. Firstly, we present the model you saw in Chapter 5 as an image.

The image we have used is that of a tree, with the 'motivators' depicted as the roots, 'character formation' as the trunk, and 'expressing love in action' as the leaves and the fruit. Secondly, we have changed the terminology: 'motivation' becomes 'Re-sourcing'; 'character formation' becomes 'Channelling'; and 'expressing love in action' becomes 'Embodying.' We explain this in more detail below.

Thirdly, in the chapters that follow on Re-sourcing, Channelling, Embodying, and Loving self, we will not stick rigidly to the themes identified in Chapter 5. As mentioned, we do not want our chapters to be nothing but a list of competencies. Rather, these chapters will use the sub-themes to *inform* the writing. We will draw on a range of influences, including psychology and spirituality, and, as a result, these chapters will reflect a diversity of sources, not simply our research.

Let us now examine the three newly termed elements of the model: 'Re-sourcing,' 'Channelling,' and 'Embodying.'

The first overarching theme relates to our deep motivators. These are the fundamental sources of our actions, and in the research they were identified as personal values, personal motivations, and a guiding set of beliefs. These deep motivators can be likened to the roots of a tree. When we access these energies, we call it **Re-sourcing** – tuning into the source of love that lies in our roots. Re-sourcing is how our managers were able to stay connected to their deeper values and principles, the presence of love within them (often stemming back to powerful childhood memories), or their own particular sense of the sacred. We also include in this the capacity to love self, which is a foundational aspect of leading with love. This relates to our original definition of love:

> To love is to act intentionally, in sympathetic response to others (including the sacred or the divine), to promote individual and overall wellbeing.

Re-sourcing enables us to cultivate and connect to our sympathetic responses to others and to act accordingly.

The second overarching theme, originally referred to as *character formation*, comprises the broad themes of 'character,' 'reflection and learning,' and 'self-acceptance.' When we have the capacity for reflective learning, we are conscious and aware of the drivers of our actions but are less hooked by them. We are able to find a way of being among the pressures of daily life, acknowledging their existence but without losing touch with our true selves. When in touch with our true selves, we are able to develop a sense of self-acceptance and self-compassion. We are also able to maintain vigilance (from the Latin *vigil*, 'awake') around our egocentric drivers and exercise a conscious and healthy control over our behaviour: we develop a capacity to *transform* negative emotions rather than *suppress* them. This enables us to open a strong and healthy channel through which love can flow freely. We therefore call this process **Channelling**. Channelling relates to our ability to align actions with intentions, i.e. *to act intentionally* in terms of our original definition of love. Using the tree metaphor again, channelling can be represented by the trunk and main branches.

The third overarching theme, originally entitled *Expressing love in action*, comprises the broad themes of leading people, and relationships and love. Love is only love if it makes an impact, if it *impacts others* and *promotes individual and overall wellbeing* in terms of our original definition of love. This means finding the best way to express love often in the face of conflicting pressures. It enables us to see people for who they are and treat them in a loving manner while pursuing the necessary goals and ambitions of our leadership purpose: the balance of love and power that we discussed in Chapter 5. We call this process **Embodying**: embodying love in the world. Using the tree metaphor, Embodying can be represented by the leaves and fruit.

All three elements are indicators of maturity, according to the theories around developmental psychology we raised in Chapter 4. The tree metaphor allows us to present the model visually, as shown in Figure 7.1.

Here is a recap of the three new overarching themes or processes:

- **Re-sourcing** helps us to access the purity and simplicity of love as a powerful force within us which, for all the reasons we have articulated so far in this book, offers the best hope of transforming all our lives for the better.

FIGURE 7.1 The tree as a symbol of leading with love.

- **Channelling** is about labouring to make ourselves and our relationships vessels capable of carrying love into the world. It reminds us of St Francis's famous prayer: 'Make me a channel of your peace.' This is about overcoming the ego and the many factors that complicate and cloud human relationships.
- **Embodying** is about expressing love among others who do not necessarily reciprocate, understand, or appreciate what we are doing. It involves leadership moments where we act in alignment with love in such a way that it sends out a powerful message to others and expresses love in and through relationships in the world.

For anyone reading this from a spiritual perspective, it is worth noting that these three core processes can be located in the Noble Eightfold Path of Buddhism:

- re-sourcing as *right effort*, *right mindfulness*, and *right concentration*
- channelling as the combination of *right view* and *right resolve*
- embodying as *right speech*, *right action* and *right livelihood*

They can also be aligned with the two basic commandments of the Judaeo-Christian faith:

- re-sourcing: *love God* ...
- channelling: *with all your heart, your soul, your mind and your strength, and* ....
- embodying: *love your neighbour as yourself.*[2]

These three processes can form the template for leading with love. For example, you can use them as a framework to ask yourself the following questions:

- What can I do each day to **re-source** myself, to touch the deeper energy of love within me, and to allow this to refresh my clarity of purpose and presence? How do I choose to remember who I really am – my values, my beliefs, what motivates me – rather than acting in response to situational drivers?
- How am I **channelling** and how is the health of my channel? How much capacity do I have to act with inner freedom and choice? What can I do to increase it? To what extent am I able to act according to my values and intentions? How do I feel about myself? Do I accept myself or am I dominated too much by the inner critic? What is the energy that is actually flowing through me as I am talking and acting? Is it love or is it something else? How can I maintain a capacity to stay aware and alert to this?
- How am I **embodying** and expressing love? What impact am I having on others? What is the quality of the connection between us? How attentive am I being to the needs of others? What can I do today to express core virtues such as compassion, courage, and generosity? Where is it most needed?

The following three chapters will expand each of these three processes in order to generate prompts and practices for shifting the balance of our leadership towards love. In addition to the research, we will draw on contemporary thinking in leadership development and psychology, as well as the wisdom of ancient spiritual traditions. We must, however, re-emphasise a fundamental point: there is no 'technique' for this. It is, by definition, a highly subjective and contextual process: the love in *you* manifested in *your* way in *your* particular context. What we can do, however, is apply some foundational self-awareness practices that increase the likelihood of your being able to tune into this love and find the strength and clarity to embody it in your own leadership moments.

Finally, because self-awareness, self-discipline, self-observing, self-remembering and, indeed, self-love are such foundational practices in this work, one more thing we need to establish before we progress is a framework and a language for understanding the 'self.'

Our framework for describing the 'self'

This is a complex subject that has been discussed for centuries in Western philosophy, religion, and psychology, as well as Eastern philosophies such as the Vedas and Buddhist texts. But it is such an important arena for our subject of leading with love that we need a simplified rendition to work with. We are not claiming that the terminology we employ is 'true.' However, we do need a shared understanding of the terms we use in the book when we refer to different elements of the self.

Our simplified framework is influenced by Western psychology (particularly Carl Jung and Roberto Assagioli), Western and Eastern spiritual traditions (mystical Christianity and Vedantic philosophy), and more recent spiritual writers such as Thomas Merton, Eckhart Tolle, Richard Rohr, and, in particular, A.H. Almaas, a teacher who, like Assagioli, has blended Eastern spirituality with Western psychoanalysis. It also reflects our own experience of working as coaches, teachers, and mentors with executives and young people and, in Chris's case, working as an organisational development practitioner. And, of course, it also reflects our personal experience of applying these ideas in our own lives. Our goal here is simply to clarify terms that will come to life as we apply them in subsequent chapters.

The framework starts from the assumption that the 'self' we experience on a day-to-day level is in fact multifaceted: at a simple level, seven facets of the 'self' can be identified. When we speak (or think) 'I' at any given moment, we may be identifying with any or all of these:

- the ideal self
- the self-concept (who I believe myself to be)
- the inner critic or superego
- the 'shadow' or repressed self
- the egoic, false, or 'habitual' self

- the authentic or 'essential' self
- the observer or 'witness'

These notions are well established in Western psychology and some can be traced directly back to Freud and Jung, but they also have an older pedigree: for example, in the Upanishads and Vedic literature.

The **ideal self** is our concept of the kind of person we would like to be or feel we ought to be. This ideal will have been absorbed by us from parents, teachers, and society (through the media, advertising, and cultural values). The ideal self is the source of many of our 'shoulds': 'I should be popular,' 'I should be rich,' 'I should be successful,' 'I should change the world,' etc.

The **self-concept** is the construct we have of ourselves and is comprised of our childhood conditioning, broader societal conditioning, and lessons we learn about ourselves from experience. We may define ourselves as introvert, extrovert, analytical, creative, entrepreneurial, open, funny, conscientious, friendly, good at numbers, not good at numbers, a team player, sensitive, etc. The definition may be 'positive' or 'negative': 'I am gentle/weak,' 'I am forceful/aggressive.' Our self-concept will be based on our experience of feedback from the world as well as the kinds of constructs that are promoted as important as we are growing up.

The ideal self and the self-concept can be sources of shame and pride in ourselves. It may be that the less we feel our self-concept matches our ideal self, the more shame we feel about ourselves. The most important point about the self-concept is that it is just that – a concept – and hence is conditioned by our experience; it can never be who we truly are because it is an idea, not a self. Our problems begin when we start labelling ourselves and others with such concepts and then believing them to be 'true'; we end up relating to ourselves and others as two-dimensional concepts (cartoons) rather than real-life beings (see Higgins 1987).

The **inner critic** or superego is the hyper-vigilant, active part of us that goads us into achieving our ideal self-concept and criticises us for constantly failing to live up to it. It is binary in nature, highly judgemental, and draws on the language of 'should.' However, more than telling us what we *should* be, the inner critic berates us, judges us, and drives us to strive towards the ideal. Its energy is 'striving,' and it pushes us towards burnout (see Earley and Weiss 2011).

The **shadow** or repressed self comprises the parts of us that we try to deny because they are so uncomfortable or so far from our ideal self or self-concept that we do not want to acknowledge them as a force within. It often contains repressed childhood experiences that we were unable to process at the time as well as instincts and emotions that we were taught were 'bad,' such as anger, rudeness, or jealousy – and, of course, sex. When we find ourselves behaving in ways that we do not want to, or are ashamed of, it is often a result of our shadow side 'leaking,' or our primal defences being triggered. Unfortunately, as we suppress these parts of ourselves, often at a very young age, we also lock away with them powerful essential qualities such as creativity, will, spontaneity, and joy.

There is a strange symbiosis between the inner critic and the shadow self. The two need each other. The repressed self will act out its urges – for example, in an eating binge – which will cause a flood of criticism and self-loathing from the critic, which will in turn reinforce the repression. Many psychological and spiritual breakthroughs come when people learn to welcome and love their 'shadow.'

The **egoic** (or false self) is the psychological system of self-concept, ideal self, and inner critic and the dynamics that play out between them. It is the force that causes us to act in pursuit of our compulsive desires and causes in us the endless 'thirst' to consume, compete, and achieve for our own sense of self. The ego is our primary point of identification in life, often referred to as the 'habitual self,' because it is the basis of our sense of stability, predictability, and control. It is often what we refer to when we say 'I' – 'I feel,' 'I want,' 'I need.' It is our default when times get tough, or we feel threatened. The more insecure we feel, the more rigid our egoic structures become and the more defensive our behaviour. The ego is in charge when we try to make reality fit our self-concept rather than allowing ourselves to grow by embracing new insights about the world. In most spiritual traditions, the goal of spiritual growth is to transcend the ego ('die to self' in Christianity; overcoming selfish desire, kama-tanha, in Buddhism; or finding the true self in the Upanishads) or, perhaps more precisely, to ensure the ego serves the true self rather than being the one in charge.

The authentic or 'essential' self

We have made an important distinction between the ego and the true self. The notion of a true self draws on spiritual notions of a soul, original 'image' or 'essence.' Psychologically we might refer to it as the higher Self (Assagioli 1990; Jung 2002).

'Internal Family Systems' therapy (IFS) distinguishes between our 'parts' (similar to what we have described above) and the 'self,' which is similar to the Vedic concept of the core self:

> IFS recognizes that underneath all of our parts, every human being has a true Self that is wise, deep, strong, and loving. This is who we truly are when we aren't being hijacked by the painful or defensive voices of our parts. With its compassion curiosity, and connectedness, the Self is the key to healing and integrating our disparate parts.
>
> *(Earley and Weiss 2011: 20)*

We can often get glimpses of our true self by remembering times in our child-hood when we were simply in the moment and experiencing the world in a vital, spontaneous, and joyful manner. It may be a memory of playing with friends, of cuddling a parent, of being in nature; whatever it is, there is no background commentary or judgement of experience: there is only the experience itself. This innocent self is not self-conscious nor self-condemning and nor does it judge itself. It just is. Just like a baby, there is nothing it has to do in order to be loved: it is simply loved for being itself. This is the self that emanates or connects to love. It is similar to the highest levels of human development, as described in Chapter 4; with the exception of a few fortunate or gifted souls, once this connection to our innocence is lost in childhood, it takes most of us a lifetime to fully achieve the complete realisation of the loving self.

An incident recounted by one of our leaders, Dan, offers an interesting example of a leader caught between these various selves and not trusting in his true self. On confronting his manager's bullying behaviour towards the team, Dan instinctively realised what was happening: his manager was trying to play a false role of 'bad cop' and this role was not working, even by his own standards. Dan contacted his manager and suggested he forget about playing that role and just be who he is. His manager replied, 'but it doesn't matter what style I use, whether I'm good cop, bad cop – nothing changes.' Dan responded as follows:

> I said, 'Well, how about if you would just be you, stop trying to be this Hollywood entity, just be who you are naturally, because the passion that you have for the product sells itself. Just be that person, and motivate us that way, rather than, you know, flicking a switch and going "Well today I'm going to be the bad cop."'

The bottom line is that the ego, or false self, cannot love – neither itself nor others. Its whole *raison d'être* is to try to make us what we are not, based on the assumption that who we are is not good enough. Our inner critic is constantly comparing us against others and our ideal self and, as a result, we become consumed by self-judgement. The more self-judgement we inflict on ourselves, the more inadequate we feel, which we then try to hide and/or project onto others. We cannot afford to be in a close and transparent relationship with others because we will become too vulnerable: they might see our flaws and this, we feel, would be the end of everything. Our inadequacies will be revealed and our hopes of achieving our ideal selves will collapse.

The good news is we are not our inner critic; we are not the ideal self-concept that we are striving consciously and unconsciously to become; and we are not the self-concept that is never good enough. They did not birth us, we birthed them; and we birthed them at a young age when we needed protection. Unfortunately, we then ceded control by identifying with them, believing that they were our true 'I.'

The witness: getting to know our true self

So how and where do we come to 'know' our **true self**. It is not with our habitual understanding; it is with a different faculty. Our true self is not a construct in the mind; the latter is only a limited representation of our being – a cartoon drawing as opposed to a real living creature. Our true self is the totality of our being. This includes the mind, which has to become the servant not the master of this process. The mind cannot figure itself out by itself. It has to let go and allow itself to be 'illumined' or to *recognise* (the root of which literally means to 'learn again') who we really are. We will talk more about this in Chapter 11 when we discuss self-love.

We are therefore seeking to develop an attentiveness that enables us to fully experience our being, without judgement, rejection, or any evaluative inner commentary. This is the role of the **observer** or **witness**, which is the part of us that is able to observe without needing to classify, attach, or reject.

The idea that we have a part of the mind (the witness) that can 'observe' all these dynamics and detach from them comes from Indian philosophical thought and is used extensively in psychosynthesis, the therapeutic system developed by Assagioli as a blend of Eastern and Western thought. The witness enables us to detach from our thoughts and emotions rather than being identified with them and hence being 'reactive.' It stops us from 'doing the things we do not want to do' and enables us 'to do the things we do want to do.' Instead of being the angry or irritated person when anger or irritation arises, we take a step back and view ourselves as an actor who is portraying the role of an angry person. We observe ourselves in that role and thereby become more balanced and choiceful.[3]

When the witness is online, awareness is free and can be directed any-where; the mind is still and can accept without condition the self that comes into awareness. This self is felt, sensed, and recognised rather than described or analysed. There is a sense of consciousness expanding along with an amazing stillness and spaciousness that enables us to perceive ourselves as true being.

The following chapters will include many references to these different aspects of the self. In particular, we will discuss overcoming the ego (Chapter 9) and the inner critic (Chapter 11), because the ego has to loosen its grip for love, which is a quality of true being, to be able to flow in the moment when it matters.

Notes

1 Swami Sarvapriyananda makes this point in his lecture to the Vedanta Society of New York: https://www.youtube.com/watch?v=A8ZnLW7tHEU&t=1609s. See also 'Why Lord Krishna did not tell Bhagavad Gita to Duryodhana?' MythGyaan, https://mythgyaan.com/why-lord-krishna-did-not-tell-bhagavad-gita-to-duryodhana.

2 Taking the definition that 'God is love' leads you to the mind-bending invitation to 'Love love with all your heart, soul, mind and strength.' And that is to acknowledge, as some do, that love is actually a bigger force than anything we can generate with our own strength. We simply need to open ourselves to it.

3 Thanks to Dr Nick Sutton of the Oxford Centre for Hindu Studies for this explanation.

References

Assagioli, R. (1990) *Psychosynthesis: A Manual of Principles and Techniques*. Wellingborough: Crucible.

Earley, J. and Weiss, B. (2011) *Freedom from Your Inner Critic: A Self Therapy Approach*. Boulder, CO: Sounds True Inc.

Easwaran, E. (2007) *The Bhagavad Gita*. Classics of Indian Spirituality. Tomales, CA: Nilgiri Press.

Higgins, E.T. (1987) Self-discrepancy: A theory relating self and affect. *Psychological Review*, 94(3), 319–40.

Jung, C.G. (2002) *The Undiscovered Self*. Abingdon: Routledge.

8

'RE-SOURCING'

Connecting to love and aligning intention

Your task is not to seek for love, but merely to seek and find all the barriers within yourself that you have built against it.

Rumi

* * *

Connecting to love as a force within us and holding it as conscious intention

First and foremost, leading with love is an intentional act. It is important therefore to infuse our intention with love. In the metaphor of our tree, this is using our roots to tap into the deep reservoir of love within us and around us. But, as we have seen in earlier chapters, our attention is easily captured by other more immediate factors and we 'forget' love, which often lives at this deeper level. There are two conscious practices we can adopt to keep love available to us as a force in our day-to-day decisions and choices. The first is actively connecting with the deep-rooted, often unconscious, presence of love within us; the second is to follow this by surfacing it into a consciously held, aligned intention that we can keep available to us in the day-to-day. As Neil puts it:

And I think that whole thing goes full circle: you know, this whole 'love' thing. I mean, when I was a kid and, you know, you read all about love and how important love is and, I think, you just don't take it seriously enough … [as a leader] … until you experience it and then you go, 'God, it is powerful.'

(Neil)

We will now explore what 'connecting to love' and 'aligning our intention' might look in practice.

Connecting to love

Broadly, there are three means by which we can connect to love. The first is 'accessing' love, which involves connecting to the source of love within us – usually in the heart. The second is rooting our leadership in our true self – our deeper identity, guiding philosophy, and values – in order to act from a deeper inner conviction – a sense of what feels 'right.' The third, which we will deal with in a separate chapter, is learning to love ourselves.

Accessing love

What do we mean by 'accessing' love? The simplest analogy is that of plugging into the mains electricity. When we are acting in love, we 'light up.' We have already asserted that love is present as a powerful force in all of us. Leading with love need not add another onerous task to our already overstretched resources. On the contrary, our task is to 'plug in and switch on.' To do that we have to learn to discern where and how love is present and then, in our conscious will, to let it flow.

We consciously choose the language of 'accessing' love rather than 'possessing' it. Love is an energy and an intelligence within our being that we 'feel' into and can choose to collaborate with – allowing it to shape and inform our perceiving, thinking, and acting. Love also has a transpersonal quality. It is shared. It is an energy that flows between people, building connection, trust, and mutuality. It only exists in relationship: our relationships with others, our relationships with ourselves, and, if you take a spiritual perspective, our relationships with the planet, non-human life, and the transcendent. Furthermore, opening up to love need not be an all-or-nothing experience (e.g. I am either overflowing with love or I am filled with antipathy). Love grows; we can connect to love by opening ourselves a tiny crack. In the practical context of the workplace, it is often the case that we allow ourselves to open to love gradually, over time.

So, how do we access love as a living energy within us? How do we attune to the source and presence of love in ourselves? There are two foundational practices: opening the heart and presencing in the heart. Central to both of these is some kind of meditative practice, which brings us to a level of stillness and awareness that enables us to do these things.

It may seem strange to talk of 'opening the heart.' Clearly, we are referring to the heart as the seat of our emotional life, not the physical organ; we are talking experientially rather than scientifically. We discussed the functioning of the heart in Chapter 6: we all know what it is like to 'open' or 'soften' and to 'close' or 'harden' our heart towards others. The hardening or closing of the heart is a deep, instinctive self-protective response resulting from our natural human sensitivity to a perceived threat. This is because the heart is the location of the most precious and tender things in our lives. It is most likely, therefore, particularly in the performativity climate that we described earlier, that the day-to-day state of our hearts is closed – we are 'getting on with the job.' The ability to keep one's heart online in these conditions is a distinctive characteristic of our leaders. As Max put it when referencing a time he went out of his way to help someone:

> If I'm the type of person that prioritises the business above all else, I probably wouldn't have done it, because I'd have been worried about my own numbers … but for me, if you prioritise people and the individual, then that leads you down that path. That to me was the right thing to do. And I would not have forgiven myself if I hadn't done it.

To open, the heart needs to feel safe. That is why so much leadership theory focuses on the importance of trust as the basis for effective team performance (Schein and Schein 2020; Zhu et al. 2013; George 2003; Altunoglu et al. 2019). In fact, the literature differentiates between affective and cognitive trust. Cognitive trust is trust in the ability, integrity, reliability, and competence of the leader. Affective trust is deeper, and emerges where there is genuine care and concern in the relationship (the 'I–thou' relationship again). In part, that is determined by our context and how much threat we experience in our environment. But if we leave it to external factors, we are following/reacting not leading/initiating. Again, it is well-documented that it is an appropriate level of vulnerability on the part of the leader that is crucial in creating higher trust contexts (Nienaber et al. 2015). Leadership is all about taking the first step.

So how do we take control of our responses and do the work necessary to keep our hearts open, even in tough contexts? First, we adopt a practice of opening the heart, of mastering the reactivity that makes us slip into self-protection. In this way, we break the cycle of low-level fear that is the norm in most workplaces.

The first step in opening the heart is to still and settle the 'worrying mind' that is forever trying to control events to protect the ego. That enables us to sense into what is really moving inside us (including love) at a deeper level below the noise of or busy minds and the outside world. One of the easiest ways to do this is to bring awareness into the body, which is always present and can radically shift our perspective of threat. We call this 'presencing.'[1] The simplest way to become present is to bring awareness into breath or the body (e.g. hands, feet, or gut, or our senses: touch, sight, or sound). We can do this by a short meditation, or even by pausing briefly to:

- ground: feel the contact of our feet with the ground, our body in the chair
- soften: relax the body, particularly softening the face and releasing any tightness in the gut

- breathe: be conscious of the breath, slowly drawing it right down into the belly, breathing in through the nose and out through the mouth
- bring awareness into the senses (touch, sight, taste, scent, sound) and/or sensation (the tingling aliveness of hands, feet, face)
- come back into breath, drawing it right down into the belly, and begin to notice the freedom you have to presence your awareness wherever you want to – to notice what you are noticing – coming back into breath periodically to re-ground yourself and stop your attention being captured or distracted.

Try this for a few minutes and notice any subtle change in your state. Many people on first doing this discover a tightness in the upper chest and shoulders, or maybe in the abdomen, which indicates a certain baseline level of anxiety and overcontrol. As you breathe and release, you may feel your chest softening as you relax and draw air down into your core. Certain kinds of breathing techniques – even the simplicity of taking slow, deep breaths – can trigger the parasympathetic nervous system, which is the relaxation response (the 'rest and digest' response as opposed to the fight-flight response) and comes into play when we feel safe, calm, and relaxed. In this state, the mind can become free from its whirring busyness and you may feel the deeper part of the chest genuinely softening and relaxing. This is often the first step to opening the heart, or 'bringing the heart online.'

Like all work in this area, presencing takes practice, so a regular meditation, even for a mere five minutes a day, can make a huge difference. As you practise, you will acquire a growing freedom to presence your awareness out of the busy mind (you do not attempt to 'still the mind': you just let it carry on doing what it does and simply bring your awareness elsewhere, usually breath or body).

Following on from this basic practice of presencing our awareness, there are a number of meditations available specifically intended to help soften or open the heart. We will talk more about this in the chapter on self-love (Chapter 11). One of the best known is a 'loving kindness' meditation, where you bring yourself and others to mind with a simple intention to love by using a repeated phrase. There are many helpful online resources, but in essence the practice involves the repetition of a phrase: 'May I be happy, may I be well, may I be at peace.' You then think of someone close to you and repeat: 'May they be happy, may they be well, may they be at peace.' You continue by repeating the phrase for someone who is neutral to you, then for someone for whom you feel a dislike. You can extend your meditation to include your organisation and the planet. Another technique, from this presenced state, is active 'consideration': to put yourself into another person's world, stepping imaginatively into their shoes and notic-ing what is preoccupying them, what they are experiencing, and how they may be receiving and interpreting this experience. You can practise this by focusing on different people every day for a few weeks, including members of your team, your direct reports, your boss, subcontractors, and people from other areas with whom you regularly come into contact.

Another simple but important practice involves getting to know your people beyond the transactional relationships that often characterise the workplace. This was emphasised by all our interviewees: they *knew* their people; they *saw* them as fully rounded human beings with challenges, desires, joys, hopes, and fears. Once you get to know an individual on a personal level, you begin to build affective trust. You see people less as threats and more as human beings who, like all of us, need a combination of support, care, and concern as well as challenge, risk, and adventure. Once we cease to view our colleagues as threats, we find ourselves shifting from a hyper-vigilant, defensive posture towards more open, thoughtful, and considered responses. In essence, we shift from the fight-flight sympathetic nervous system to the parasympathetic 'rest and digest' response, thereby bringing psychological and health benefits to ourselves and to our relationships.

Having learned to free ourselves from the reactive mind, to feel safer, and to bring the heart online, we can go a step further and actively presence our awareness in the heart and sense into what is flowing there. This involves bringing awareness out of the busy mind and travelling the 'eighteen inches' to place it in the centre of our heart – which we can actually experience as a physical location at the centre of our chest.

The human heart is full of mirror neurons, which pick up on people's feelings and needs, infusing compassion and our 'sympathetic response to others.' It is also a source of our deepest values, and contributes to the activity of our conscience, the source of our moral emotions (Haidt 2012): the quality that whispers constantly to us when we risk violating our inner principles. As we become adept at presencing in the heart, we learn to discover these deeper places in our being and become able to access them more freely in the day-to-day.

The heart communicates itself energetically/somatically before it emerges into cognition – 'the inarticulate speech of the heart,' as the songwriter Van Morrison coined it. Another advantage of presencing in the body before accessing the heart is that it activates our somatic intelligence, which enables us to feel these subtle movements within us. Over time, we can learn to listen to our hearts by feeling into them. We may actually feel a pain in the chest, a tightening, a lump or a blockage, or warmth or coldness, or some kind of flow or pressure within. As we bring our attention to it, we can feel the energy and emotion it contains.

This takes practice. It involves paying attention to the actual sensations being experienced in the heart (in the chest area) and the actual felt experience of emotions physically flowing through us (to begin with, you might benefit from the assistance of a coach). This practice of placing our awareness in the heart allows us to notice what is really moving us to action, including love. In this way, we can cultivate the art of listening to the voice of love in our hearts so that it is available to us when we most need it.

As an example of this kind of inner inquiry, try bringing awareness out of your mind and into breath (take a few deep breaths and focus your attention on the physical sensation of breathing), gently place your hand on your heart (the middle of your chest above the sternum) and allow your awareness to drop into your chest; then, write down spontaneously and without editing what occurs to you. What is your heart telling you right now? You can also try placing your hand a little lower, more towards your belly, and notice if anything different comes up, maybe from your deeper heart or (even lower) your gut.

As we practise placing our awareness in the deeper heart, we can start to experience the movement and energy of love at work in there – and other transformational emotions such as compassion, joy, and peace. This is an art, and you may need the support of a good coach or spiritual director to fine-tune it. Becoming present to physical sensation in the body allows you to detect what is happening in the heart by actually *feeling* it rather than trying to analyse or label it. You can sense what is really moving in you and allow it to flow.

As you learn to feel into the 'knowing' of your heart, you can gradually develop the art of accessing this more readily in the day-to-day. What does the voice of love within your heart have to say to you about the situation you find yourself in? This can be done quickly by taking a deep breath before doing or saying something and consciously opening up the heart – where love is always active and flowing. Dan expresses this in his interview: 'to make the human side come out ... I think it's very easy for people in leadership positions to be abstracted from who they are as a person.'

Besides love, we find other things present in the heart:

- immediate, pressing emotions such as fear, excitement, worry, doubt, urgency, anticipation, and frustration, all of which may be distorting or capturing our thinking
- deeper emotions such as hope, courage, determination, and trust
- the energy of our values, which can inspire
- the felt aspect of conscience, which can highlight the gap between what we truly want to be and how we find ourselves behaving.

As we bring the heart online and sense into the felt experience of it, we are able to access the deep knowing it contains and bring this into our choices and actions. We can ask the conscious question and feel into the knowing of the heart for the answer: 'How is this love within me moving me to respond in this situation?' This intentional leading with love can radically affect our decisions and choices as leaders, as was so clear in the interviews.

One simple reason why this heart enquiry is so important is that we simply 'forget' to sense our love for the people around us. Or else we are too embarrassed to even acknowledge it, let alone express it. As a coach, when people express appreciation for the qualities or actions of someone else, Chris always asks, 'Did you tell them? It is staggering how often the reply is an embarrassed 'No.' They noticed but forgot to say it. If we neither (a) notice it nor (b) express it, love dries up. If this sounds soft and indulgent in an organisational context, consider that Gallup research into organisational health has highlighted the importance of 'having a best friend at work' (Mann 2018) and the work of Lencioni and others has highlighted the importance of deeper, trusting relationships in high-performing teams (Lencioni 2002).

As we gradually open the heart and learn consciously to presence our awareness in its centre, we find ourselves able, at work, not only to tune into love in ourselves but also in others (and the transcendent). We notice the effect others are having on us in our hearts and, when we can do this, it is remarkable how quickly the heart tells us whether love is at work, or some other energy. Love from others tends to 'feed' us: it strengthens, empowers, makes us feel more confident, valued, and deeply 'seen.' It also has a warming effect – or the opposite when forgotten. When we refer to someone being 'warm-hearted' or 'cold-hearted,' we are not in fact referring to their hearts but to the effect they have on ours. When we receive love, our hearts soften and expand and we become more capable of generous loving action ourselves.

If we are in touch with our hearts and our deepest values, we also find the qualities of 'consideration,' 'empathy,' and 'resonance' kicking in. When the heart is soft and open, we are able to engage with others with undefended, unconditional enquiry – 'Who are you?' – and to see them as the real, full human beings they truly are, albeit hidden behind all their defences. We sense into the mystery of the other person we are relating to: from being 'known' and categorised they become unknown and curious. The consequence of the energy of love at work is always connection – with our true selves and with others. It is a connection that goes far beyond mutual convenience or day-to-day collaboration and it often defies rational self-interest. This ability to connect to others as complete human beings with lives outside of work, dreams, hopes, and ambitions was the most important theme raised by our interviewees, being mentioned by them all as central to their leadership philosophy. It is only when you build these connections that the real conversations can take place, in trust, which make the crucial difference in personal and organisational life.

We acknowledge this is not easy, particularly when working in environments that do not cultivate or value love but rather encourage competition, fear, and the devaluing of the individual (as seen in the examples in earlier chapters). But every individual reading this book has the choice and the capacity to lead with love and can claim the physical, emotional, and mental benefits that go with this choice.

Rooting ourselves in our true values

So, to prime our intention, as we have shown, we begin by learning to attune to the energetic presence of love as flow within us. Next, we consciously connect to our deepest values, the things that are most dear and precious to us in life. As we consciously 'remember who we truly are' this stirs positive energy within the heart which can give us the courage, passion, and clarity to make bolder and more loving choices rather than those merely dictated to us by events.

At one level, this is foundational leadership work, which would have us reflect deeply on what Simon Sinek (2017) calls 'our why,' our core purpose, or 'calling.' It may be our personal 'why,' what we stand for as a leader, our organisational 'why,' our organisation's higher purpose, our societal 'why,' or the good we are trying to do in the wider society. Whatever its manifestation, it was a clear theme across the interviews.

> So, I always try to have good business karma. Even though you're trying to make a tough decision that people aren't going to agree with, but, you know, if you've been true to your values and yourself, and you're going to make the good, mostly good decisions.
>
> *(Ann)*

A more radical reflection is to tune in to what we sense as 'sacred' in life. You cannot think about what is 'sacred' to you without your heart coming online. It concerns the most precious and important things in your life. As the gospel writer Luke states, 'Where your treasure is, there is your heart' (Luke 12:34). As a core practice, we would encourage everyone contemplating leading with love to spend some deep reflective time answering this simple question: **'What do I hold as sacred in my life?'** Just take a blank page in your journal, write down spontaneously what comes to you, and see what emerges. As you do this, notice the quality of the energy that arises within you and where it stirs. It may be a tenderness in your heart, for example, a stirring in your gut, or a feeling of bright clarity in your head. If you can remember this somatically as well as cognitively, it will strengthen your ability to access its true energy when you find yourself challenged to embody it in everyday life.

Again, this reflection is likely to take us beyond the individual into the collective and/or transcendent. The psychologist Carl Jung described what he calls the 'collective unconscious': a layer of our unconscious mind which connects each of us to the history of thought and behaviour of all of humankind. As we tune in to what is deeply sacred, we may access what Jung would call 'archetypes': embedded wisdom structures that shape our deepest intuitions and responses. The most obvious of these are 'family' and 'young life,' but there are others such as a deep love and reverence for nature; our appreciation of order, justice, beauty, art, music, and creativity, and respect for key human qualities such as courage, generosity, and integrity. Different people will, of course, come up with different things when they explore the sacred, but what we find sacred gives each of us a valuable clue about our own identity and place on the planet. Bill Plotkin (2008) defines the notion of 'soul' in these terms: the unique space that we are each meant to occupy in the ecology of the world. Environmentalist Joanna Macy picks up on this idea when she invites people to 'act your age':

> Now is the time to clothe ourselves in our true authority. Every particle in every atom of every cell in our body goes back to the primal flaring forth

of space and time. In that sense you are as old as the universe, with an age of about 14 billion years. This current body of yours has been prepared for this moment by Earth for some 4 billion years, so you have an absolute right to step forward and act on Earth's behalf. When you are speaking up at a city council meeting, or protecting a forest from demolition, or testifying at a hearing on nuclear waste, you are doing that not out of some personal whim or virtue, but from the full authority of your 14 billion years.

(Macy 2014).

For those that have a faith or a spiritual perspective, the question of 'what is sacred in your life' will take you into your religious or spiritual precepts. How do you live these out in the context of your working life? This may be about the conscious application of simple rules – 'Thou shalt not steal' – or the practice of virtues such as kindness and generosity, but most spiritual traditions emphasise deep prayer and meditation as a way of opening the heart and responding to the movement of love within; in other words: 'Thy will be done, not my will.' The Hebrew Psalmist says, 'Search me O God and know my heart … and lead me in the way everlasting' (Psalm 139); the Sufi tradition focuses on accessing the subtle energy at work within us in the Lataif, the highest of which is the Qalb-e-Shaheed – 'the witnessing heart.' Christianity, Hinduism, and Sufism focus on the 'work' of the purification of the heart as the basis for true discernment. 'Blessed are the pure in heart, for they shall see God' (Matthew 5:8).

The measure of aligned intention is, in most of the world's spiritual traditions, the quality of peace. Thomas Merton, writing in the contemplative tradition, describes this as follows: 'God speaks in the silent depths of the spirit. His voice brings peace. It does not arouse excitement because excitement belongs to uncertainty. … [I]f He moves us to action we go forward with peaceful strength' (Merton 1994: 185–86).

Whichever level you work at, or whichever tradition you espouse, we propose that the outcome of the process of discerning and clarifying your deep heart identity is always that sense of clear, peaceful, purposeful conviction that Merton describes. You just 'know' in your head (clarity), in your heart (peace), and in your gut (conviction) that it is the right thing to be pursuing. You can do no other. It may not be *the* truth, but it is *your* truth, for this season in this place. Others may have their truths which may be different, but this is the basis on which you will engage with them. You have found your deep heart's 'why' and you are at peace with it.

Aligning our intention to our source

Well I think that, you know, I think knowing who you are and what your values are and how those work within an organisation are so, so important.

Know your non-negotiables, learn how to communicate impactfully and effectively, and understand different communication styles, because you're going to have to adjust along the way and not everybody is going to adjust to you.

(Ann)

For us to move beyond self-reflection into action, all or any of the 'sourcing' suggestions above need to be anchored in a clear intention: 'this is how I want to live my life; this is the kind of leader I want to be.' This is a crucial step in the process: opening up the **will**, as well as the heart and the mind, to the presence of love and our deeper values. Framing this and holding it consciously in our mind helps keep this love 'online' and alive in our day-to-day attention and choices. We would therefore encourage anyone who is seriously contemplating leading with love to have some kind of personal statement to help them keep it in mind. This may be a permanent 'personal mantra' or it may be more specific to a particular time or situation. Max had a very clear, simple personal precept that he used to great effect in this leadership: 'if something feels morally wrong, it generally is, and don't do it.'

A more specific example might come from a colleague of Chris. Alan was in a new role and found himself losing his bearings somewhat. He conducted an activity to re-root himself in his personal values and remind himself why he took on the role. He came up with three precepts to guide him on his way forward: 'No passengers,' 'Everybody matters,' and 'No fear.' He had to put these to use almost immediately in a difficult confrontation with a board member who castigated him for a project that was going badly and insisted Alan fire the project leader.

I was on the back foot and mentally going through who I would replace the guy with, when I suddenly remembered my precepts. I knew this guy was not a passenger; he was a good guy. Then I realised I was afraid. In a flash, I saw that this was everything that was wrong in this company: the culture of fear causing people to bury bad news until senior managers eventually uncovered it and ripped into people. I knew in that moment I had to make a stand.

(Alan)

Alan pushed back against the board director and actually got him to apologise to the individual he had picked on. It was a culture-changing moment and rippled across the business, stimulating much greater openness and trust between top-tier and mid-tier leaders. 'I would never have done it,' he said, 'if I hadn't done the work to clarify those precepts.'

Pursuing the electricity metaphor alluded to earlier, you might view this tangible framing of our intention as the 'plug' we use to connect ourselves into the source supply. A clearly held and articulated intention helps us, even if things get difficult, to retain our clarity stemming from the deep energy of love flowing through us.

So, how would you want to frame your own intention? Just a simple phrase, maybe, or an image or a symbol – something that can help you keep in mind what really matters to you. This is a fundamental practice in this work of leading with love. We call it 'self-remembering.' We all need some kind of conscious framing to help us 're-member' amidst all the distractions and pressures of daily life. Most of us who fail to lead with love do not do so deliberately; we just forget. These foundational techniques for presencing our awareness in what is really flowing through us and priming our intention are the main things that keep us from forgetfulness.

> What I try and do is look for the good in people all the time. ... I try to look, to have a very empathetic view to life in general. ... [O]ne of the things I teach people when they join, in their induction programme, is the rule of reciprocation. ... [B]eing nice to people you get kindness back.
>
> *(Neil)*

Note

1 'Presencing' is a word already in use in the leadership literature, having been coined by Scharmer and Senge (Senge et al. 2005; Scharmer 2018) as the key to 'learning from the future as it is emerging,' as opposed to 'learning from the past.' The key elements in their definition are 'open mind,' 'open heart,' and 'open will.' Although we are using the term more specifically and in a more limited context, our use of the word is congruent with theirs.

References

Altunoglu, A.E., Sahin, F. and Babacan, S. (2019) Transformational leadership, trust, and follower outcomes: A moderated mediation model. *Management Research Review*, 42(3), 370–90.

George, B. (2003) *Authentic Leadership: Rediscovering the Secrets to Creating Lasting Value*. San Francisco, CA: Jossey Bass.

Haidt, J. (2012) *The Righteous Mind: Why Good People Are Divided by Politics and Religion*. London: Penguin.

Lencioni, P. (2002) *The Five Dysfunctions of a Team: A Leadership Fable*. Hoboken, NJ: John Wiley.

Macy, J. (2014) Five ways of being that can change the world. *Films for Action*, 6 July 2014. https://www.filmsforaction.org/takeaction/five-ways-of-being-that-can-change-the-world/?fbclid=IwAR1P_PJFc9eggPfgNNiKlzhsmhK874eNCRgp0NvWIDWkIpQwpxxbuf9m8QE (accessed 18 September 2020).

Mann, A. (2018) Why we need best friends at work. *Gallup*, 15 January 2018. https://www.gallup.com/workplace/236213/why-need-best-friends-work.aspx (accessed March 2020).

Merton, T. (1994) *The Ascent to Truth: A Study of St John of the Cross*. London: Continuum.

Nienaber, A., Hofeditz, M. and Roneike, P.D. (2015) Vulnerability and trust in leader–follower relationships. *Personnel Review*, 44(4), 567–91.

Plotkin, B. (2008) *Nature and the Human Soul: Cultivating Wholeness in a Fragmented World.* Novato, CA: New World Library.

Scharmer, O. (2018) *Introduction to Theory U.* May 2018. https://www.youtube.com/watch?v=11jnAHNdnSc (accessed February 2020).

Schein, E.H. and Schein, P.A. (2020) *Humble Leadership: The Power of Relationships, Openness, and Trust.* Oakland, CA: Berrett-Koehler Publishers.

Senge, P., Scharmer, C.O., Jaworski, J. and Flowers, B. (2005) *Presence: Exploring Profound Change in People, Organizations and Society.* London: Nicholas Brealey.

Sinek, S. (2017) *Finding Your Why: A Practical Guide for Discovering Purpose for You and Your Team.* New York: Penguin.

Zhu, W., Newman, A., Miao, Q. and Hooke, A. (2013) Revisiting the mediating role of trust in transformational leadership effects: Do different types of trust make a difference? *The Leadership Quarterly*, 24, 94–105.

9

CHANNELLING
Self-observation and self-examination

'Channelling' is in many ways the harder, more conscious work of leading with love. It is easy to use phrases like 'opening the heart,' 'connecting,' and 'trusting.' But it can be so hard in practice. To do these things, we need a level of clarity, openness, confidence, courage, and wisdom that allows us to be vulnerable and to let go of our dysfunctional egoic needs and insecurities. We also need the capacity to see situations and people with greater objectivity rather than through our own preconceptions, fears, and filters. If love is the 'sap' running through the tree, channelling is about developing the tough, yet subtle, trunk and branches that let it flow. We need strong bark to protect against disease or threat, yet at the same time the trunk needs to be permeable to enable water and nutrients to flow between the roots and the crown. The trunk represents the channel that connects our values and sense of self to our visible actions in the world. A weak channel leads to a disconnection between our values and our actions – we fail to live authentically. A strong channel keeps the connections strong and enables us to flourish in a way that is conducive to our own health and the community as a whole.

Transforming the ego

The work of channelling involves us becoming increasingly more aware of our own egoic structures and how these help or hinder us in expressing the love we find within us. At one level, it may simply be a matter of understanding our patterns and learning not to let them take over. At a deeper level, it may involve us radically transforming the ego by letting go of patterns that are negatively distorting our perception and our behaviour – in other words, being less driven by our self-protective needs.

But, as per St Paul's dictum quoted in Chapter 7, this is hard. We find ourselves not 'doing the good I want to do but instead doing the bad I do not want to do' (Romans 7:19). The deep conditioning of our egoic nature unconsciously drives our leadership behaviour. We are subject to all sorts of pressures that exert a more powerful hold over us than the subtle voice of love. These include basic survival needs for security, subsistence, acceptance, and belonging, as well as self-esteem needs such as to 'get a result,' to achieve, to be liked, to be in control, to be right, to be 'good,' to be valued, recognised, respected, etc. We have all constructed our lives in such a way as to enable us predictably to meet these needs; when these are threatened, we become defensive and self-oriented. There is nothing wrong with these needs, and part of learning to love ourselves is recognising their validity. But these needs can hijack our behaviour and/or become ingrained as long-term patterns in our personality. Not only do these self-protective egoic structures inhibit our capacity to love, they inhibit our capacity to access and express our true selves and also our capacity to relate fully and effectively with others. So, sooner or later, we come up against the contradictions in them and have to learn to free ourselves from them.

Opening the channel by self-observation

There are two key tasks in this work of transforming the ego: self-observation and self-examination. Self-observation, which is based on the capacity to 'presence' as described in the previous chapter, is the ability to 'witness' our own reactions and responses to situations and to begin to understand why we behave the way we do, especially when we find ourselves behaving in ways that are contrary to what we want or value. Ann described this very clearly: 'so, I can choose in this moment how I'm going to react. ... [I]s it going to be a way that I'm going to be proud of, or is it a way that I'm going to be disappointed in myself.'

The first step is to notice *how* our attention gets hijacked, how our defences are triggered, how we get 'caught' by reactive emotions, and, eventually, *what* seem to be the underlying triggers for these. This can be achieved by a simple process of reflective journaling, maybe at the end of each day. When did you find yourself 'caught' today? What was it like? And what was it that put you there? Conversely, when did you find yourself behaving in a way you were 'proud of,' to use Ann's words? What was it like being in that state? In particular, try to notice the physical sensations of these opposing states (tightness in the chest, knotted tummy, etc.). Such journaling will gradually develop your ability to notice in the moment when you are being triggered and enable you to choose not to go with it.

A useful skill, which Tony Schwartz has powerfully demonstrated in his 'Energy Project' (Schwartz and McCarthy 2007), is to discern the quality of the energy flowing through us. Is it a 'surviving' energy, which always has a negative quality (fear or doubt), or is it a 'thriving' energy, bringing life, purpose, passion, and love? Developing our 'somatic awareness' – noticing the actual physical sensations of frustration, tension, doubt, worry, joy, peace, and love in our body – is very useful and important here.

It takes practice to create enough space away from our habitual responses to access our inner 'witness' and be capable of self-observation. A significant step is to learn to differentiate between the (neutral and curious) 'inner witness' and the (judgemental and self-protective) 'inner critic' or superego. The latter is the inner voice that defends our egoic patterns and is a powerful agent working to keep us stuck in them – even in the guise of trying to overcome them. It is characterised by the constant chatter in one's head about self-evaluation and judgement – usually with a tone of recrimination, blame, or self-doubt, or else displaced into self-justifying blame and anger towards others or our context. This is the voice that berates us when we fail to get to the gym as we had intended (rather than be curious about why we didn't feel like going this particular day), undermines our self-belief, causes us to feel like a failure, and may eventually persuade us to give up going to the gym altogether. Its energy is a false drive to perfect ourselves to show up in the world in a way that we think we are expected to – as our 'ideal self,' usually picked up from parental conditioning and early schooling. It is what we call a 'should energy,' and it has all our attention focused on ourselves and/or how we think others are perceiving us. It therefore has little room for love.

To combat this, we need to draw on our practice of presencing once again, which enables us to detach awareness from whatever is preoccupying our thoughts (usually our egoic or instinctual drives) and to become 'present' in our fuller awareness, or 'witness.' We can then decide to 'respond' rather than react. By 'responding,' we mean making a conscious choice to behave in a more loving manner, congruent with our true intention, as developed in the previous chapter. It is a lifetime's work to cultivate the ability to respond thoughtfully in highly emotional situations rather than react emotionally, but we get better with practice.

To cultivate our 'witness,' we therefore first have to disidentify from all the head chatter of the ego and superego. This is where a meditation or grounding practice can help: anything that enables us to recognise we are more than just the chatter in our heads. Bringing awareness into the body and consciously relaxing the body is one of the most effective ways of doing this. Most of our egoic concerns are expressed as tension in face, neck, shoulders, back, and gut. Sensing into these and relaxing the muscles has an effect as we release them. Focusing our awareness on the body, the breath, or the senses has the effect of bringing us into the 'now' and away from the chatter of the head. It is not a case of silencing the head – although some mistakenly enter into just such a futile struggle – it is a case of disidentifying with it: bringing awareness into a different place. This is how we presence and strengthen our inner witness.

Also helpful in self-observing are:

- having a clear intention, as described earlier; this sharpens our attention and makes us alert to when our behaviour runs counter to our intention
- learning to disidentify with the superego (which we cover in Chapter 11)

- having a daily practice or rhythm (grounding, gratitude, fresh air, exercise, etc.) during which we can observe ourselves, with simple curiosity
- setting 'boundaries' for ourselves, e.g. in time management, relationships, or eating and drinking
- journaling and self-reflection: looking back over the day to notice when we were closest to, or furthest from, showing up as our 'best self'
- meditation and/or prayer

Freeing up the channel by self-examination

A second important task, often the precursor to self-observation, is purposeful self-examination, for which we may need a little quality 'retreat' time in order to take a step back and look at our lives. This is about thoroughly examining our motives and drivers, particularly (from self-observation) those that seem to be leading us into disrupted or distracted states of being. Where do we find ourselves striving too hard, trying to prove ourselves? What are our sources of deep unhappiness or frustration? With whom do we find ourselves losing patience? Why? What is this hooking in us? The importance of reflection cannot be overemphasised and was constantly referred to by our interviewees:

> And I guess it was, at that stage, I probably realised actually what I do is I do look back. And I am reflective of what I've done, how we've done things, but I'm also reflective of what others do. I'm not judgemental, but I watch what other people do right and try and build that into my, sort of, my sponge-like mind, as it were.
>
> *(Neil)*

Often these will be things that we need to stop doing: things that are wasting or distorting our energy, like an overwhelming need to earn approval, be in control or achieve goals in order to feel good about ourselves. These egoic drivers need to be seen for what they are and let go of. Some of the biggest breakthroughs we encounter in our leadership coaching are when people let go of a need, such as to 'prove themselves.' The freedom and relief they find is palpable; they become less obsessed with their own performance, more able to prioritise what they know to be important, and more able to listen and attune to others.

Another important task in freeing ourselves from our egoic constrictions is to embrace rather than repress, or act out, negative emotion. We tend to view anger, fear, doubt, jealousy, envy, and anxiety as 'bad' and therefore to be avoided. Emotional intelligence is the ability to notice and experience our emotional states to access the intelligence they contain: 'What is this really telling me – about myself and about the situation?' This again involves presencing our awareness first in the body, which acts as a point of stability for us, and then into these negative emotions – allowing ourselves to feel them and fully experience them. The ego will try to avoid this because it fears annihilation; remember: one of its primary purposes is to create routines that help us avoid uncomfortable feelings. It takes courage to sit in one's fear, grief, or anger and to see them for what they truly are – usually the shadow of powerful positive energies such as creativity, love, and justice.

Otto Scharmer refers to this as the capacity to 'see our seeing' (Scharmer 2018); it is usually a prerequisite for transformation. Instead of seeing things through the filter of our existing constructs, patterns, and feelings, which keep us stuck, we learn to let go and step fully and honestly into what is truly present to us right now in our lives. It is hard to do this kind of self-awareness work alone. Our leaders often sought out a coach, an objective friend, or a learning set of people from outside their organisation by whom they could be supported and challenged around their leadership practice.

As we engage in these practices, we gradually build a new purity of perception and reception – how we handle our experience of reality. This means being able to receive and welcome everything that happens for what it is, and work with it as it is, not how we fear or want it to be. Most importantly, it means not denying anything we are experiencing: from practical problems with a plan through to unwelcome emotional responses such as anger, shame, or even panic. We accept everything and allow ourselves to experience it fully. Our egoic channel is much clearer, cleaner, and stronger and hence there is more room for love. In fact, it is only when we do this that the powerful presence of love can bring its transformational agency. Adam Kahane powerfully describes one such moment in peace and reconciliation talks in Guatemala with the 'Visión Guatemala' team. The team worked together for over two years and contributed to major changes in Guatemalan society through the implementation of peace accords, fiscal agreements, and an anti-poverty strategy, as well as in teaching and in local development policy. Kahane noticed how the Visión Guatemala team had succeeded in exercising collective generative power, so he interviewed members of the team some years after the project had ended. Many of them pointed to one five-minute incident that had occurred during their very first meeting.

> One evening after dinner, the team had gathered to tell stories about their personal experiences of the Guatemalan reality. A man named Ronalth Ochaeta, a human rights worker for the Catholic Church, told the story of a time he had gone to a Mayan village to witness the exhumation of a mass grave from a massacre. When the earth had been removed, he noticed a number of small bones, and he asked the forensics team if people had had their bones broken during the massacre. They replied that, no, the grave contained the corpses of pregnant women, and the small bones were of their foetuses.
>
> When Ochaeta finished telling his story, the team was completely silent. I had never experienced a silence like this, and I was struck dumb. The

silence lasted a long time, perhaps five minutes. Then it ended and we continued with our work

(Kahane 2007: 5)

This five minutes of silence was unforgettable and made a deep impact, giving the team the strength to do the tough work they went on to do. One of them explained this to the researchers: 'A very moving experience for all. ... If you ask any of us, we would say that this moment was like a large communion.' Another said, 'I understood and felt in my heart all that had happened. And there was a feeling that we must struggle to prevent this from happening again.' Kahane saw clearly that what he was encountering was love powerfully at work in the hearts of these leaders:

> What I hear in these words is the language of love. By love I mean the drive to re-unify that which was once united and that was then separated or torn apart. ... Elena Diez Pinto, the project's organizer mentioned to me that the sacred book of the Mayan Q'iche people, called the Popol Vuh, contains the following text: 'We did not put our ideas together. We put our purposes together. And we agreed, and then we decided.' Love is how we know collective purpose. Love makes power generative.
>
> *(Kahane 2007: 5–6)*

This, of course, is an extreme case, but it makes the point so powerfully. It is only when we are willing to step into the darkest places of our experience that a true transformation in mindset is possible. As we pointed out in Chapter 7, leading with love cannot be accomplished by developing a set of competencies but instead emerges from a profound shift in consciousness. Kahane's example depicts such a shift occurring as a group of people with opposing viewpoints sat down, listened to each other, and opened their hearts to clear the channel, enabling love to flow through.

Effectively, everything we have described in this chapter is about 'purifying' the channel: optimising our conductivity – to continue with our electricity metaphor from the last chapter – and removing unnecessary resistance, blocks, and bad connections to the flow of love within us and between us. In the early stages of our growth, we will find ourselves only able to do this in moments, though of course each moment matters hugely. Gradually, as we start to strengthen our inner witness and habituate ourselves to presence and feel rather than avoid and react, we start to develop a more sustained capacity to live and lead in this way. Key to this is learning to love ourselves, about which we will say more in Chapter 11. Before that, we will look at the fruition of all this inner work of resourcing and channelling: the embodying of love in action and relationship.

References

Kahane, A. (2007) The language of power and the language of love: Solving tough problems in practice. *Reflections: The SoL Journal on Knowledge, Learning, and Change,*

8(3), 5–10. https://www.solonline.org/wp-content/uploads/2018/08/sol-reflections
_8.3.pdf (accessed November 2019).

Scharmer, O. (2018) *Introduction to Theory U*. May 2018. https://www.youtube.com/
watch?v=11jnAHNdnSc (accessed February 2020).

Schwartz, T. and McCarthy, C. (2007) Manage your energy, not your time. *Harvard
Business Review*, October 2007. https://hbr.org/2007/10/manage-your-energy-not
-your-time (accessed December 2019).

10

EMBODYING AND EXPRESSING LOVE IN ACTION

If re-sourcing enables us to tap into love as the sap flowing from the roots of our tree, and if channelling is the trunk and branches, then embodying represents the fruits and canopy – the expression of love in word, deed, and relationship. When this happens, love is a sustainable source of energy, endlessly replenishing. It does not drain us, as happens when we get caught up in our own striving. According to Mother Teresa,

> the success of love is in the loving – it is not in the result of loving. Of course it is natural in love to want the best for the other person, but whether it turns out that way or not does not determine the value of what we have done.
>
> *(Mother Teresa 1995)*

There are so many forms and permutations of loving action that we cannot attempt to enumerate them here. You will have already seen several examples from the research in Chapter 5. However, we would like to pull out three key themes that may be helpful when you start to consider how you express love in action:

1. the willingness to see people for who they are rather than who you need them to be – to see their positive intentions, not judge them for their egoic flaws
2. the willingness to trust and to handle the risk of this
3. the strength and resilience to act purposefully with the power system

The willingness to see people for who they are rather than who you need them to be

The foundation of expressing and enacting love in the world is the ability to 'see' others more for who they truly are and less for how we want them to be. The former takes us into a world view of 'promoting overall wellbeing'; the latter takes us into an instrumental one. This was the most pronounced and most consistently recurring theme in the interviews: treating people as people ('I–thou'), not as objects ('I–it').

> I mean, when I look at philosophies, it's just kind of like that, treat people how you want to be treated. It kind of goes back to that … ask people how they want to be treated, but sometimes they don't get that. Be inquisitive; know your employees. So, I think it's a little bit about, you know, a little bit about that personal connection, it's not all just business.
>
> *(Ann)*

This only really becomes possible when we work on minimising the filter of our own egoic needs and judgements from the interaction. All the work in Chapter 9 of transforming the ego and letting go of our own needs is central here. The simplest mechanism for identifying when we are falling out of leading with love is to notice the nature of the judgements we find ourselves making of others. Is our heart softening, with connection, understanding, and compassion, or is it hardening in judgement, withdrawal, frustration, and blame? If we have developed our capacity for self-observing and can catch ourselves in this, the next response is curiosity: what is it – about me, them, or the situation – that seems to be behind this hardening? What questions might I ask to seek to understand rather than judge? Naomi expressed this in the interviews:

> I always remember the vast majority of people come to work to do a good job; work, volunteering, whatever it is, they're trying to do a good job. If they aren't, in your view, you should try and find out why, from their perspective, not from 'Well, they're not doing a good job because they're an idiot and they don't care what they're doing,' but 'Why are they trying to do it?' … 'Why are they approaching it the way they are?' Because – lo and behold – they may well be right.
>
> *(Naomi)*

This is not to say that leading with love requires us to be soft and to refrain from challenging people. Indeed, we will find ourselves witnessing, or on the receiving end of, ego-driven behaviour from others, who may be a long way from even thinking about leading with love. We will have to learn to confront or challenge this while retaining a compassionate understanding. Leading with love does, however, enable us to be clear in our motives: acting for the good of others (including the company and other stakeholders) rather than out of our own frustrations, prejudices, or selfish needs.

This is really an extension of the principle of channelling, but with an interpersonal, rather than an intrapersonal, aspect: the channel of love between us, not just within us. It is the discipline of healthy open relationships where we can 'speak the truth in love' (Ephesians 4:15), where nothing important remains unsaid or hidden lest someone takes it the wrong way or reacts badly. There is a host of skills and practices necessary to underpin this, and much has already been written in this area by the likes of Kahane (2000, 2004) and Isaacs (1999), but fundamentally this is a vigilance about the quality of the conversations we find ourselves having. Are they 'real'? Are they moving us forward? Or are we in an elaborate dance of avoidance and defending? Authenticity and openness were key qualities in our leaders, and there were many instances where, because of the trust they had built up, they were able to have quite challenging conversations: 'we had a phone call the next day, and I put my position across again, firmly' (Dan).

Every relationship we have is channel – we can be attentive to what is flowing through this channel and, if there is enough love and trust present, challenge each other and hold each other accountable for the quality of the flow. It is an inevitability in complex organisations that the 'resistance' in the wiring of human connection is very high. There are so many factors that can impede communication – to do with culture, language, structure, power, upbringing, and personality, as well as a simple misunderstanding. It is a pure percentage game, but the gains are massive when communications and information flows happen with ease and trust.

The willingness to trust and to handle the risk of this

Trust was a very big theme in the interviews. Our leaders consistently chose to give people lots of headroom, which often played through into significant performance benefits.

> I think you have to start from a position where you trust people. You trust them to get done what they need to get done, and I think especially in a professional environment like this, it … Yeah, so, you know, if things do go wrong, and sometimes they will, then you know you made the decision to give them that independence, then you've got to be prepared to stick with it, and support them through that, and, you know, they'll learn from it, and, you know, most of the time people don't make the same mistake again. That it's just part of the learning process. And that's key, and I think if people know that you've got their backs … And deliver, and delivery is all. But I think most of the time, you know, and people have differing strategies about what they think delivers results. And, you know, can see that there are different techniques that work.
>
> *(Max)*

Our leaders seemed to be able to let go of control because of their trust firstly in their knowledge of their people – who would surface any issues should they come up – and secondly in their own capacity to deal with the fallout, even at senior levels, if things did go wrong.

The strength and resilience to act purposefully with the power system

> If you want to be able to make a difference, then you have to have and assert your power. So, therefore, you've got to find a way of doing that that's within your values.
>
> *(Neil)*

Finally, we come to action, although that is where our definition of love begins: 'to act intentionally.' We end here, because 'right action,' in Buddhist terms, flows from the kind of inner alignment we have been describing above. If our attention is primed with loving intention, and if we are presenced in conscious love, then our action will stem naturally from this source. But, of course, this is somewhat idealistic! The hard part is *sustaining* loving action in the face of the many systemic forces and pressures that can push us back into expediency and compromise. The Buddhist eightfold path also includes 'right concentration,' 'right effort,' 'right speech,' 'right thought,' and 'right livelihood,' all of which emphasise that the real challenge is not initiating action but keeping it going.

We can apply the same principle of 'channel' not only to relationships but also to the systems in which we are functioning, noticing the quality of the energy flowing through them and the impact they have on the people operating within them: love or fear, generativity or instrumentalism. The natural loving response is so often denied by the system architecture – particularly the widespread application of quantitative targets, performance measurement, and monitoring technology, all supported by a reward-and-punishment culture. Our challenge, then, as leaders is how to intervene intelligently in the system to reduce some of the factors that are inducing fear and self-protectiveness in others.

It is a dead certainty that if you make the choice to lead with love, you will come up against significant and sometimes very strong forces of opposition. Matthew described this very clearly, in political and cultural terms:

> So, for the first two years, lots of battles. … I had fight after fight and endless conversations about the social contract, about how important to help people just to understand that, you know, we want to be fair and this is how we want to be fair, but I couldn't construct a real 'this is how we want to be fair' because it wasn't really there. So then the job became, as new individuals came into other roles, to make sure that we had a shared interest, that people really understood the damage that was being done and to look at the benefits if we did it differently.
>
> *(Matthew)*

This tends to be the case because of all the systemic factors we highlighted in the earlier chapters of this book, such as expediency, performativity, and instrumentalism. It is also likely because of emotional factors –fear, anxiety, manipulation, cynicism, distrust, and anger – buried not far below the surface in many of our organisational systems. The response of such emotional states to love is always initially hostile, and love has to be able to 'hold its space' long enough to allow for the discharge of these emotional states and for more positive states to emerge.

So there is another paradox: leading with love requires the development of a thick skin! The Gospel writer Matthew referred to this as the ability to be as 'wise as serpents and as innocent as doves' (Matthew 10:16). Leading with love will invariably bring disruption, and so much of the wisdom of leading change will apply as we step out to lead in this way. In our work with change agents, we talk about 'clear mind, firm hand, soft heart' and emphasise four basic processes for strengthening your capacity to sustain intention and momentum in the face of 'resistance':

i. doing the inner work: to be clear on your 'why' and align around this in head, heart, and gut
ii. knowing your strength: developing a personal practice that enables you to access your inner resolve and to step into conflict boldly and calmly
iii. never going it alone: finding the significant other(s) who are in it with you and building deep trust and connection with them
iv. patience: reading the times you are in and being prepared to hold your own discomfort and frustration until the times are right.

Doing the inner work

We have already covered much of this in the sections above on intention and presence. The only thing to add when we come to embodiment is to learn to cultivate the ability to gain a studied detachment from the passionate energy that is inspiring you into action. 'Teach us to care and not to care. Teach us to be still,' as T.S. Eliot says,[1] and this is to be wise about the limits of our agency – the great wisdom of humility. Often it is small, significant actions that make the greatest difference – not grand schemes and interventions. Mother Teresa points out, 'Don't look for big things, just do small things with great love. ... [T]he smaller the thing, the greater must be our love' (Kolodiejchuk 2012: 34).

A feature of passionate action is that the heart can become overexcited and disconnected from head and gut. This is why we emphasise the importance of alignment – being deeply grounded in the truth of what you are addressing, which you feel in your very core, your 'gut,' just knowing that it is the right thing to do; and because of that you can be patient and do the groundwork needed. Susan described this clearly in the research:

> So, it's just being honest at the moment. In the last couple of years, it's me trying to hone that in, the social enterprise, to say, 'Here's how you're part

of the collective, here's all the resources, but you have a go yourself, it's not waiting for me to come to your area to deliver stuff, because I might never come.' I say no more than I say yes to stuff, because I have to, because there isn't enough hours in the day, so, trying to be honest with that as well to people. But also saying like, 'It's all there, just go for it, like this isn't about me, this is about you.'

(Susan)

Knowing your strength

Related to the above, this has an inner element to it and an outer realpolitik. The source of your strength is that deep gut conviction that the path you are choosing, founded in your knowledge of love, is the right one. The other inner aspect of this is knowing your talents (and your limitations). Anita Roddick, founder of The Body Shop, for example, was an inspirational campaigner of deep gut conviction, but she needed to give space to others to build a stable business around this – the more practical operational embodiment of love in action.

The outer aspect is your ability to understand and work with power. Some expressions of leading with love are in the moment: just saying something that needs to be said. Even these require us to be confident and clear about our own power base: what gives us the right to say this, to make this challenge? Will we be listened to? Do we have the quality of relationship? Have we earned our place at the table?

But some expressions of leading with love are much longer term, changing the culture in an organisation, for example, from one of fear and blame to one of joy and creativity, as one manager we know is pursuing. He quickly learned that simply proclaiming 'this is wrong' – even making a rational business case for why it was wrong in terms of the costs of poor decision-making – was not enough. In fact, it merely confirmed the culture of fear and the sense of inadequacy that lay behind this. He discovered his main task was to build confidence – at surprisingly high levels within the business hierarchy. It took two years of patient work proving the power of this in his own team and some smart networking with some key stakeholders before he suddenly found himself with access to the people who needed to hear him. Matthew in the research described 'Two years of battles' to get a shift in mindset before he could get change taken seriously.

Never going it alone

Again, related to the above, this seems to be a golden rule of all successful leadership interventions. On our own, we will *always* lose perspective. Full stop. Either consumed in our zeal or buried in our doubt. Individual human beings, however much inner work we do, do not have the emotional and spiritual capacity to stand up to the powerful forces at play in the world around us. We will always get caught emotionally and have our attention hijacked. The nature of love is to bind people together, and the nature of leading with love is to bind people together in a shared cause or course of action.

So, whenever we feel moved to act, particularly in pursuit of some bigger work, the first question has to be 'Who is in this with me?' 'Who shares my heart for this?' And, of course, how do you find out?

Dave Logan at the University of Southern California (USC) (Logan et al. 2011) has done some fascinating work on 'triads' as the driving energy behind successful organisational transformations (the triad seems to be the smallest group in which we can be genuinely objective). There must be strong mutual trust and shared purpose between all three triad members, which is particularly important when you are in an exposed senior position in the inevitable politics of senior organisational or public roles. Isolated, we are at the mercy of the 'social dominants,' motivated by the pursuit of power in and for itself, who naturally tend to rise to the top of organisations but who have often not learned to attune their wills to the movement of love within and around them. We all need people who 'get us' and can 'watch our back'; when we are leading on the basis of love, this is even more important. Logan's work is a fascinating testimony to the truth of the ancient proverb 'a chord of three strands is rarely broken' (Ecclesiastes 4:12). Matthew in the research described how he benefited from this:

> [W]e try and encourage everybody to form a three, just on the basis that in a pair it is very easy to assert something or to get away with not being held to account for what you have said; in a three it is much harder because you are outnumbered in the first instance and one of the two of them will remember what you said and what you were going to try and do and I think it's great.
>
> *(Matthew)*

So, as you set out on a leadership journey, it is always good to ask 'Who are the others in my triad?'

Patience

Finally, as an inevitable consequence of the three points above, there is patience. The famous phrase from Paul's letter to the Corinthians comes immediately to mind: 'Love is patient.' Indeed, it is worth quoting the passage in full because it expresses so much of what we have been saying in this chapter:

> Love is patient, love is kind. It does not envy, it does not boast, it is not proud. It does not dishonour others, it is not self-seeking, it is not easily angered, it keeps no record of wrongs. Love does not delight in evil but rejoices with the truth. It always protects, always trusts, always hopes, always perseveres.
>
> *(1 Corinthians 13:4–8)*

Knowing when to intervene and when to let something go, when to speak and when to keep silent, is a core characteristic. The knack of simply sowing a seed and trusting that it will blossom in the fullness of time can sometimes be all that is needed:

> [A]s new trainees are coming in, I don't declare I'm going to do this and be your mentor now. ... I just would naturally make sure they're okay: 'How are things going? Do you need any help?' and just start that very basic process of leading and encouraging individuals forward. So, that was kind of, I guess, the bedrock of everything.
>
> *(Dan)*

> [A]nd when you have done the baseline, then you put the philanthropy on top, it all builds, and I think that's where we have done so well, not grown to be the biggest company in our sector, but, you know, twenty-four years consistently, safely giving a good place to work and believing in what we believe in and, of course, then customers believe in you, so it is much easier to win customers, so we have effectively no sales force.
>
> *(Neil)*

Leading with love may require us to take brave and radical steps in the moment, but, if we choose to take up the invitation, we can do ourselves the service of recognising we are in it for the long game. There will be many setbacks, much hurt. We will come up against forces and contexts more powerful than we are, and we may often feel unappreciated, misunderstood, and like we are making little progress. But the power of love is its unstoppability:

> I would encourage other people, you can't stop love. ... What's that phrase someone once said? You're on a trip to London and you get stuck for two hours at Hindhead. What, do you never go to London again? ... You just find a different route.
>
> *(Neil)*

It is not down to us. Ultimately, it is a bigger force than we are and we do not need to attach our ego to it and worry about success, profile, or popularity. We give it our all, as wisely as we can, and let events unfold. We learn to wait, to watch, to sense when the moment is right. We learn to do the little things of which Mother Teresa spoke with the greatest love we find ourselves able to muster; we do not worry about their significance or impact: we trust that this is enough.

At its simplest, leading with love focuses on the inputs. Business and the pressures to perform will make us focus on outputs, and there is nothing wrong with that. It can do no other. But the measure we use when we lead with love is the input not the output. We then accept the challenge of living with this tension and reconciling it – with patience, forbearance, and understanding. Fortunately, love changes us in the process: we become less concerned with our ego-drives, with our need to prove our worth or justify our place on the planet.

One of the most powerful expressions of this was a letter from the American writer Thomas Merton to Jim Forest, a young activist struggling in the protest against the Vietnam War:

> Thanks for the letter and for the awful, and illuminating, enclosure [about the civilian casualties in Vietnam]. I can well understand your sense of desperation. And the 'bleak mood.' And also I am glad that you wrote about it. As you say, there are no clear answers, and you can guess that I don't have magic solutions for bleak moods.
>
> Actually, I would say one thing that probably accounts for your feelings, besides all the objective and obvious reasons, you are doubtless tired. I don't know whether you are physically tired or not but you have certainly been pouring your emotional and psychic energy into the CPF and all that it stands for, and you have been sustained by hopes that are now giving out. Hence the reaction. Well, the first thing is that you have to go through this kind of reaction periodically, learn to expect it and cope with it when it comes, don't do things that precipitate it, without necessity (you will always have to).
>
> And then this: **do not depend on the hope of results**. When you are doing the sort of work you have taken on, you may have to face the fact that your work will be apparently worthless and even achieve no result at all, if not perhaps results opposite to what you expect. As you get used to this idea you start more and more to concentrate not on the results but on the value, the rightness, the truth of the work itself. And there too, a great deal has to be gone through, as gradually you struggle less and less for an idea and more and more for specific people. The range tends to narrow down, but it gets much more real. In the end, as you yourself mention in passing, it is the reality of personal relationships that saves everything.
>
> Nevertheless, you will probably, if you continue as you do, begin the laborious job of changing the national mind and opening up the national conscience. How far will you get? God alone knows. ... As for the big results, these are not in your hands or mine, but they can suddenly happen, and we can share in them: but there is no point in building our lives on this personal satisfaction, which may be denied us and which after all is really not that important.
>
> *(Forest 2014)*

Note

1 'Ash Wednesday' (1930) (Eliot 2015: K:38–39).

References

Eliot, T.S. (2015) *The Collected Poems of T. S. Eliot*. Ed. C. Ricks. London: Faber & Faber.

Forest, J. (2014) Thomas Merton's letter to a young activist. *Jim and Nancy Forrest*, October 2014. https://jimandnancyforest.com/2014/10/mertons-letter-to-a-young -activist/ (accessed January 2020).

Isaacs, W. (1999) *Dialogue and the Art of Thinking Together: A Pioneering Approach to Communicating in Business and in Life*. New York: Doubleday.

Kahane, A. (2000) *Power and Love: A Theory and Practice of Social Change*. San Francisco, CA: Berrett-Koehler Publishers.

Kahane, A. (2004) *Solving Tough Problems: An Open Way of Talking, Listening and Creating New Realities*. San Francisco, CA: Berrett-Kohler.

Kolodiejchuk, B. (2012) *Mother Teresa – Come Be My Light: The Revealing Private Writings of the Nobel Peace Prize Winner*. New York: Random House.

Logan, D., King, J. and Fischer-Wright, H. (2011) *Tribal Leadership: Leveraging Natural Groups to Build a Thriving Organization*. New York: HarperCollins.

Mother Teresa (1995) *A Simple Path*. New York: Ballantine Books.

11

LEADING WITH SELF-LOVE

I guess you have to have good self-esteem, and I think that that's one of the things about, you know, having confidence in yourself.

(Ann)

I'm in a place now where, you know, I do like who I am as a person.

(Dan)

It's about yourself, being yourself. It's about self-respect. It's about just caring for people.

(Max)

And so I think there is a direct correlation between happiness, contentedness, comfort in your own values that then lead you to make better decisions and to be the better you.

(Matthew)

I think respecting myself is very important, and I think that's partly what drives the 'do the right thing', and the reason that's got stronger over time is because if I am not doing the right thing, then I don't have respect for myself.

(Naomi)

So I'm quite comfortable with the way I manage people, you know, I enjoy, I really enjoy managing people. I enjoy relationships, I enjoy business ... I don't consider work ... 'work' ... I'm comfortable with, I think, the way that the way the business runs and the way that I interact with the people; and I like coming to work and I don't mind being around people.

(Peter)

You know, for the first thing I've had to come to understand about leadership ... and about the way I look at and behave with other people and treat other people, it's how I look after myself. And how I see myself. And how I accept myself, with all, you see, I am my own best critic and worst critic. I don't need anybody to tell me how bad I really am, because I'm good at that. In fact, one of the things I used to work on hard with me was to stop saying negative things about myself. So, the negative part of that is that I can also quickly see the flaws in other people ... [when I was] on the staff, the students told me that I had the gift of discouragement. Well, you know, what I assumed to be okay, because I did to myself, I pointed out ... mistakes and told them.

(Charles)

* * *

Brene Brown, renowned researcher on shame, authenticity, and self-love, in her book *The Gifts of Imperfection: Let Go of Who You Think You're Supposed to Be and Embrace Who You Are* wrote the following:

Of this, I am actually certain. After collecting thousands of stories, I'm willing to call this a fact: A deep sense of love and belonging is an irreducible need of all women, men, and children. We are biologically, cognitively, physically, and spiritually wired to love, to be loved, and to belong. When those needs are not met, we don't function as we were meant to. We break. We fall apart. We numb. We ache. We hurt others. We get sick. There are certainly other causes of illness, numbing, and hurt, but the absence of love and belonging will always lead to suffering

(Brown 2010: 25).

According to Brown, if we do not feel lovable, not only is it difficult for us to receive love, it is difficult to offer it. She states plainly that 'we can only love others as much as we love ourselves' (Brown 2010: 26). What Brown found, in her ten years of researching thousands of personal stories, was that many of us simply do not believe in our own worthiness; we do not believe that who we are, right now, in this moment, is enough. We do not love ourselves. As a result, we strive to acquire those qualities that we think will provide us with a sense of worthiness. These qualities might include success, wealth, being a good parent, love, losing weight, expertise, status, power, popularity, being seen to be helpful or good, courage, sobriety, attractiveness, strength ... the list goes on. But they all have us striving for something 'other' than what we are right now in the moment.

Brown's research also revealed that, on the other hand, there is a group of people able to live life to the full: to love and be loved, to be joyful, empathic, compassionate, assertive, strong, full of gratitude, creative, calm, intuitive, playful, and trusting. They have cultivated a sense of purpose and meaning in their lives. Such people seem to have achieved the highest levels of human development that we saw in Chapter 4. Brown termed this phenomenon 'wholehearted living' and she found that those who had achieved this had a deep sense of their own worthiness and had grounded their lives in a real felt sense of love and compassion – both giving and receiving. Those who cannot embody 'wholehearted living' are more likely to experience fear, shame, and conditionality ('I am only worthy if ...') and tend to look outside themselves for external goods which appear to promise self-esteem but rarely deliver.

Our own research participants acknowledged as much, noticing that they were more effective at leading when they felt good about themselves. Some indicated that their capacity to lead with love increased as their levels of self-acceptance and self-worth rose.

So, how *do* you learn to love yourself?

To address this question, we begin with an ancient parable, 'The Hymn of the Pearl'.

> One day, a young prince, still a child, was summoned to his parents. The time had come, they told him, to leave home and go to Egypt to seek the one Pearl. This Pearl was in the middle of a sea, nestled by the side of a loud-breathing serpent. If he could bring back the Pearl, he could come home and claim his right to be heir to the kingdom. At this, his parents took from him his beloved glittering robe and purple toga which had been tailored especially for him. But, before setting off, they provided him with an abundance of treasures for the journey (gold, silver, rubies, opals and agate) and a guide.
>
> The young prince travelled to Egypt and, having been warned not to trust the people of that place, disguised himself in Egyptian clothes. But the Egyptians discovered that he was not one of them and tricked him into eating their food. The prince then forgot he was a son of kings and, believing he was an Egyptian, he served the King of Egypt. He lost all memory of the Pearl and fell into a deep sleep.
>
> Eventually, his parents found out what had happened to him. They wrote a letter reminding him of his true identity and of his quest for the Pearl. On reading the letter, the young prince remembered his true identity, that he was a king's son. He longed to reconnect with his true home and he remembered the Pearl and his parents' promises once more.
>
> So, newly invigorated, focused and determined, the prince successfully lulled the serpent to sleep and snatched the Pearl. On arriving home, he

reclaimed the glittering robe and purple toga and wrapped himself joyfully in their folds. The prince had done what he had promised and had brought back the Pearl. His parents rejoiced and welcomed him back to his kingdom.

This is a basic summary of the story, from the gospel The Acts of Thomas, which we recommend you read: it is short and very beautiful. We chose it because it presents self-love as the outcome of a journey that we all must take in order to find our true selves and claim our inheritance as human beings. It is a profound and complex text which has many levels of meaning, but a simple expounding of the story will help us understand what our journey of self-love might look like.

The prince in his palace at the beginning of the hymn represents our original soul or childhood innocence. But he cannot stay in this state: he has a task to perform. The prince is sent out into the world to find the one Pearl (symbolising insight). He is equipped with treasures (personal qualities and gifts) and helpers (mentor and allies), but ultimately the task is his. The serpent represents our defences, our attachments, and everything that prevents us from accessing our true selves. As the prince enters the material world, he is distracted and forgets his true nature and his purpose for being there. This state of awareness is termed 'being asleep' in the spiritual literature. This is where our ego dominates and we identify with the 'false self' we have constructed to fit into the norms of the world (the prince's disguise). Eventually a 'wake-up call' reminds him of his quest and of his royal nature: he is a prince, as are we all; we are rulers of our true selves rather than slaves to our egos, living according to somebody's else's story. The prince eventually grasps the Pearl, having defeated the serpent (his inner demons), and, returning home, he reacquires his robes. The robes represent the dignity, wisdom, and grace of his true self. He has grown bigger and wiser with the knowledge of the Pearl in his hand. He has completed the quest and is worthy of taking up the royal mantle. He has overcome the temptation of living a false life; he is fulfilled and at one with his true nature which consists of all the aforementioned qualities: love, strength, peace, joy, creativity, peace, gratitude, wisdom, etc. This is the Pearl (and peace) beyond price, the treasure that qualifies us to lead others.

* * *

You may ask why we need to refer to an ancient text to enquire about self-love when we have modern psychology supported by scientific research. Importantly, the ancient text reminds us of something that we often lose sight of in modern times: that life is a journey of the soul, not just a path to 'success'. We use the word 'soul' to refer to the unique essence of who we are, our true self. 'The Hymn of the Pearl' describes the journey of 'becoming' (coming into being of) our true identity.

According to this, and many ancient traditions, the road to self-love consists of:

1. waking up from our identification with the world (Awakening)
2. conquering our inner demons, overcoming our egos (Self-knowledge)
3. recognising and embracing our true selves (Self-acceptance)
4. returning 'home', where we can simply be ourselves and make our unique contribution to the world (Self-expression).

We have talked about these ideas in previous chapters in relation to how we relate to others. Here we will use them as a framework for finding self-love. We will also draw on modern psychology, reminding us once again of Brown's observation: 'we can only love others as much as we love ourselves' (Brown 2010:26.

Waking up from our identification with the world: Awakening

Many of us are like the prince. We are asleep: we identify with the pressures and distractions of our contexts and forget or even suppress our true selves – as shown in the parable we used earlier in the book, that of Zumbach's suit.

By conforming to the world's beliefs, norms, and values, we distort ourselves and feed the inner critic that tells us we are never good enough. We forget to listen to our inner voice and end up striving to be something we are not. When we strive to achieve external validation or attempt to be something we are not, we cannot love ourselves. We end up in the living hell of self-criticism, low self-esteem, and using all our energy to attain something that never fulfils us. Organisations are very good at making us feel we (our core selves) are only as good as our last performance review or the results of the last job or task we completed. We are lulled into believing that we are only acceptable and 'successful' if we climb the corporate ladder, and that those at the top are somehow better than those on the front line. We believe that if we are to be acceptable we must do better in the race to the top. Even highly successful people often feel that they have wasted their lives; that, in some way, they are not good enough.

If we are to love ourselves, we have to embrace, at some stage during the process, the radical truth: that all human beings are valuable and sacred just because they are alive. Life is not a competition, a game designed by Social Darwinists where the few who gain the prizes are more worthy (though some – particularly the winners of this particular game – are willing to promote this idea). No one is 'better' than anyone else; you may be more (or less) intelligent, wealthy, popular, happy, but you are not better (or worse). You do not need to prove yourself or show others that you are valuable or attempt to justify your existence: you are intrinsically valuable because you are alive.

This first step on the journey to this realisation can be the most difficult: that is, 'waking up' to a recognition that we are not living a 'full' life or, as Brene Brown would put it, we are not living wholeheartedly. This is scary: we might feel as if everything on which we founded our identity is effectively 'up for grabs'. We may have been misguided in what we have sought to achieve and how we have defined ourselves. This kind of recognition often comes about as a result of a 'mid-life crisis', but a crisis does not have to be the catalyst (Psaris 2017). As we 'wake up', we start the process of getting to know who we truly are and to realise that there is so much more to us than we thought.

Many of the practices involved in this stage have already been covered in Chapters 7 and 8, and do not need to be expounded again here. These include meditation, presencing, self-remembering, reflective journaling, self-inquiry, and working with a coach or spiritual director.

We are not necessarily in control of when we 'wake up'; remember that the prince in the story had to be awoken by an external force: a letter. External forces or events are often the catalysts that wake us up from our identification with the world, but they have to be knocking on a door that is ready to open. Such events do include crises (job loss, failure, divorce, illness, and death of loved ones) but possibly also a sudden realisation, having become successful and achieved all you had hoped for, that you are still not happy. Perhaps you have reached a realisation that life has become stale; you no longer feel energised and engaged but instead feel boredom, alienation, or apathy. A simple recognition such as this can be part of a psychological awakening.

In her book *Hidden Blessings: Midlife Crisis as a Spiritual Awakening*, Jett Psaris (2017) explores these themes in depth and portrays the process of awakening to our true selves as a journey comprising twelve stages. Awakening can be dramatic but it is the start of something important which ultimately leads to the wholehearted living that Brown so vividly describes.

Conquering our inner demons, transforming our egos: Self-knowledge

As we awaken into a greater consciousness, we become more aware of the dynamics of the ego and, in particular, the inner critic, which has the function of preserving our egoic structures from threat: it is most commonly experienced as a powerful voice inside our heads maintaining a self-judgemental running commentary on our performance.

We have described the workings of the inner critic already in Chapters 7 and 9. Earley and Weiss, who work with Internal Family Systems therapy (IFS), define it as the 'part of us [that] is responsible for our feelings of worthlessness.' They add: 'When we feel ashamed, hopeless, inadequate, or just plain awful about ourselves, it's because our Inner Critic is attacking us. When we believe its words, we often feel worthless, ashamed or depressed' (Earley and Weiss 2011: viii). The inner critic is represented by the serpent in 'The Hymn of the Pearl', and it is probably the element in the psyche acting most strongly to inhibit our capacity for self-acceptance. It is responsible for ensuring we identify with and strive to attain the ideal self that we were conditioned into accepting by the authority figures in our lives. It is probably society's most powerful tool for keeping us all in check. As soon as we learn that we are too loud, lazy, stupid, bossy, demanding, stupid, fat, naughty – whatever messages we may have internalised when we were too young to counter them – the inner critic embedded in our psyches will begin to tell us we are not good enough. When we are adults, the voices become more sophisticated: you are not talented enough, you are not experienced enough, you are not clever enough, you are not charismatic enough … try harder. *The inner critic's job is to make us conform to somebody else's view of what or who we should be; it is the main reason why we silence our true self and find ourselves unable to love ourselves.*

Sometimes, the inner critic is subtle and offers insights into how to survive in the 'real world'. It whispers, 'You can't trust anyone: they will betray you,' 'There is danger all around: you need to protect yourself,' 'You must be liked by others, otherwise you will be alone,' 'You must achieve, otherwise you won't be respected,' 'You must gain power, otherwise others will take advantage of you,' 'You must acquire lots of knowledge so others can't manipulate you.' These all appear true because we have learned to see the world in this way. We believe the inner critic because it seems to be protecting us against failing in the world. As one of our coachees once said, having been given excellent confirmation of her talents in a 360°-feedback exercise, 'They say I am a really good leader, but I don't believe them.' She did not believe them because she believed her own inner critic more.

So what can be done to address this? We believe that everyone can benefit from skilled help in this area, and access to a coach or counsellor would be beneficial. We also recommend IFS, in particular the book by Earley and Weiss. It will help you to recognise your inner critic (they divide the inner critic into eight different types) and to respond in a more effective manner. They remind us that our inner critic emerged from a need to protect ourselves when we were young. We needed security, to be accepted and loved, and when we found that these qualities were not automatically available to us, we developed strategies to obtain them. At this time, our inner critic was our teacher, showing us how to people-please, to be clever, to be funny, to achieve, to be self-sufficient, or whatever strategy we learned to keep ourselves safe and acceptable in the eyes of others. Some simple practices for overcoming the inner critic include:

a) Learn to recognise, and label, the 'voice' and tone of your inner critic. You can identify it because it does not speak to you with love. It is usually harshly, not constructively, critical, or fills you with self-doubt and fear; for example: 'You are going to look stupid,' 'Who are you to be in charge of this?', 'Don't look weak,' 'Be polite,' 'Don't be so serious.' Some are able to locate their inner critic at a particular point in the body, often to the right of their neocortex, or ear, or on their right shoulder. It is useful to locate its position for when you come to recognise its voice later.

b) Learn to recognise your most common worries and strivings and the energy that lies beneath these, e.g. a fear of loss, pain, or rejection.

c) Learn to recognise and manage your typical reactions to your inner critic. Three typical reactions are: to rationalise, to give in, and to act out. Rationalisation comes from the mind when you try to argue with your critic, which just gives it more power. Giving in comes from the heart; you accept the messages the inner critic is conveying and fall victim to them. The third strategy comes from the gut where you feel an urge to act on your feelings and engage in self-destructive behaviour doing things that are harmful to yourself and others; the underlying message is that we don't care if we harm ourselves because our lives don't matter. These are all maladaptive reactions to the inner critic and simply do not work. Our next practice, self-acceptance, is important in overcoming these.

d) Finally, you might like to learn about the Enneagram, which is a tool to identify the self-sabotaging inner voice and find strategies to address it. However, we recommend you undertake this with a skilled practitioner: it is a powerful tool with many hidden meanings and can easily be misunderstood.

Recognising and embracing our true selves: Self-acceptance

Self-acceptance seems one of the most obvious and simple principles in the world: to accept ourselves as we truly are. But, in reality, it is a subtle and significant developmental process. It is easy to be lured into thinking 'I am fine just as I am' when, in fact, all we are doing is reinforcing the false, ideal self. This simply provides more ammunition for the superego as we fail to live up to it. Self-acceptance, therefore, involves a deep, compassionate acceptance, not only of our weaknesses but also the 'darker' and more 'shameful' parts of ourselves that we keep locked away or buried in our 'shadow.' (These terms have been explained more fully in Chapter 7.) Below, we describe three key practices for the kind of true self-acceptance that enables us to love ourselves for who we truly are:

- self-compassion
- self-enquiry
- letting go

Self-compassion

Self-compassion is the inner equivalent of compassion for others. If friends or family members suffer due to setbacks, challenges, or mistakes they make, we invariably respond with kindness and want to help reduce their suffering. If only we could respond that way to ourselves! We are often far harsher and crueller to ourselves than we would ever dream of being to others.

What is more, as soon as we venture into the exposure of leadership, with the eyes of the world upon us, we are in danger of our inner critics going into overdrive. We need self-compassion to calm us down, relieve the pressure, show humanity to ourselves. Interestingly, in 'The Hymn of the Pearl' we see self-compassion through the *absence* of certain behaviours. On waking up from his slumber, the prince does not berate himself or blame himself for falling asleep: he simply remembers who he is and gets on with the job without a hint of self-recrimination. It is vital that leaders in particular learn to access their self-compassion. This can be a difficult process but it contains its own reward.

So how do we cultivate self-compassion? According to Kristin Neff, a leading researcher and practitioner in this area, there are three components: cultivating mindfulness, acknowledging our common humanity, and demonstrating loving-kindness.

Cultivating mindfulness is a huge topic in itself and we have alluded briefly to it in the section on self-observation in Chapter 9. In effect, we need to recognise what state we are in, particularly when we are being cruel and judgemental to ourselves and holding ourselves to impossibly high standards. This can be done through a process of practising self-observation and regular, daily meditation. Other activities that support mindfulness include being in nature, resting in a quiet space, or anything that brings you back to the body. The opposite of mindfulness is being 'hooked' or 'caught' by the messages running through your head. If these messages are judgemental, intolerant, harsh, or critical, they will invariably be triggering the fight–flight response and inducing stress and ultimately ill-health. The most invidious trigger of self-judgement is social comparison and, again, mindfulness can help us to recognise when we engage in this destructive habit. Mindfulness is the first step towards recognising how cruel we are to ourselves. Only then can we intervene to address the problem.

Acknowledging our common humanity involves recognising that you are human and (thankfully!) imperfect, which means that you deserve kindness and compassion as much as the rest of humanity. You are not alone. Everyone struggles with some kind of pain and this is a part of being human. So, if you make a mistake, put your hand up and accept your own humanity: people warm to a leader who is open about his or her mistakes. This comes across clearly both in the interviews and in research on humility in leadership (Nienaber et al. 2015; Regoa et al. 2017). Having compassion for yourself when you make mistakes enables you to show compassion to others when they do the same. If we judge and condemn ourselves, we will do the same to others. This is not a trivial point. If a leader is harsh and judgemental, she or he will, aware of it or not, be cultivating a climate of fear. Being self-compassionate introduces compassion and acceptance into our workplaces. This was a consistent theme across the interviews: a patient understanding of others and their patterns led to real wisdom about how best to engage with them. For example, Charles realised that, because he judged himself harshly, he judged others similarly. Furthermore, it was as he learned compassion for others that he began to learn compassion for himself.

Loving-kindness is the third element of self-compassion. It is perfectly acceptable to feel a sense of 'loving-kindness' for ourselves and our inner battles: to feel compassion when we are weary, scared, or just feeling a bit down. In the West we usually find this difficult; the ubiquity of the phrase 'feeling sorry for ourselves' is an indicator of how we are generally dissuaded from practising self-compassion. If such a feeling is ever allowed in, we are likely to say to ourselves something like 'For goodness' sake, pull yourself together. You're lucky: you have a home/family/good job … and you have no right to feel sorry for yourself.' But we have every right to feel kindness and compassion for ourselves – life is hard! Some ways of enacting loving-kindness to oneself are presented here as a stimulus for you to think about what works for you.

- **Physical**. How do you look after your body in a way that feels compassionate? For example, exercising, walking in nature, taking a bath, booking in a massage, taking a break and a cup of tea.
- **Mental**. How do you care for your mind? For example, meditation, watching a movie, reading a book, practising positive self-talk.
- **Emotional**. How do you care for yourself emotionally? For example, keeping a journal, sharing your feelings with a best friend or partner, engaging a coach or a counsellor.
- **Relational**. How do you relate to others in ways that bring you genuine happiness? For example, meeting with friends, spending time in shared activities, playing sport, sharing a hobby.

Training in loving-kindness meditation has been shown to lead to improvements in relationships, motivation, pleasure, self-acceptance, and satisfaction with life (Shonin et al. 2014).. If this is an area that you find difficult, do visit Kristin Neff's website where you can find a series of self-compassion meditations and exercises. You may be able to find courses on self-compassion near you which will enable you to go into more depth on this fascinating topic.

As we develop self-compassion, we develop more compassion for and insight into others.

Self-inquiry

The practice of self-inquiry is at the heart of all the other practices. Embedded in all of them is the assumption that there are important questions that we want answers to: how do I attain self-acceptance? How do I find my true self? How do I gain a sense of meaning in life? These are the kinds of questions that characterise spiritual seekers; they are, in effect, what catalyses the spiritual quest. The word 'quest' ultimately comes from the same root as the word 'question' (Latin *quaerere*). All stories are founded on a question: how do I find love? How do I rescue the prisoner? How do I find the murderer? How do I defeat evil? 'The Hymn of the Pearl' is driven by the prince's quest for the Pearl; it is only when he falls asleep that he stops asking questions. So it is with us.

When it comes to the question of self-love, the quest is inward and our questions are directed inwardly. So, instead of assuming you know yourself, open a self-inquiry and ask 'In what way might I be limiting myself?' 'If there is more to me than I know, how can I find out more about myself?'

When combined with self-observation, you can open some very powerful self-inquiries:

- Why did I react like that when she mentioned that topic?
- What caused me to feel that way in the meeting?
- What is it in my interactions with Jo that makes me feel so defensive?
- What made me feel so calm and in control in that situation?

Crucial to effective self-inquiry is compassion and appreciation. We are inquiring into ourselves in order to explore this amazing inner territory. We cannot explore and open up if we end up judging ourselves. For example, if you shout at someone, you may feel shame, embarrassment, or aggression. To handle these feelings you may find reasons why you are so bad as a leader/mother/friend or, alternatively, why they deserved it. But this does not help. Compassionate self-inquiry is founded on the bedrock of non-judgement. If you cannot look at yourself without judging yourself, self-inquiry will not work.

Done with compassion and appreciation, self-inquiry can be fun! You can open up an inquiry about any aspect of yourself and your reactions: physical, emotional, and cognitive. *You* open up the inquiry so you are in control: you don't have to dive deep straight away; you can start with a relatively superficial inquiry and take it as far as you like, e.g. 'Why do I like Caroline so much?' You identify characteristics of Caroline that you admire. Why do I admire those characteristics so much? Which do I recognise as present in myself? What is it like to feel and experience these qualities within me? You may pause, access your heart, and actually feel the positive presence of them flowing within you. They may be part of your values, taught by your parents and you believe in them. And you experience gratitude for this. What are the implications of this? As you reflect, you notice that you only trust and listen to people who share these values. Again, you ask, 'What are the implications of this?' You may realise that you dismiss too quickly those people whom you feel lack these values. This causes you to reflect on the diversity of the people you allow to influence you: what might you be missing out on? What would be the benefit of being more open to such different perspectives? And so on.

It is important to ask questions that are meaningful and motivational. Questions take you on a journey, and we need to feel equipped for the journey and motivated to embark upon it. So, if we decide to open an inquiry, it is important to craft the question well. How you craft the question will depend on the purpose; as stated above, you might like to start with a relatively easy question but recognise that this might take you deeper quite quickly.

Inquiry, when done authentically and with compassion, commitment, and resilience, can open doors to self-acceptance and self-love. It can bring peace, contentment, and fulfilment and all the qualities mentioned by Brene Brown of wholehearted living. However, in this work it does help to have a skilled guide.[1]

Sometimes we are forced into inquiry against our will, through a crisis in our lives. Then the inquiry is full of pain, disappointment, and anger, and we need self-compassion as we work our way through. This is best illustrated by an example.

Cheryl was a senior manager in an insurance company and had risen very quickly in her career due to her consistent performance, and her ability to turn businesses around and to generate results. She was confident, ambitious, and an incredibly hard worker, regularly putting in ten hours a day and working at weekends. She could quickly size up a situation, see what needed to be done, and then implement new systems and processes quickly and efficiently. Her interventions always generated excellent financial results and she was proud to think that, in her time, while having made some difficult business decisions, she had saved failing businesses and ultimately preserved jobs as a result. She was confidently looking forward to a place on the board but was shocked to be told, in a meeting with the chair, that she was not ready. While her results were brilliant, her brusque manner had alienated a number of her peers and even some board members, who did not relish working alongside her. She was known for 'taking no hostages' and not suffering fools gladly. As a result, she was told, people were scared of her; her manner did not encourage the level of trust and openness that were vital at board level (and which the board had worked hard over the past few years to achieve).

Cheryl felt deeply distraught on hearing this feedback. Everything had appeared to be going so well: she was successful, wealthy, respected, and admired; it had seemed that she ticked every possible box but now, for reasons she could not comprehend, all her hopes had evaporated and she was left feeling like a failure.

The shock caused Cheryl to take time out to reflect. She decided to hire a coach. This had been suggested before but Cheryl had not wanted to. She knew the coach would ask uncomfortable questions that would force her to inquire into some parts of her life that she sensed were not working but to which she had not been ready to open herself up.

Through her coaching sessions, Cheryl came to realise that she defined herself completely in terms of her worldly achievements. She learned that, throughout her childhood, the only way she had been able to gain her parents' approval was to work hard and achieve. For Cheryl, dedication to results, hard work, achievement' and success had become means by which she earned respect and admiration – substitutes for love. An interesting effect of this dynamic on her leadership style was that she was always looking upwards; her focus of attention was on pleasing her boss and getting his or her recognition. She had placed her bosses in the position of parents, striving to please them but paying much less attention to those reporting to her – unless they were of a similar mind-set to her and prepared to work day and night to achieve results. She had become a taskmaster and had no time for the human side of her job.

It will be clear from this vignette that opening up to inquiry can sometimes bring you deep into the realms of the ego and can trigger some intensely uncomfortable insights. Cheryl had developed a strategy for getting what she needed, based on learning she had acquired as a child. This had seemed to work quite well into adulthood, too. But, in retrospect, she realised that she had ignored the warning signs: she had had plenty of feedback about the downsides of her leadership style but she had been too scared of facing the issues. She refrained from inquiring into the areas of her life that needed her attention primarily from a fear of what she would find.

In choosing to do the work at this depth, Cheryl would learn self-compassion, understand the egoic drivers resulting from her wounded, inner child, and learn to forgive herself. She would change her interpersonal style with her work colleagues and get to know them on a deeper level. She would also learn to love herself and others in a spontaneous, free, and heartfelt manner.

Cheryl's journey involved some pain. And she is not alone: in making this journey, she has followed many before. However, it is by inquiring into our own sufferings that we start to experience something quite rare: tenderness. And tenderness allows us to tolerate pain, both in ourselves and others, to feel it rather than to shut it down or try to fix it, and that in turn helps us to become kinder and to show more love in our lives. It is here that the core practice of presencing which we discussed in Chapter 8 is so important: simply being with ourselves as we are and welcoming every emotion, even the darker ones, as our friend and helper.

Letting go

The process of accepting ourselves involves us letting go of the 'alternative identities' that we have in some way over-attached ourselves to. This could be a role – 'doctor', 'leader', 'protective father', 'dutiful wife' – or an aspect of our self-concept, such as 'caring', 'hard-working', 'clever', 'fun', 'beautiful', 'plain', 'boring,' or 'lazy'. Or it could be any other 'I am...' statement that we choose to make true about ourselves and then inhabit.

If we return to Cheryl's example, one element she had to let go of was her attachment to work and her need for achievement. Cheryl had used achievement to prop up her identity, to provide her self-worth and to judge others. She had believed, and often overtly stated, that all those who were not as successful as she was were either lazy or simply did not have the talent. Cheryl was deeply attached to her career and, if she was going to achieve any degree of happiness, she would have to let go of this attachment. This did not mean giving up her role or even her desire to get on the board. It means that she had to *let go of its role in her psychological life* as a measuring stick to evaluate both herself and others. She has to reach that point where she is *prepared* to give up her career without it affecting her self-esteem. Cheryl can then allow her sense of self-worth to be based on the simple fact that she is a human being, alive on this planet connected to and dependent on all the other lives who occupy this planet at the same time.

Self-acceptance at its core is the acceptance that the purpose of life is life itself – not acquisitions, achievements, honours, prizes, qualifications, fame, wealth, popularity, power, or status. According to Carlo Strenger (2011), we have a deep fear of insignificance, a fear that is reinforced, if not cultivated, by our materialistic Western values. This fear of insignificance generates needy, judgemental, and unhappy selves that have to justify their existence by means of external prizes and symbols. Letting go means reaching that point in life where we accept ourselves just as we are, living breathing beings.

One of the most insidious drivers, common among leaders, is 'responsibility': 'If I don't do it, then it won't get done.' Like all our ego-drivers, it is an asset, up to a point. It gets us on in life and makes us effective. But it soon becomes a colossal burden, especially in leadership where we unintentionally disempower others by doing too much ourselves. Learning to let go of that and to encourage responsibility to sit where it truly belongs is one of the most liberating steps in the journey of leadership development. It is painfully difficult to begin with as we suffer the agony of seeing things not done as we think they should be, and yet gently amusing when we look back and see that, somehow, the organisation managed to carry on and we were released to become more effective.

Breakthroughs in this area can be sudden or gradual, but people often describe a feeling of waking up one morning feeling free, able to breathe, with a deep peace, and self-acceptance: 'I'm OK,' 'I can trust myself to do my best and that is enough,' 'I don't know the answer to this right now, but I know it will come,' 'I don't know what decision to take right now, but I will know when I the time comes.' Or, as our interviewee Matthew expressed it, 'I think there is a direct correlation between happiness, contentedness, comfort in your own values that then lead you to make better decisions and to be the better you.' Invariably, it takes a skilled guide or coach to help us through the process of letting go.

Returning 'home', where we can simply be ourselves, and make our unique contribution to the world: Self-expression

The final element in our model is self-expression. As Howard Thurman, mentor to Martin Luther King, puts it: 'Don't ask what the world needs. Ask what makes you come alive, and go do it. Because what the world needs is people that are alive' (Thurman and Harding 2010).

As you walk this journey, you will gradually find that the inner critic begins to let go its hold and you find yourself worrying less about your own 'performance'. You become more capable of being present and accepting and trusting yourself for who you are, just as you are, where you are. Then you are free: to be your most effective, to express yourself, and to be in genuine connection with others.

This fourth stage of self-love is about valuing the distinctiveness and significance of who we really are: the particular passion, talent, and wisdom we bring to the world, unique for each one of us. The energy that flows from this place is a positive, creative energy. We don't have to strive to express it; we just clear the way and let it flow. It has an intelligence of its own, it is self-optimising, and it will show us the way if we are willing and able to trust it. It is interesting how many of our nominated leaders were also entrepreneurs: freeing their own creative passion and energy as well as encouraging others. 'Is the life I am living the same as the life that wants to live in me?' is the provocative question that Parker Palmer (1999) asks us in order to help us engage our true self. Also relevant is the question we posed in Chapter 8: 'What do I hold sacred in my life?' The nature of the response to this is almost always towards service, creativity, or generativity of some kind: the promotion of 'general wellbeing' that is part of the definition of leading with love outlined in Chapter 2. The greatest joy we experience as human beings is not to consume, it is to contribute. All we have to do is trust it and be brave enough and clear enough to let it live within us.

The energy of our true self is subtle and essential, stemming from our deep life force, not compulsive or driven like our ego. Learning to tune into this qualitative difference in our inner energy is an important practice which helps us notice whether we are leading from love or from some other force. This is the practice we called 'self-remembering'. Being our true self does not necessarily square with what the world demands of us, and we have to have a deal of self-love and courage to trust that this is what we are here to bring to the world. There are those who wake up to their true identity and endure the challenge of realising they are in the wrong role, or indeed the wrong relationship(s). They find themselves feeling stifled by, or find it harder to find true motivation in, the 'old things'.

Most of the time, however, it will be a matter of making our role fit us, rather than the other way round: bringing our own perspective and truth to the situations in which we find ourselves, doing it our way in a gentle, non-compulsive, but firm and persistent manner. We learn to recognise that, of course, there is no one particular role that is ever going to be the perfect fit and we learn to express our true self in different ways, in different contexts, and in a balanced life, with fruitful personal, family, and leisure interests.

This is a constant challenge; the world and the organisational system we are in will try to pull us into a different way of being. We will get caught by pressures, 'issues,' and other people's 'stuff', and we will forget who we really are. So self-remembering is important: pausing to breathe, to ground ourselves in our true intentions in our heart and gut, and to remember our deeper identity, as we discussed in Chapter 8 – 'No, this is who I really am and this is what I will choose.' We saw this in the interviews – managers chose to stay true to their values, despite the risks incurred – and we see it again in the fuller case studies we describe in the next chapter.

In the final stages of self-love, we learn to let go of more and more, to surrender our desires and cravings and trust what is flowing through us, especially as the deeper heart and the higher mind starts to open and we come into the full resources of our nature. We are awake, aware, and conscious in our full being;

heart, soul, body, and mind. We are aware of love as a force within us, working through us, and we realise we don't really need much else. Our practice moves from self-remembering to self-emptying. We just don't matter anymore, except as a channel for what is flowing through us. We develop an effortless capacity to 'see' others as they are and have the love, wisdom, and humility to engage with them where they can meet us, rather than where we want them to be. We give way and make space in the world for others which can be better filled by them than by ourselves or anyone else. There is no need or striving to be 'sacrificial' in our service. We do it because it is the natural thing to do. We recognise and have tolerance for the imperfections of the systems around us and are awake to the windows that open up where our interventions can make a difference, and where they won't. We do what we do anyway. We don't worry about success or failure. We trust. We are living at the highest levels of human development. We are leading with love.

We finish with a quote by A.H. Almaas, who describes the state of consciousness that flows from this kind of self-acceptance.

> One is not self-centered, although one is unique. One is completely selfless, loving, compassionate, real, generous and human. How else can one be? His [sic] nature is Being. He is pure consciousness. He is an integration of love, kindness, joy and all aspects of Being. And he is fully aware of all these aspects and dimensions, without much preoccupation with them. He is fulfilled but is concerned with the fulfilment of others. He is satisfied and contented, and he is concerned with the satisfaction and contentment of others. He is personally fulfilled, satisfied, contented and happy, living a personal life that is completely and unselfconsciously devoted to the service of humanity. There is no self-sacrifice, not a hint of personal renunciation, but he is not selfish, not self-centered and not preoccupied with himself. His service is the expression of love, compassion, and truth. But he does not necessarily feel that is why he serves. He does not even think that he is serving. Love, compassion and truth are the constituents of his personal beingness. He is all of Essence, and so does not need to think of it or of acting according to its values. That is what it means to be a person of Being, the essential person. He is a precious pearl, rare and incomparable ... These aspects of Essence are universal, in the sense that all human beings have the capacity to experience and know them
>
> *(Almaas 1996: 113).*

Note

1 Both of the authors work with a coach skilled in the Diamond Approach, which is spearheaded by A.H. Almaas.

References

Almaas, A.H. (1996) *The Pearl Beyond Price. Integration of Personality into Being: An Object Relations Approach.* Boston, MA: Shambhala Publications.

Brown, B. (2010) *The Gifts of Imperfection: Let Go of Who You Think You're Supposed to Be and Embrace Who You Are.* Center City, MN: Hazelden Publishing.

Earley, J. and Weiss, B. (2011) *Freedom from Your Inner Critic: A Self Therapy Approach.* Boulder, CO: Sounds True Inc.

Nienaber, A., Hofeditz, M. and Roneike, P.D. (2015) Vulnerability and trust in leader–follower relationships. *Personnel Review,* 44(4), 567–91.

Palmer, P. (1999) *Let Your Life Speak: Listening for the Voice of Vocation.* San Francisco, CA: Jossey-Bass.

Psaris, J. (2017) *Hidden Blessings: Midlife Crisis as a Spiritual Awakening.* Oakland, CA: Sacred River Press.

Regoa, A., Owens, B., Leal, C., Melo, A.I., Cunha, M.P., Goncalves, L. and Ribeiro, P. (2017) How leader humility helps teams to be humbler, psychologically stronger, and more effective: A moderated mediation model. *Leadership Quarterly,* 28, 639–58.

Shonin, E., Van Gordon, W. and Griffiths, M.D. (2014) The emerging role of Buddhism in clinical psychology: Toward effective integration. *Psychology of Religion and Spirituality,* 6(2), 123–37.

Strenger, C. (2011) *The Fear of Insignificance: Searching for Meaning in the Twenty-First Century.* New York: Palgrave Macmillan.

Thurman, H. and Harding, M. with Beckwith, A. (2010) The Living Wisdom of Howard Thurman: A Visionary for Our Time by Howard Thurman (Audio CD).

12

LEADING WITH LOVE IN PRACTICE

Five case studies

There is no simple formula for leading with love: it is a subtle and gradual process of inner and outer transformation. It is about the interaction between human beings and their context and what flows from one to the other – love, or something else? Leading with love requires us to embrace crucial leadership moments, which spring up unpredictably and test us, often in times of deep transition when we can feel most vulnerable. In such moments we face a choice between closing down or allowing something different to come through. In choosing love over fear in each of these leadership moments, trust and wisdom increase, enabling us to mature in our leadership and capacity for love. As we have said before, leading with love requires a shift in consciousness and this emerges over time through constant practice. In time, you realise that you have experienced a profound transformation in the way you see the world and in how you wish to show up in the world.

Because the process is so contextual and differs from person to person, we decided it would be helpful to present in this chapter real-life examples of a number of people who have taken practical steps on their journey into leading with love. The characters are composites of people we have worked with but the dilemmas they face and how they reacted to them are real. These cases, taken from different stages of the leadership journey, differ from the 'raw material' of the research, in that the subjects have all been through a process of conscious development to increase their capacity to lead, and in most of them, we can observe an increase in love, as per the analysis of Chapter 7.

We look at the situations in which they found themselves, how these impacted them, the choices they faced, how they responded, what they learned, and how they grew (or did not grow) in their capacity to lead with love. Why did some hold back? And what did it take for others to step into leading with love? You may recognise elements of your own experience in these examples, but, such is the diversity of opportunities to bring more love into the world; it is difficult to be comprehensive. Nonetheless, we will pull out some general themes, principles, and tips which can help you to follow your intention to allow more love to flow in your leadership (and your wider life).

With the exception of the last, the case studies are composite ones; although based on real leaders and their circumstances, they are fictionalised in order to protect the identities of the people concerned.

Cases 1 and 2: Awakenings

Sheila and Jeremy are both high-performing individuals in senior professional roles in large commercial organisations. Both have consistently excelled at what they do and have been rapidly promoted as a result. They are regarded as successful, high-potential individuals; they earn top rewards, achieve outstanding performance figures, and work exceptionally hard and to high personal standards. They are both what Daniel Goleman (2000) would describe as 'pace-setter' leaders, inspiring and driving performance by personal example. They expect a lot of themselves and others and, as a result, become impatient with 'underperformers' and can appear intimidating – although this would never be their conscious intention. Both, however, found themselves facing the prospect of failure: for the first time, their approach was not working and results were not going their way.

Although Sheila was still personally successful in the market, there was an issue with the mood and performance of her team. A lack of cooperation and an increasingly unpleasant atmosphere led to tensions, mistakes, blame, and a decline in sales. As the tension and poor behaviour worsened, results declined further, creating a vicious cycle. The critical incident was losing four high-performing members of her team in quick succession to competitor businesses. As a result, senior managers began questioning her approach and her suitability for a leadership position. They did not want to risk losing her, however, because she was such a kingpin in the market. Instead, a gradually intensifying whispering campaign of disapproval and disappointment started to build.

For Jeremy, the critical incident was the relationship with a major client, for whom his team had to provide an integrated service. This was a new role for him, very visible at exec level, and a big step up for him. The client relationship steadily deteriorated over the subsequent six months to the point where the client complained to his boss and asked for him to be taken off the account. It was such a significant client that the managing director became involved, which was humiliating for Jeremy who saw it as a major blemish on his career. He became aware that some members of his team had been contributing to the issue, complaining about him to members of the client team; and the mood in *his* team was now being cited by the client as one of the reasons why he was not suitable for the account. This was very hurtful and left him feeling undermined and angry at their disloyalty.

These were significant moments for both these individuals. They had both attached their egoic identity so strongly to their career success that they became deeply distressed and emotional at the prospect of failure. This is a good example of what can happen when an egoic leadership style that appears to deliver success finally runs into its own limitations. It can feel like the threat of personal annihilation. In psychoanalysis this is known as an ego-alien condition (as opposed to ego-syntonic in which the ego is confirmed by events). It can manifest in various forms, some quite predictable: the leader who likes to be liked having to make people redundant; or the entrepreneur who has to take her hands off day-to-day operations and hand it on to people who can put more process into it. It is the moment when the very thing that makes you successful starts to have the opposite effect.

These ego-alien moments can be profoundly generative. As we saw in the last chapter, they can provoke moments of 'awakening' – *if* there is a holding created where the individual can face into them. If so, this when the person's true self, and the love this contains, can flow through the cracks in the ego and establish a more rounded, mature, and loving identity. The Japanese art form Kintsugi is one of the best-known metaphors for this, where cracked pottery is repaired with laquer infused with gold, making the finished work all the more beautiful in its broken imperfection. In terms of our framework, it is like a severe shaking of the tree, which forces us to root deeper into the earth (our deeper 'source') and to renew/strengthen the trunk (the 'channel').

Sheila's emotional response was deep frustration and anger. She felt unsupported by senior managers, by her peers and by her team. Presencing in her anger, however, she uncovered a deep sadness and sense of isolation and loneliness beneath it. Two of the people who had left were high-flyers whom she had encouraged and considered friends. She felt betrayed. In her opinion, she had helped establish them in the market; she was shocked at their lack of loyalty or appreciation. It was like they had no sense of a relationship with her but were responding purely instrumentally. She was becoming increasingly conscious, with the atmosphere of criticism growing around her, that she was alone. There was no one who 'had her back' 'after all she had given to this business.' She felt deeply let down and this fuelled her anger all the more. She could tell that, although people were saying nice things to her face, there was no one who was genuinely concerned or interested in helping and supporting her at this difficult time.

That was because Sheila was not the kind of person to ask for help – or to signal vulnerability in any way. Her intense ego-drive, inherited mainly from her father, for competence and achievement made such behaviour feel like a weakness. In talking to Sheila, and observing her understanding of the human dynamics playing out, it was clear that in fact she had a highly developed empathy. Indeed, it was this that made her so successful with clients. She had the potential to become a very skilled, motivational leader if only she would access this empathy more and ease off the achievement drive. As she relaxed and became more 'human,' she would build connection and trust and be able to give support and ask for it – and focus on helping her people win, rather than just winning herself.

The key to unlocking this was allowing herself to be vulnerable – to love herself enough to be able to ask for help and to give others the opportunity to express support and compassion for her. However, this was an anathema for her ego.

A member of the senior management team was wise enough to recognise Sheila's predicament. He listened, expressed an understanding of her position and offered to help broker some crucial conversations. She was appreciative and relieved that someone understood. But, in the end, she refused to go there. She backed away. She knew she needed to reach out but she could just not bring herself to do it. It was just too painful, too humiliating. In the end, she took the classic way out in such a situation: she left and joined a competitor.

We have begun with this case because it is a common story in which the defensive ego wins. Sheila knew what she needed to do, knew that it would be good for her and the business, and was seriously contemplating stepping into it. But she had ready access to an escape route, and the psychological discomfort of the wiser choice, and her fears and doubts about the likelihood of success, outweighed the potential benefits. For her own growth as a human being, this was a crucial opportunity which might never come her way again. Simon Mitchell (his real name) was one of our early interviewees and his story is described below. He makes this point beautifully:

> [it] is simply the fear of letting go of our old selves, of our old ways of relating and organising. It is essentially a resistance to part of our identity dying; it's hard. But with an open mind, open heart and open will … we increasingly have let go of the ways of the past and have the courage to allow a new paradigm to emerge, one that is rooted in the present, is congruent with our deepest values and allows us to reach our full potential.

Unfortunately, many senior leaders do not have the courage to do this.

This level of avoidance, as we shall see later, is common in those in exposed leadership positions, where the perceived risks of being 'out of control' (i.e. stepping out of established habits and patterns) is so much higher … and where it is relatively easy to leave and find a different position elsewhere.

Jeremy's response to his situation was anger, shock, and a growing depression. His whole identity to that point had been centred around being a high-potential, fast-track leader, making rapid progress towards the top; this was a very visible and palpable reversal. There were many complex variables at play in a situation in which to some extent he was being scapegoated. Many of these variables were political and part of wider dynamics between the two organisations, but some were attributable to his own pace-setting leadership style and his failure to pick up on emotional nuances in his own team and that of the client. When the issue broke, he was naturally afraid that it would damage his career and so immediately set about trying to manage and justify the situation. At a deeper level, however, his inner critic was in overdrive: 'I should have seen this,' 'What if I am not capable of functioning at this level?' 'Have I been over-promoted?' 'My career is ruined,' 'What will I do with my life now?'

Jeremy, in contrast, did look for help: he approached HR, who allocated him a coach. As he took time with his coach to ground himself and his presence in these difficult emotions, he began to find a calmer and clearer point of awareness. He began to 're-root' himself. 'Why is this such a big deal? This is just work. Why am I so obsessed with work?' He also began to look more objectively and calmly at the situation, to realise that there were many factors in play that had led to this. He also realised that, ironically, it was his own concern and drive to make a success of the role that had created some of the problems. He was so focused on the numbers and deliverables that he was alienating people in his team and the client's.

But, more importantly, he began to ask himself some fundamental questions. 'Why is this such a catastrophe for me?' 'How did I get to the point where my performance at work is the be-all and end-all of my life?' Jeremy went on a retreat to take stock of himself and his life. He began to self-remember: 'This isn't me ... I am actually a kind, empathetic, creative and fun person. I care about people and yet here I am treating them as functionaries.' His passion at college was drama; he had always been warm, popular, engaging, and inspirational. How had he got to this place? The immediate outcome of this was a decision to rebalance his life. He began with self-care, realising that he was at his worst when he did not get enough sleep. He put in place a conscious rhythm of life, including time for meditation and exercise. He also re-prioritised social activities and seeing friends.

This led to substantial change in his ego structures, which in turn allowed more love to flow through into his awareness and into his behaviour. The first thing was a new sense of calm. He began adopting a different tone. He sat down with four of the key people in the situation, took responsibility for his part in it, asked for their analysis of it and, in the light of this, for their help in turning it around. This enquiry revealed some important structural and commercial issues in client relationships that had been hitherto buried or ignored. He also invited 360 feedback from the client organisation as well as his own, shared it openly, and took steps to listen, understand and reset some key relationships (where the relevant parties were amenable; not all were, of course). His managing director, who had taken a personal interest in the issue, was so impressed by Jeremy's mature response that the incident probably did him more good than harm in the long run.

So, whereas Sheila stepped back from the vulnerability of inner work and open dialogue, Jeremy stepped into it. The baseline for him was learning to love himself again – for who he truly was, not what he thought he needed to be. It has been a challenge to maintain his new rhythm of life, but it does not seem to have adversely affected his work: on the contrary. He comments, smiling, 'I am much more focused and productive … and I am a lot quieter in meetings nowadays.' He has also found himself 'seeing beneath' the behaviour of others and being less judgemental, more understanding. We can be confident that, if he can retain this calmer/clearer perspective, he will be a better leader for it – assuming that he continues to dedicate his life to leadership in a large corporation, which is no longer a given.

Case 3: Leading with love at the top of the system

We have already mentioned how hard it can be in the most senior roles to take the risk of 'letting go' and letting love in. Sonya was a leader who took the necessary risks associated with vulnerability and change, again in very testing and exposed circumstances. She was the managing director of a business in a sector that was consolidating rapidly in the face of massive technological, economic, and regulatory changes. She entered the job as a divisional director as decisions were being made by her parent company to reshape her division to make it an autonomous business unit ready for potential sale. Her priority was to build a strong leadership team with a much bolder and clearer market focus – which was a challenge in what was previously a very functional, siloed culture. This played to her strengths and she rapidly built a cohesive, loyal team who were excited by the new challenge. However, the pace of change, the complex politics of the external context, and the need to make some quite tough, radical decisions internally caused her to take too much upon herself and to start shutting her team out of her thinking and decisions. She controlled and ran the whole change process, which her intellectual capacity, knowledge of the business, and speed of thought enabled her to do. But she became, unwittingly, increasingly insular and her team, even her closest allies, began to view her as a cold, remote, arrogant, and arbitrary leader, finding themselves on the receiving end of decisions of which they had no prior warning. As a strong, determined leader she was able to enact the change successfully to become the MD of the new business with its new owner.

Immediately, she found herself facing further changes: a major investment in new technology that would transform the operating model; plans to acquire another business; and a shift in her own role that required her to be much more present externally in the market and regulatory environment as an industry leader. As she looked into the scale of what she was about to embrace, she experienced a moment of absolute clarity: 'I am absolutely not doing it that way again!' The initial thought was probably purely one of survival. She was aware of her weariness and the complete absence of joy and excitement as she looked at the road ahead; what could have been the pinnacle of her career felt like complete drudgery.

She realised she simply did not have the capacity to manage this level of complexity in the way she had before. As she paused and presenced in her weariness and flatness, she began to realise to her horror the kind of leader she had become.

Taking time and space for herself, she began to bring her truer self online. She saw how, as a leader, she had been violating some of her deepest values and principles – most tellingly, the abuse she had visited on her team by initially mobilising and enthusing them, then ruthlessly cutting them out. This was another powerful 'ego-alien' moment, driven both externally in terms of capacity, and internally in terms of values. As she enquired more deeply, she realised how her values around leading with care for others had been distorted into what came very close to deception. 'I was trying to shield people from things I thought would upset them or be too hard for them to handle. I was afraid of the potential emotional reactions. It was the exact opposite of what I deeply believe in, which is trusting in my team.' The way she was working was not working. 'I was so determined to get it right I had locked down my capacity to care. I realised I didn't really like myself any more … and I was hardened to people I once liked and trusted.' Something new was needed – and she didn't have long to find it.

In terms of our tree metaphor, what Sonya needed was nothing less than a replanting: a period of rapid growth and transformation to be able to flourish in the much bigger and more exposed context in which she now found herself. An analogy can be made with the true story of a fallen oak tree, as reported by Kew Gardens in London, in which a huge oak was toppled over by a gale, but then re-rooted itself. Not only did it survive but it emerged stronger, healthier, and free of disease. It transpired that the ground around its roots had become compacted. By being toppled, the earth had been loosened and air was able to get to the roots, refreshing and renewing the life of the tree. As a result, a technology has emerged to aerate tree roots and strengthen trees (BBC 2020).

The work Sonya did was similar: a re-basing of her leadership in her true values. She re-engaged the team, conducted a frank review of 'learning from the recent change' and, after some time, as people gradually came to trust her again and to be more open, she accepted some very discomfiting feedback about her role in it. But her curiosity was directed mainly on how she had come to lose touch with herself to such an extent and without really noticing (or admitting) it. As she reflected, she realised that the key issue was lack of trust: not trusting herself and not trusting her gut. She analysed and overthought everything, relying completely on her intellectual capacity. She recognised this as a pattern from way back in her childhood, one that had got her successfully through life so far. When times were tough, she withdrew into her head, shut others out, and sorted things out herself.

This required some classic channelling work on transcending the ego: substantially changing the way energy flowed through her. She realised that she had to learn to trust more and focused on learning how to presence in the body and access her gut-knowing. In exploring it, she realised that her gut instinct was right most of the time – when informed by her heart as well as her head – and that, at her best as a leader, she was able to combine sound, strong judgement in her core with deep connection and valuing of those around her: as long as she trusted. She also realised how she had been actively repressing her gut- and heart-knowing, to the extent that she was suffering irritable bowel symptoms and extreme, almost debilitating, tension in her neck and shoulders.

As Sonya began practices to help her make more contact with her body, she found herself making interventions on the basis of this gut sense – which created more space and capacity, cognitively and emotionally, as well as time. She began to recognise the occasions on which she did not need to say anything, to understand what to let flow from others and when/how to intervene more subtly to bring things back on track.

It was most immediately noticeable in the relationship she built with her new chairman, in which she found herself being 'unusually forthright' and much happier to give her subjective view on matters. A highly experienced chair, he soon came to appreciate the wisdom Sonya was bringing. It also enabled him to coach her more effectively and give her the occasional steer in areas where her gut was less reliable. Most importantly, as she presenced her centre of awareness more in her body, her heart became more available to her. She was able to offer more compassion and empathy, along with her more inspirational qualities. The team dynamic evolved and trust began to rebuild. This was just as well, because their responsibilities began to grow rapidly and they all found themselves stretched in ways they did not expect. Sonya made it her priority to sense into the state of her team, realising how she needed to depend on them. It was not easy, and there were lots of tense moments and challenging conflicts to resolve. She was able to use her emotional intelligence to see when people needed support, as almost everyone did at some point.

Case 4: Seeing the system and remembering why we are here

A large charity that addresses poverty and ill-health was enjoying success, expanding and, in the face of a wider appreciation of the scale of the issues it dealt with, attracting more funding. It was recognised that its informal, slightly chaotic, decision-making structure needed to become more strategic; a more intentional approach to allocation of resources was required, in order to serve the greatest need and create the largest impact – a focus on 'value,' in other words, underpinned by more robust decision-making processes. A new CEO, Colin, was appointed to lead this. This led to a major change programme which had significant implications for the wider team.

The outcome was a perfect storm in which workload and demands on the charity increased, staff felt unsettled, hurt, upset, anxious, or angry at the change process, and decision-making became temporarily harder as roles and processes changed. Extensive efforts at consultation – a core value of the organisation – backfired, with complaints coming from staff about not feeling involved. A lot of blame was discharged towards the 'exec' – not so much about the 'what' of the change, the need for which was recognised, but about the 'how,' and vehemently so. An opinion survey at that time scored very highly in general but not on those questions beginning 'Senior leadership....'

For Colin, and indeed other members of the exec, who were close and who related well as a team, this was surprising and hurtful. They felt this indicated nothing more than a lack of appreciation and became frustrated with the 'whingeing,' 'immaturity,' and 'lack of accountability' in the wider management team. A schism emerged between the exec and the next level of leadership.

Colin was exasperated and hurt. The survey results wounded him.

> I have done everything they asked me to do. The whole point of what we are doing is to empower people to get on, yet they seem to push everything back up to me and blame me for their 'not being allowed to do' the very things I want and need them to do.

In a way, it was true. Colin *was* doing all the right things. But he and the exec were becoming the lightning rod for the pent-up emotion in the organisation. This is not uncommon in charities (and public health) with an active operational presence on the 'front line' of need. People often choose to work in such organisations out of a deep vocational commitment and are fully focused on relieving real and sometimes desperate need – and the need is always greater than the resources available to meet it. People work hard, with little expectation of reward, and they expect others to do the same. Frustration can easily become the predominant emotion, and a perverse consequence can be negative attitudes towards the organisational system and/or their colleagues in other teams, which come to be seen as 'blockers' rather than enablers, preventing them doing their necessary work. In what is primarily a work of love and compassion, serving those in need, what tends to receive very little of that love and compassion is the organisation that has been established to deliver it. People are unforgiving towards the inevitable imperfections that manifest in every organisational system. It is a predictable systemic emotional pattern. In church circles they call it a 'hardening of the oratories.'

For Colin, a man of principle who had left a highly paid commercial career to dedicate his life to the charity sector, it was both exasperating and soul-destroying. He eventually verbalised it: 'I can't do this. I have no doubt the strategy we have put in place is the right one and I know I am doing all the right things in change management, but nothing is working.' He felt deeply and personally responsible for the negative emotional climate that was building, but everything he tried to do to improve it seemed only to backfire.

It was a personal friend who took Colin into his moment of presencing and breakthrough, by helping him access the voice of love, which had remained present, but unheard, beneath all his strategising. 'Why are you doing this work, Colin?' he asked. 'Why are you all doing it? Is it the money? Is it recognition? Is it status? Is it love?'

'None of those,' was Colin's reply, the deeply rational, principled man that he is. 'I just believe in it. And I want to serve – to put my skills and experience to good use in the world.'

'Why?' replied the friend. 'Is it recognition? Is it significance? Is it to feel good about yourself? Or is it love?'

Silence.

— 'Is it about you? Or is it about them?'

— 'It's about them.'

— 'Then it's love. What does the voice of love have to say about your own managers?'

A lengthy pause.

— 'That they are hurting, angry and pretty exhausted.'

— 'What does the voice of love tell you that they most need?'

— 'Space … to find some calm, get perspective … actually to love themselves a bit.'

— 'What is your role as the leader here, then? … And, by the way, what does the same voice tell you that you most need?'

Colin decided to take a day out on a personal leadership retreat. It began with a long walk to ground himself in nature where he always felt most free. 'Why am I putting myself through all this?' was his initial thought. 'I could be living a quiet, simple life here in the countryside.' As he allowed himself to breathe and to presence in the emotion that lay behind the thoughts, he began to access some of the beliefs and assumptions that underlay them.

> I realised that I was just taking myself, and it, too seriously. We all were. Not the work, which we all care deeply about, but our role in it. Like, if we didn't do it, then it wouldn't get done. As I looked at the natural world just carrying on around me, I realised somehow that it would get done, despite 'me,' not because of 'me.' I really didn't matter.

It is not unusual, in these journeys of transformation and release into leading with love, to have an occasional epiphany such as this. The battering to his ideal self-image as a leader and the prodding of his friend had opened up a space inside him which, when allowed simply to 'be,' filled with something new. It was a profound release. Colin described tears of relief flowing. 'I'm OK. I can do this,' he thought.

> The strategy we were pursuing was entirely the right strategy, as were the changes we were putting in place. We all knew that. It could have been anyone half-sensible doing my role and they would be doing exactly the same thing. It was inevitable. I had slipped into the trap of taking personal ownership for the strategy and the change, as had my colleagues on the exec. The more responsible we felt and the more we tried to fix it, the worse we made it. Our job was not rational, it was emotional, or even spiritual – to

restore the true heart of the charity – and to engage with change from this shared heart. Because from that place the change is obvious.

This is a good point to quote again the lovely line from T.S. Eliot's poem 'Ash Wednesday,' which captures this wisdom elegantly: 'Teach us to care and not to care. Teach us to be still.' To care, perhaps, about the right things, including ourselves, but not to care about our image, our reputation or our 'success.'

Colin changed his whole leadership approach. Instead of being the visible leadership champion of the change, trying to sell it and engage people with it, he began behaving as though it was both inevitable and irrelevant: their change not 'his.' He framed his personal leadership intention as two completely new principles: 'remembering who we are' and 'patience.' He started speaking from the heart about his deep care and concern for the climate in the charity, cleared his diary, and spent personal time with his leaders at the next level just to listen. He organised a leadership retreat purely to give people permission to 'be still' – connecting and getting to know each other better – and he gave them space to vent emotion and get below this to a remembering and appreciation of who they really are and why they are in this work. He insisted that they give similar space to their own teams. 'If this is a work of the heart, then I want us to do it with a heart.'

The relief in the charity was palpable. The leadership retreat in particular seemed to shift the whole basis of relating: people visibly relaxed and were more open, more constructive, and less edgy with each other. Conversations that had seemed impossible a month ago started happening and the anxiety about the change dissipated. It became accepted. Even those whose roles were substantially affected, including two who were made redundant, acknowledged positively that it was the right thing to be doing.

For Colin, the learning was all about humility – and the joy and freedom that can flow from this. 'We really are so much less important than we think we are. I view my role so differently now – about creating space to allow good things to be done by people who really care. It is a privilege, however tangled it can sometimes become!' His learning about patience and deeper understanding was also important. This enabled him to embody a leadership approach that steadfastly refused to allow things to get personalised, while still allowing them to be deeply human – recognising that most of the emotional challenges in the organisation stemmed from wider systemic and social forces. He began to see his role as one of keeping the organisation alive and free from the negative effect of these forces, which would inevitably filter through and burden people by the very nature of the care they were trying to provide. He never articulated it this way but it was basically an organisational version of 'loving yourself' – so the organisation is then resourced to be able to love others.

In this case study, the core theme is clear: creating space for people to breathe and to truly 'see' each other – and the goodness inside. This is what allowed the lifeblood of the charity to flow.

Case 5: Inner transformation leads to outer transformation

While the above cases are composites to protect anonymity, we will close with the story of Simon Mitchell, former CEO of LinuxIT (2012–2015). This is a true story that Simon narrated to Karen and is also taken from an interview with Professor Emeritus Chris Mabey whose research interest is in spiritual leadership. We are telling it in full because it clearly shows the linkages between our 'inner state' as leaders and the 'outer state' of our organisations. Simon, who gave consent for us to use his real name, found himself in a position where his organisation was crying out for a different kind of leadership and he was someone who could provide it. But,

> In 2012 LinuxIT was on the brink of administration. There was a palpable sense of fear, insecurity and mistrust; key workers were leaving in their droves; and the senior management team were in conflict. It was clear to all and sundry that LinuxIT had no higher purpose beyond profit maximisation for shareholder gain. It had become an opportunistic, money-making enterprise and the vacuousness of this approach had left LinuxIT in a similar place to me personally: broken, inauthentic and concerned only with what it could take from the world. Although I was not leading the company at that point, it was clear that my personal imbalance was somehow echoed in the business.

This 'wake-up call' for Simon has clear echoes of the young prince coming to himself in 'The Hymn of the Pearl.' How had he 'sleepwalked' into this position? It led him into a deep process of self-inquiry.

> As a young adult, I had found myself very clearly on the wrong side of the tracks. Until my late teens, I had conformed to a fundamentalist Christianity preached by my church. This was a church made up of many beautifully kind, charitable and selfless people but underpinned by a doctrine that, perhaps unwittingly, manipulated fear and guilt, denigrated self and the world, and avoided any challenge with an infuriatingly closed system of logic. When I started to reject it, I scrapped everything that goes with it: spirituality, God, religion, ultimate purpose, deeper meaning, etc. I threw it all out with the bathwater. My life became an insatiable and reckless pursuit of happiness through carnal pleasures. One way or another, I had to keep the excitement going, chasing the next high, whether that was induced by drink, drugs, sex, violence, money or whatever; it was all about chasing that high ... In reality, I was wracked with fear, anxiety and shame, which I tried to hide from the outside world by projecting a carefree, rebellious and wild persona. I was deeply inauthentic which made life incredibly stressful.

Simon found himself deeply questioning his own way of life, just as his once successful business was asking the same question.[1] He went into counselling and began to study psychology to explore his own drivers, but it was a Transcendental Meditation programme that was the turning point for him.

> The decision to try TM was not an easy one. It conflicted with my ego on so many levels. I did 'science' not 'spirituality'; 'tough guy' not 'hippie'; 'high energy' not 'sat about on cushions humming.' However, practising TM[2] … utterly transformed my life. Practising TM daily, I love the relaxation and solace associated with the meditation itself, but it's the changes in me and the world around me that have had the greatest impact. It is as though I am plugged into a source of love, warmth, courage, creativity, wisdom, hope and forgiveness.

His TM work gave him a new perspective on himself which was transformational.

> I can now see who I am beyond this flawed ego and litany of selfish mistakes. Being present more often has then led to the development of a sense of equanimity.

It was this developing quality of equanimity that enabled him to look very differently at the business and to have the courage of his convictions to assert that the business had a future, but with a very different culture.

> In 2013 I became CEO. It looked for all intents and purposes as though I had inherited the captaincy just in time to disappear with the ship under the waves. We were in financial and cultural ruin and it was going to need a miracle. But I hadn't given up hope. If I could turn my personal life around, maybe I could do the same here. My mission was to explore how I might, as leader, help to bring my new-found personal balance and meaning to the organisation.

One 'leadership moment' led to what eventually became seen as a critical moment in the establishment of the new culture in the business: whether to take on a payday loan company as a managed services customer.

> On the one hand, we desperately needed the money to stay afloat; but on the other we were unable to dismiss our concerns about the unethical nature of their business and felt it would at least be incongruent with our personal values to support them.

It caused Simon to have to face directly into the new ethos he was bringing to the company. It was a very difficult decision financially, especially given the indebtedness of the business and the pressures arising from this. But he was clear that the future of the business lay in its values – and he trusted that this would reignite the passion, commitment, and belief of his people. The whole ethos of the Linux OS and the people who worked in it were values-based.

When I became CEO, I brought everyone together and assured them that I wanted to allow positive change to happen. I told them that I believed there was a shift happening in our company consciousness and that I was committed to helping LinuxIT to become a values-driven learning organisation that we can all be very proud of. I wanted us all to get more from our jobs than money. I wanted to help create a place where we could bring our whole selves to work and find meaning, fulfilment and joy in our work. I also explained that I didn't expect them to take my word for it but that the proof would be in the pudding.

This stance was put to the test almost immediately with this latest business decision. It proved to be a turning point.

> I was expecting cynicism. I have been cynical myself at times, catching sight of myself and what I was now espousing, and thinking, 'What is this hippie shit? Who have I become?' But I believe this is simply the fear of letting go of our old selves, of our old ways of relating and organising. It's hard. But with an 'open mind, open heart and open will,' as Senge put it, we increasingly let go of the ways of the past and have the courage to allow a new paradigm to emerge, rooted in the present, congruent with our deeper values.

Simon saw his leadership as about providing a safe environment within which his colleagues were encouraged to listen to their deeper sense of purpose and to connect with their colleagues in different way. This was all about the new future that was emerging in the Linux world, not about maximising their own sales.

> We made radical changes at all levels of the business, from the spiritual to the mundane and everything in between. We started by getting consultants in to evaluate where we were on our spiritual journey both individually and as a culture. We de-layered the organisational structure. We brought everyone together on one floor to bring down barriers to communication and flow of information. We introduced a games room and spent more time having fun together. We standardised pay, reduced the differential between top and bottom earners and provided every employee with an interest in the company. Basically, our business model was now founded on the delivery of increasing value to our customers rather than purely on profitability.

They did this by honestly assessing their ability to deliver real value to potential customers – and the customers' congruence with their own vision and values – before taking them on.

After a couple of years of employing this approach, LinuxIT was an entirely transformed organisation. On a purely financial level, the company had turned around completely with no debt, unprecedented sales, reduced costs, and an extremely bullish forecast, which led eventually to the successful integration of the business into the wider Claranet holding as the market grew and consolidated – but still maintaining its distinctive ethos.

> Most importantly, LinuxIT was rich in meaning ... The conversation meta-morphosed from themes of fear, insecurity and mistrust to belief, optimism and togetherness. We had a real sense of purpose and a culture buzzing with creativity, commitment, caring, mastery, trust, laughter, ambition and belief. New ideas and opportunities were abounding like never before. Suddenly, everyone seemed to be noticing us for all the right reasons. Relationships that had become fruitless were revitalised. We won industry awards and public accolades.

What was most striking from the interview with Simon, however, was his almost bemused realisation that a struggling business in a very tough, rapidly evolving, and competitive marketplace could be so transformed by what he termed 'spiritual' practices – leading with love.

> LinuxIT is a truly wonderful, happy place to work and just about every-one who comes into contact with us tells us they have rarely seen or felt anything like it. I am proud of what we built and I believe, as far as my leadership is concerned, this outcome would have been entirely incon-ceivable to me had I not learnt TM and found my way to a more spiritual leadership.

Simon's story highlights many of the themes presented in this book. We rec-ognise, of course, that the circumstances he and the business found themselves in combined to make the effects of this approach spectacularly visible. As we have said before, seeds sown when leading with love rarely bear such rapid fruit. But Simon's example clearly illustrates how the practices we refer to can release not just an individual leader from deep-rooted egoic patterns but a wider organisation. Rather than looking outside to fill the gaping holes in his psyche, Simon focused on his personal practice and looked within – to find that he already possessed everything he was looking for. His release from anx-iety and shame on the inside is mirrored in what takes place on the outside. There is a flow from his higher level of consciousness (no longer fear-based but love-based) to that of his staff. Suddenly, no longer acting from fear, he and his company accessed a richer way of being and acting in line with their deeper values.

Simon's personal work plugged him into a source of love, courage, creativity, wisdom, hope, and forgiveness. These are all signs of a higher level of emotional maturity and spiritual development: Tornstam's 'gerotranscendence,' as described in Chapter 4. This is a place where it may be impossible *not* to lead with love. But the encouragement we take from his story, and the previous case studies, is that his journey into leading with love benefited so many others.

In summary: the practical learnings

There are a number of core themes to draw from these case studies:

- The 'breakthrough moments' which trigger people into the 're-sourcing' phase of our model: when people access something deeper in themselves, what we refer to as their 'true identity' – the 'me I didn't have time for,' a more resourceful, integrated, loving self that exists at a level below or beyond habitual awareness. For some, this was a transpersonal experience: a connecting to something spiritual, 'bigger than me,' which they experienced as 'flowing' through them.

- The experience of a high degree of vulnerability prior to these breakthrough moments, often associated with an 'ego-alien' experience or setback in which they encounter the limits of their current level of ego-functioning and come to see and challenge the insecurities driving it (need for control, achievement, harmony, etc.). This provides the impetus for work on 'freeing up the channel,' if people are willing to step into it – which they are not always. This is the crucial moment: when people choose either to let down their defences or to go back into them.

- The willingness to step into this, and risk the loss of control that comes with it, requires people to be vulnerable enough to access support from others or a coach, who can provide a 'holding' that enables people to go there.

- The use of presencing techniques, such as 'grounding' in the body, meditation, or on retreat in nature, to access the heart and discern the authentic voice of love in their deeper selves.

- A much higher degree of self-acceptance or self-love arising from this… which provides the basis for a different pattern of engaging with those around them: more patient, accepting, enquiring, more able to trust, but equally able to 'call things,' and be demanding without being anxious or making others defensive.

- A new clarity around priorities and what really matters to them. A shift to seeing the bigger picture beyond their immediate role.

- An increase in both humility and power. A new peace and equilibrium which allows more joy in their work and leaves them less caught up in unnecessary drama without diminishing their effectiveness and presence and, on the contrary, increasing it.

- A struggle to establish a rhythm to sustain their clarity. Forces were 'pulling them back.' The high of an initial breakthrough (in most cases) was followed by the hard part of sustaining it: 'self-remembering.'

- The gradual stabilisation of these new qualities and behaviours into a self-fulfilling pattern, which can best be described as a leadership flowing from 'being' rather than 'striving.'

As with the previous chapter, we will finish with the words of A.H. Almaas:

> Achievements are not looked at as ways to gain recognition, love, self esteem, success, fame, power and so on. They might bring such things, but they are not for such ends. They are merely the natural expression of being oneself, living and functioning authentically. One does not care about gain from success in the world; success in the world can happen, but only as a side consequence of gaining one's authentic being. In other words, one does not gain value from one's accomplishments; these accomplishments are, rather, the expression of one's self-existing value
>
> *(Almaas 1996: 349).*

Notes

1 Simon was a founding member of LinuxIT in 1999, established to support the expanding presence of the open-source Linux operating system. The business grew rapidly but then hit significant difficulties in 2011/12.
2 Simon describes TM as a simple mental technique which is practised twice daily for twenty minutes while sitting comfortably with your eyes shut. By using a mantra, the mind settles down towards the source of thought, your own inner self. This place is a reservoir of energy, intelligence, creativity and bliss. Everyone has it but most of us are unaware how to access it.

References

Almaas, A.H. (1996) *The Pearl Beyond Price. Integration of Personality into Being: An Object Relations Approach*. Boston, MA: Shambhala Publications.
BBC (2020) The oak tree in Kew Gardens that taught the world a lesson. *BBC News*, 29 January. https://www.bbc.co.uk/news/av/stories-51282656/the-oak-tree-in-kew-gardens-that-taught-the-world-a-lesson (accessed 24 September 2020).
Goleman, D. (2000) Leadership that gets results. *Harvard Business Review*, 78(2), 78–90.

13

CONCLUSIONS

This book has been over three years in the researching and writing. As we begin this final chapter, we find ourselves in a time when the call to lead with love is stronger than ever. Writing these closing remarks in July 2020, as the COVID-19 virus reaches its peak in the United Kingdom, has a particular poignancy. We hear countless everyday examples of people leading with love: connecting, supporting, sharing, and supplying those in need. Now, in the context of the pandemic, the phrase from our definition, 'overall wellbeing,' takes on a whole new meaning: it feels like our awareness has expanded and the number of people that we include in our circle of concern has grown, to include strangers and 'distant others.'[1] What's more, the ugly underbelly of racism has shown itself once more, and people all over the world are grieving for an American, George Floyd, who died as he was pinned to the ground by police.

On the one hand, much remains the same. The forces that gave rise to the dynamics of instrumentalism and dehumanisation that we described in the early chapters of this book are still as present and powerful as ever. However, much has changed. Our society (which means all of us) has begun to inquire into how we can best utilise the world's resources, how we work, how we communicate, how we relate to others, and how we manage ourselves for the benefit of all people in our communities. Many have experienced our profound interconnectedness. We have seen how impossible it is to isolate ourselves from events in countries both near and far from our own. In short, we have, as a society, begun to question.

As we pointed out in Chapter 11, the word 'question' ultimately has the same root as the word 'quest' (Latin *quaerere*, 'to ask, seek'). The word 'quest' has come to embody ideas such as 'adventure,' 'expedition,' 'journey,' or even 'pilgrimage.' And our use of 'question' in this context incorporates the idea of 'quest.' A question can imply the beginning of something, perhaps the beginning of an adventure or journey because it also implies a search for answers – maybe even to questions that we have not yet fully articulated. This can involve a feeling of excitement and adventure: where will our questioning take us? What answers will reveal themselves? Will we agree on anything at all? Will we make radical decisions that take us in unexpected directions requiring qualities such as courage, perseverance, and, of course, compassion, empathy, and love?

Many people are asking foundational questions, and asking them as nations, possibly for the first time since World War II. How shall we live? How shall we cooperate? What changes do we need or want to make? The scenarios ahead of us are many. It would be easy to polarise: either a new low-growth economy of sustainability, care, and cooperation or a reversion to individualism and competition as we ratchet up the old engines of economic growth. This kind of polarisation rarely helps. We will need some kind of economic growth to support the many millions of people all over the world who are out of work. But what kind of economic growth? And how should we pursue it? What ideals should underpin our actions and decisions in the post-COVID era?

It is, of course, encouraging, and necessary, that we ask these questions, and other complex questions that are emerging in these times – and we will all have our own views about what the answers may be. But, in order to reach good conclusions, rather than dive straight into the questions per se, maybe we need to step back and ask 'How?' rather than 'What?'... *How* are we going to ask and answer these questions? Who is going to be doing the asking and who will be invited to respond? How will we reach some kind of acceptable consensus and what values will underpin our responses?

Can we really have the same people who led us into this dehumanising and destructive system leading us out of it? We need leaders with a different level of consciousness. Because everything that we value – economic security, fulfilment of everyone's potential, thriving healthy communities, a flourishing planet and ecosystem, people taking responsibility for their lives – these are all outcomes of a system that is led by people who lead with love. And that, potentially, is all of us.

So, what will shape our response to this crisis and any others that may follow? What do we really want? What do *you* really want? And, while we may not all want the same things, there is a sense that the vast majority of us are questioning whether we really want to live instrumentalised lives in the dehumanised organisations we have been working for.

We are aware that this book has looked at leading with love at the individual level and, of course, we have to 'be the change we want to see,' so the starting point is always to look at our own lives. However, in addition, many of us may now be seeking to embody new ideals within our organisations, communities, and societies in order to be part of a wider change. Significant change at the systemic level requires individual change but also requires more than that. How do we learn to lead with love at the individual level in such a way that it scales up into organisational and even societal change? It is this question we now address as we bring this book to a close. We examine each level in turn.

Leading with love at the individual level

This book, from both theory and practice, has sought to explore the dynamics of leading with love. At its heart the proposition is very simple. Listen to the voice of love within you and act upon it. By doing this, you will mature, psychologically and spiritually. You will also benefit personally, for it is through the maturation process that you learn to live a wholehearted life – a life of peace, joy, contentment, and love. Through the research we found a set of people who were able to do this – and to do so on a sufficiently consistent basis to be recognised for it. Somehow, these people, all working in highly pressurised environments, in the face of the same powerful systemic forces that we all face, were able to carve out the space and inner freedom to embody love in their leadership. These individuals possessed a quiet psychological and spiritual maturity, a groundedness, which helped them to withstand the huge pressures to instrumentalise others.

The examples that our interviewees gave us were often such seemingly small things: small acts of kindness and thoughtfulness; patient interventions into organisational systems or cultures to sow seeds for future change. At one level we may look at these and ask, 'Is this enough?' How will these small acts ever counter the powerful forces we described in the early chapters of the book? But the reality of leading with love is that it is always in the small things: it is about developing the habit of responding intentionally with love in all situations. Then, when the big decisions come, the loving response is natural and well founded, however risky it may feel.

These leaders offer us hope that change at the individual level matters and makes a difference in people's lives. Probably the simplest thing that distinguished our leaders with love is that they just *remembered* that love mattered, in the face of all these systemic forces that would have most of us forget. We may think we forget because we are too busy – and then blame ourselves that in some way it is *our* fault. But, as we have seen, one of the secrets of instrumentalisation is that it robs us of the luxury of thoughtful, heartfelt responses simply by giving us impossible targets or workloads which cause us to react in stress and fear. Another reason we forget to lead with love is that we reify the instrumentalising forces as 'the way the world is.' Either through shame or fatalism, we shut down the question of whether it could be any other way. It is settled; there is no question – we go back to sleep, like the prince in 'The Hymn of the Pearl,' and simply react to what we see as 'reality,' drawing on our survival responses to help us through. How beautiful it was to discover and interview people who remembered that there was a bigger and simpler truth, that everything we are doing in our own workplaces and economies is not for its own sake, but to 'promote overall wellbeing,' and that 'overall wellbeing' begins with the person in front of you right now.

It is the wisdom that St Teresa passed on to us: we cannot all do great things, but we can all do small things with great love. It is, of course, ultimately a percentage game: less a case of 'how to lead with love,' and more *how many of us will remember to lead with love and how often will we remember?* The battle is for our perception and awareness. We all know love and we all can embody it. But our heads get full of other concerns: crudely, our perceived 'survival' needs and ego-needs. And our society today, and the way we run our organisations, seems 100% geared towards fixating us on these needs. We forget to love because we are programmed to forget to love.

This is what we have tried to explore at some depth in this book. How to 're-member' and 're-mind' ourselves of what really matters to us and how to rise above the organisational and societal programming that keeps us busy, preoccupied, and stressed. We have looked at some of the forces that cause us to forget – both the external, systemic forces and the internal, egoic ones – and how to overcome these. We have looked at ways to help us refresh and 're-source' ourselves by accessing and cultivating the presence of love within us and around us. We have also looked at the foundational importance of 'loving self' as the basis for loving others. We have hopefully drawn inspiration and encouragement from the example of others doing small things with great love to remind ourselves that we can do this too – and to trust that, indeed, this is enough.

But, if we are to take the proposition in this book seriously, there are some further questions we need to address. Is it reasonable to expect that each of us can find the confidence and resourcefulness needed to let love flow through us? Is it fair to expect individuals to act with loving leadership when the majority of those around them do not? Are we putting unrealistic pressure on people to act in ways that go against the dominant, instrumentalising forces that have been increasingly taking over our organisations? This is the spectre that inevitably haunts a work such as this: is it enough? When we look at the loving actions of our leaders in Chapter 5, they can seem so small and isolated in the face of the huge structural and systemic forces we document in Chapter 3. Will 'small acts with great love' ever really be enough? More insidiously, might we even be encouraging people to overcome their egoic fixations and lead with love all for the benefit of corporate profitability – the benefits of which, in our currently unequal world, flow straight to the top 1%?

These are important questions and, while no lasting change can take place without change at the individual level (otherwise we just get new egoic leaders taking over from the old), we recognise we do need to start a conversation about change at the group and societal levels too.

Scaling up: leading with love at the group and organisational level

One of the leaders in our sample was approached recently to lead the LGBTQ+ group within a global IT organisation. He is a straight, white male and did not feel at all qualified for the job. However, the request came from a number of people at all levels of the organisation, of different genders and sexual orientations. Their reasoning was that he was widely respected (for leading with love!) and he was senior – he had an influential voice. Having been persuaded to accept, he has since organised conferences and given platforms to a wide range of speakers. In addition, to support Mental Health Awareness Week, he spoke about his own issues with mental health, including an honest and personal account of his struggles with male body image. He was invited to speak into similar conversations in several other organisations and his leadership presence, along with that of the people he has mentored and supported, has grown substantially.

This is the power of the collective. When individuals come together around a shared commitment, in the workplace but beyond the day job, individual change gets scaled up. What was once personal, private, and difficult becomes shared, open, and transformational.

What is personal need not be individual. Indeed, it cannot be. All the research into significant movements for change highlight the importance of shared leadership, people coming together and finding a quality of connection that makes them, and the ideals they embody, more powerful and transformational than the atomised norm we have come to accept in the dominant mythology of the individualised 'heroic' 'transformational leader.'

This is doubly true when it comes to leading with love. It cannot be otherwise, since love is in its very essence a relational thing. You cannot do leading with love alone, by definition. It is a shared quality. More purposefully and positively, however, love is infectious: as trust and confidence build, so it grows. The key is in those two words, 'trust' and 'confidence,' and these can only be built over time and tested through shared, and often challenging, experience.

The work of Dave Logan at USC is particularly illuminating in this area, and we would commend this to anyone thinking about what it really means to lead with love in a way that leads to sustained and sustainable change (Logan et al. 2011). Drawing on social movement theory, his focus is on how 'tribes' cohere as an engine for organisational and social change. In his paradigm, a group of people cohering around leading with love would be a 'level 5' tribe ('Life's great'), the most evolved and with the highest potential for progressive social change. Perhaps the most interesting facet of his research is the importance of 'triads,' which we discussed in Chapter 10, in the genesis of such a 'tribe.'

As we explained, a triad is a group of three people who share similar values inside a system and have 'got each other's backs' to the extent that they will look out for each other and call each other out. According to Logan, successful change, which requires us in some way to 'take on the world,' will nearly always 'start from the gut' (i.e. the deeper values) and will always have close triads at its heart. A powerful leadership triad will often comprise people with very different skills and energies, so there is a high level of mutual complementarity, but will be characterised by close relationships and some kind of shared higher purpose. We observed at first hand a very effective triad at work in a large professional services firm. This comprised a classic 'figurehead' leader who eloquently espoused clear and compelling values, a senior colleague who was an astute power operator and able to drive through some of the tough behind-the-scenes decisions that were necessary to embed deep change into the firm, and a third, who was highly entrepreneurial and able to make some very bold moves in the marketplace. The solidity of the triad had been formed in a particularly challenging project they had worked on earlier in their careers, so that when they emerged into senior leadership positions where individually each would have been critically exposed, they were able to support each other. This was not a Machiavellian power play; it just happened quite naturally as a feature of the trust they had built up. They empowered each other and this climate of confidence spread into other relationships. Collectively, they became a force at the top of the system that transformed the culture of the firm at a challenging time and took it through one of its most successful periods in its long history.

One important feature of a triad is that it is less liable to collusion than a couple. Another is that each member not only cares for each of the others, but also for the quality of the relationship between the other pair, so that, if misunderstandings arise, they actively mediate these and resolve differences productively. The other crucial feature is that triads become 'nested'; they multiply when a person from one triad builds connection with a person in another. In this way, triads grow exponentially to become a tribe and change moves from possibility to inevitability.

So an important question to ask as we start to engage on the project of leading with love is: 'Who is my triad?' Who is in it with you – *really* in it with you – and who is in it with them? How are you deepening connection, common purpose, and complementarity between yourselves? If you cannot find your triad, where might you look and what might you do to build it? It is perhaps the simplest practical wisdom of leading with love: start close to home, with key relationships and let it multiply from there. If you do not have your triad, you will be on your own.

Scaling up again: leading with love at the societal level

Thinking about collective leadership raises questions about what we want as a society. Of course, not everyone wants the same: some benefit from the current arrangements and many think they do, even if they do not. We are led by politicians all over the world, many of whom do not lead with love and yet are voted in time and time again. This brings us back to the dilemmas raised in Chapter 4:

1. Those who want power may be social dominants who want it for personal and egoic reasons (in our opinion, these are the people least qualified to lead)
2. Those who seek to rise to positions of leadership but who find it difficult to resist the pressures to instrumentalise people (both themselves and others)
3. Those who lead with love are either deterred or excluded from leadership at the highest levels because their face does not fit; they embody different values and are seen as threats

4. Many of us who want to live lives of love, compassion, freedom, peace, and joy do not want to take (potentially compromised) positions of leadership in organisations.

What gives us hope is that the numbers of people who answer to the latter categories by far outweigh those in the first. Furthermore, we hope that the ideas in this book can provide some support for those in the second category, helping them to develop the character that is needed to lead in these tough times. Perhaps in time, maybe a generation or two hence, to lead with love will be the socially accepted norm. It will become as socially undesirable to lead with selfishness and fear as it is to litter our planet with plastic, to engage in the slave trade, or to exhibit prejudice based on a person's gender, sexual orientation, religion, or race.

Such an outcome requires us to come together to change the narrative about what constitutes 'acceptable' and what 'unacceptable' leadership. Most freedoms have been won by communities battling the forces of the status quo, and it will probably be the case for this battle, too. Too many leaders benefit from fear because it is simple. It is easy to gain compliance by intimidating people. This is the dirty secret that business schools never talk about: you will not find 'management by fear' in a business textbook despite its widespread use.

One of the most important aspects of any leadership role is the power of patronage: the ability to shape how other roles around us are occupied. Some of us indeed have a formal responsibility in this: to identify and nominate successors for key roles in our organisations. How would it be if we engaged the heart more, alongside the head, in this process – looking not just for a 'track record of results' but also the ability to inspire trust, confidence, and followership? We get the leaders we deserve. We all know that the qualities that make a high achiever are not necessarily the qualities that make an effective leader.

Because we, as a global community, are on a quest for new visions for our world, we need a movement led by elders who lead with love. Elders can be of any age, for 'elder' signifies wisdom; some of our elders, such as Malala and Greta Thunberg, are very young. These elders would put in place some kind of movement or community that honours leaders who lead with love in all organisations in all societies. This community will recognise leaders who truly lead with love and will encourage all of us to nominate these leaders for awards. This movement will also recognise those people who inspire others to lead with love. Soon we will start to see these people rise to places of influence: in business, politics, charities, and government. It will become completely unacceptable to lead with fear, bullying, or vicarious intimidation via intrusive systems and surveillance. We will decide that working for twelve hours a day plus commuting on top is destructive of families, communities, and relationships. We will arrange our societies so that our organisations serve us rather than us being forced to sell our souls to organisations. The Social Darwinist survival-of-the-fittest business cultures will become a curious manifestation of a particular period in history when we forgot who we were and what we were here for.

We will be led by leaders of psychological and spiritual maturity, able to make difficult decisions in a loving way, mindful of our common purpose which is to act intentionally in sympathetic response to others, including the sacred or the divine, to promote individual and overall wellbeing. This community needs organising and it needs to be led, and here lies the danger: if it becomes powerful enough, it will attract people who are not mature enough to lead with love. This, then, is the challenge and the invitation: How can people who want to lead with love come together to realise a vision where leading with love is the norm?

Note

1 This reminds us of the picture experiment in Chapter 1, where only love expanded our circle of concern to include 'distant others.'

Reference

Logan, D., King, J. and Fischer-Wright, H. (2011) *Tribal Leadership: Leveraging Natural Groups to Build a Thriving Organization.* New York: HarperCollins.

INDEX